**International Architecture
Biennale Rotterdam**

Berlage Institute

Visionary Power

Producing the Contemporary City

NAi Publishers, Rotterdam

Preface
What about the Lifeboats?
George Brugmans
8

Prologue
The Power of Architectural Thought
Vedran Mimica
10

The City as Political Form
Pier Vittorio Aureli and Martino Tattara
16

Astana versus Almaty
IND (Inter.National.Design)
33

Cadavre Exquis Lebanese
WORK Architecture Company
41

Moscow Prefabricated
Alexander Sverdlov
51

Public Architecture and the Social Framework of Power
Sharon Zukin
59

Power Paradoxes
Martijn de Waal
67

The Zone
Keller Easterling
75

Moore's Law Meets Sustainability
INABA
87

The New City of Luoyang
Yimin Zhu
95

Garden State / Backyard City
Princeton University Center for Architecture, Urbanism and Infrastructure
103

In Praise of Discontinuity
Gabriele Mastrigli
113

Power Urbanisms
Martijn de Waal

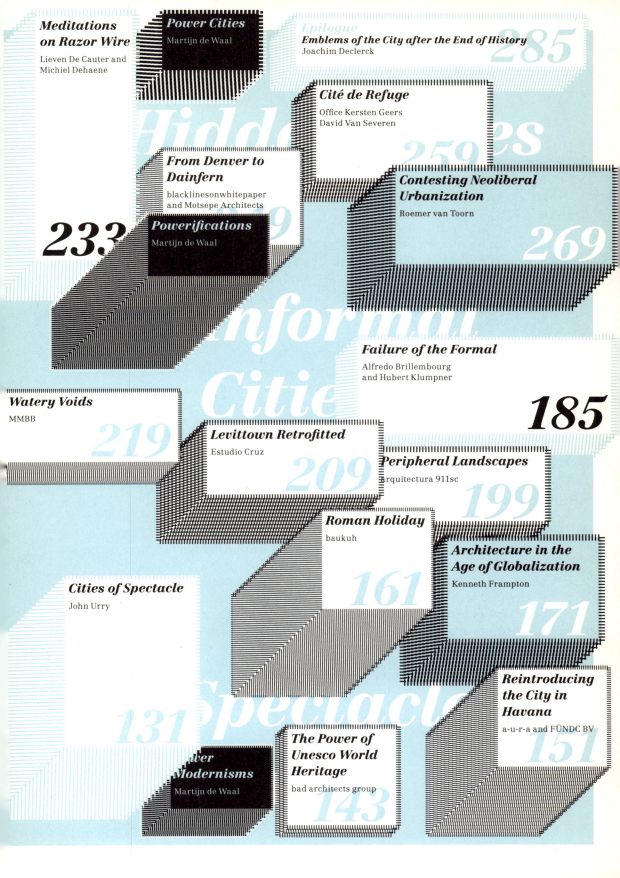

What about the Lifeboats?

Preface

The third International Architecture Biennale Rotterdam, *POWER – Producing the Contemporary City*, focuses on the city; an apt choice in the very year that more than half of the world population has become urban.

Most of us have grown a tad tired of yet more statistics, figures, maps and clever diagrams representing the global growth of cities. 'So what?' we think, or at best: 'hmm, nice design'.

But there is one figure that still really gets to me. The statistics – once I had internalized what they stand for – are mind-boggling: every single day over 150,000 people escape the countryside and pour into the overcrowded lifeboats represented by cities. Unlike earlier waves of migration to the city, this one brings migrants who are not so much hoping for a better life – even when they are looking for it – as they are *literally on the run*: the city, they pray, will whisk them away from a countryside that for them represents nothing but disaster and defeat.

150,000 a day: that's another Rotterdam in five days, another Lagos or Los Angeles in just three months.

Something is happening to the world. It's not only warming up, it's also urbanizing much faster than originally predicted: cities will account for most of the future world population growth, an estimated four billion people between now and 2050.

Most escapees disappear into 'informality', without tangible hope for a better life than the one they have just deserted, a harsh truth that proves no more able to stop the influx than the apparent inability of the lifeboats to cope with these multitudes. As it is, most of this rampant growth will happen in developing countries with slum growth outpacing urbanization per se. Between 60 and 90 per cent of urban growth takes place in slums: largely self-regulating informal cities, their survival based on the minimum component cost. Within a generation, more than half the people living in cities will be squatters.

Will these urban expansions really be cities, as we understand the concept? Does unbridled urbanization equal the rampant growth of cities?

Cities, it can be said, are human civilization's most complex manifestation. If so, the current speed of the urbanization process mirrors the ever-increasing complexity of our civilization, and we should be able to formulate an equivalent of Moore's Law to demonstrate this process; an empirical observation that the complexity of urbanization in regard to the minimum component cost doubles every so many months.

We would hence be conceding that in the age of globalization, the growth of cities is driven by progressively more complicated and often self-regulating forces, most of which – if not all of them – are completely beyond the control of scientists, politicians or planners, let alone architects.

What we would actually be admitting is that it is the intelligent design of the urban global web that will be critical to our survival as a civilized species in this new urban world.

However, in my opinion that does not seem to be a very comfortable or enlightened position. To stand in awe of the statistics, admire the clever design of the 3D diagrams and see them as symbols of something beyond our real grasp – that is, intelligent design – begs the hard question. What about these lifeboats? Can we shrug off our misgivings about whether they are really waterproof and leave it to 'intelligent design'? Are we really ready to step into the urban age 'just pasting feathers together hoping for a duck', as a US Army general recently said when appraising America's Operation Iraqi Freedom?

That operation, if I'm allowed a short detour, was and is a mess for many reasons, not the least among them the fact that it is the first war in American history prepared with the help of PowerPoint presentations. Rumsfeld and Wolfowitz must have loved the clever diagrams, entire war manoeuvres represented by just a few neat bullets; they must have loved it so much that they forgot to make a real plan.

Which proves the point I am trying to make: that we cannot stand in awe of clever presentations or revert to wishful thinking when aiming for 'duck'. We have to go 'beyond mapping' and concentrate on the nitty-gritty, the fundamentals; we have to go out into the city and make a plan to make sure those lifeboats are as waterproof as we can make them.

The International Architecture Biennale Rotterdam is a research biennale. To ask the hard question it invited as its curator for this edition the renowned Berlage Institute, a globally orientated postgraduate laboratory for education, research and development in the fields of architecture, urban planning and landscape design.

What about the lifeboats? That, however modestly, is what *Visionary Power* – the exhibition, the conference and this book – is about: identifying those architects who are committed to work on the lifeboats, and showing the power of their visions.
Visionary Power is a platform for young contemporary architects with a plan, with the will to take control of the idea of the city again, and to respond to a call-to-arms for advocacy and real engagement in the urban process.

George Brugmans
Director International Architecture Biennale Rotterdam

Prologue

The Power of Architectural Thought   Vedran Mimica

In this era of globalization – more than ever before – the city is the space where cultural, economic and political forces interact, where various powers and phenomena compete or collaborate in continuous evolution. This reality confronts us with the questions of who is producing the city and envisioning its future and what visible and invisible powers are shaping its production. This publication is the result of the quest by an international selection of leading scholars and emerging architects and researchers to position themselves vis-à-vis these issues. By exploring the global political and economic conditions and powers defining the development and liveability of today's cities, this younger generation of architects focuses on how tactical urban strategies and architectural interventions can concretely contribute to the contemporary discourse on the city.

The twenty-first century is the age of urban migration and movement, a time when people, rich and poor alike, flock from south to north, from east to west, from country to city, in search of prosperity and security as part of our inevitable existence. As the stage upon which cultures meet and civilizations clash, cities are now the hubs of networks through which the fast flows of global capital surge, and the focal points for an unrelenting media blitz. They bear the brunt of new world wars and are the aims of international terrorism. With the experience and entertainment economies in fast mode these same cities accommodate huge streams of consumers, shoppers and tourists, on a daily basis.

The city is the platform where all of these forces come into play, where different and indiscernible powers confront and interact with each other. The impact of the force of commercial capital or the power of government on the fabric of the city is perhaps easily identified. But the powers of fear, desire, religion or law are just as strong in shaping the city. Consider the way governmental facilities in Brussels currently shape the need for security; the way zoning laws affect the development of Manhattan as much as that of Shenzhen; how a cartoon of Mohammed may reshape the architecture of future embassies; how the fact that immigrants will soon account for as much as 40 per cent or more of the population of cities, such as Amsterdam and Rotterdam, emphasizes the need for a rethinking of their urban planning; or how 'powerless' individuals themselves create huge squatter cities, the *favelas, barriadas, katchi adabas* and *bidonvilles* of this world.

Investigating Five Forces

This publication is structured around five types of city conditions and their respective powers – representation, global capital, tourism, migration and fear – that are significantly reshaping urban development. The consequences of complex power systems, these forces define the present and future of our cities. Eight researchers have documented and investigated how they operate as producers of different contemporary cities.

The *Capital Cities* chapter addresses the fact that the need for cultural and geopolitical centres has not been eliminated by the demise of nation-states. The new global geography is defined by cities that are emblematic for their economic significance as well as for their cultural and political importance. In view of this development, Pier Vittorio Aureli and Martino Tattara argue the necessity for rethinking the contemporary city as a representative and symbolic entity – or as social, political and political centre – rather than the result of flux and flows.

Throughout the world, the section on *Corporate Cities* maintains, particular urban areas located within cities are transforming themselves into exclusive business or shopping districts. Understanding that this phenomenon undermines, and even colonizes, the central and public functions of the city, Keller Easterling demonstrates that these enclaves are subject to global political and economic forces that form new free economic zones, thereby creating a new urban paradigm. While commercial parties aim to create introverted worlds that are seemingly neutral, these areas become more powerful than the cities themselves and subsequently often lead to local cultural conflicts. The respective cities try to counter the homogenization of these districts by stimulating functional variety, or by activating them as structuring elements for urban growth.

In today's 'new world order', *Spectacle Cities* postulates that cities may only be taken seriously as cultural and political entities by creating museums, festivals, sporting events, universities and especially iconic buildings to sustain themselves. In an age where former sites of labour are being transformed into sites of visual consumption, John Urry points out that this is necessary in order for cities to compete in the global race for recognition. At the same time, cities copy each other's formulas and specific characteristics at the expense of the identity of these cities. By this thematic zoning, the essential role of cities as centres for revolution, individual development, new ideas and sociocultural representation of different groups is eliminated. The urgent question is how to reconcile the spectacle city with the real city.

Informal Cities references the informal social, economic, political, architectural and urban practices in relation to the more formal physical and spatial aspects undertaken to engage in urban life. The result of massive urban migrations, these spontaneous manifestations have rapidly exploded around the formal urban cores in South-East Asia, Africa and Central and South America. Alfredo Brillembourg and Hubert Klumpner maintain that the organizational, ecological and economic potential of these developments should be embraced and enlisted as an urbanization model to be further developed in close collaboration with the inhabitants/builders. This blending of formal and informal urban elements could potentially lead to a new and inclusive city geography.

The growing fear caused by globalization's by-products, such as illegal immigrants, is explored in *Hidden Cities*. According to Lieven De Cauter and Michiel Dehaene, the two urban paradigms appearing in the contemporary city are *heterotopia* and *camp*. The former is understood as offering protection by serving as a vehicle for urban development; while the latter defines a spatial condition that deprives people of their fundamental human rights. Both of these spatial organizations operate according to their own regulations, causing them to be isolated from normality.

Beyond Mapping, Projecting the City

Within the complexities of these global phenomena, the city becomes central to the contemporary architectural debate. As Saskia Sassen stated in a 2004 public lecture at the Berlage Institute, 'City space is the key zone where a lot of the power projects of global corporate capital play out, and where the new political interventions of even the poorest organizations can also be enacted.' And then more recently at the Urban Age conference in Berlin: 'Architecture needs to confront the massiveness of urban experience, the overwhelming presence of massive architectures and massive infrastructures in today's cities, and the overwhelming logic of utility that organizes much of the investments in cities.' Yet, as Rem Koolhaas pointed out in another public lecture held at the Berlage Institute in February 2006, architecture has reached an *impasse*: the concept of the city is disintegrating.

Presented throughout this volume are a series of projects by a younger generation of architects and urbanists that bridge theory and practice to investigate today's urban conditions. These ambitions – merely mappings of contemporary trends – depict how architecture and architects can initiate a transformative impact on the production of the contemporary city. As Kenneth Frampton instructs us, 'One is tempted to suggest that the great nemesis of our time is maximization irrespective of whether it is a maximization of profit or firepower. You may well ask where does this leave architects of our time? This is a question that here as elsewhere is painfully difficult if not impossible to answer in a satisfactory way. One can only say that the responsibility of being an architect is as much one of being constantly engaged in political discourse and advocacy as it is one of being involved in the design and realization of built form.'

By not searching for statistical truth, these proposals allow us to lucidly see the world as it currently exists as a means to empower us – as architects – to take action. From arguing that cities like Beirut should create new networked city-state paradigms by exploiting their inherent social and cultural differences to unmasking the urban interiors of Johannesburg, these projects unfold and unpack 'reality as is' by direct engagement with the real world.

Projects – like the one for Rome, investigating the ability of architecture to achieve the coexistence between tourism and heritage, or the use of Havana as a tourist attraction to develop a new global identity – call for a renewed commitment of architectural imagination. The research into Mexico City's unrelenting urban expansion, or the presentation of the seemingly neutral transitory spatial conditions along the border of Ceuta, reject the prevailing tendency to view the growing complexity of our urban environment as a pretext for an end to the relationship between architecture and the city.

The time for universal urban models may be over, but the need for new strategies – like using energy-management methods to urbanize Busan – for the city is no less acute. In order to equip a new generation of architects to develop these strategies, a new and in-depth knowledge of the powers and forces that drive development is required. Each project presented takes a stance, to reveal the similarities and differences between cities and cultures to offer how architects and urban designers can influence and improve our future. By clearly understanding how these forces operate, these proposals – such as the scenario for blurring political power with market hegemony in Luoyang, or the reshifting of corporate activity from the metropolitan centres to the suburban peripheries as in the case of Jersey City – show how to intelligently subvert by working with, and around, these conditions.

These projects go beyond the current obsession with mapping and pose direct questions to the architectural discipline by directly engaging in the quest for changing reality or elevating society to a different level of existence.

Architecture as Power, or the Return to the Discipline

It is clear that this current *impasse* in architecture is related to the inability of the architectural profession to form a clear idea about the contemporary city. Urban projects, like Lyotard's grand narratives, are long gone – along with the times when architects were making rigorous attempts to understand and project the city. As Koolhaas also pointed out in his recent lecture, the writing of architectural manifestos ceased in the late 1960s – at precisely the moment when urbanization exponentially increased on a global scale.

This loss of engagement with the city, as a conceivable collective entity, produces a breaking point between architecture's theory and practice. In today's world, we believe that architecture should no longer attach itself to other disciplines, such as sociology and philosophy, or through sophisticated computational techniques or other state-of-the-art processes, in order to reactivate itself. The position throughout this book is that architecture must be connected to reality through its own disciplinary tools, possibilities and performances. In order to truly take action to change our world, we must make architecture a discipline that other disciplines relate to, instead of architecture always looking to other disciplines to revitalize itself.

The architect is a figure who – through his or her professional performance, intellectual capabilities and research investigations – is able to fundamentally understand the forces shaping contemporary urban reality. Throughout this publication we show how architecture must be connected to reality through its own tools and possibilities. By delivering a juxtaposition of ideas and positions, these projects precisely implement an architectural reaction to found urban conditions by re-imagining our world. This is the power of architectural thought.

The [C]
as P[o]
Form

The City as Political Form

Pier Vittorio Aureli and Martino Tattara

The only maxim of art is not to be imperial. This means today: it does not have to be democratic, if democracy implies conformity with the imperial idea of political liberty.
Alain Badiou, 2005

City

Let us start from the outset by stating that the concept that *makes* the city is the potential for centrality – the granting of significance to a location, assuming it marks the centre of a particular territory, or any urban, political, cultural and geographic framework. From time immemorial the potential for centrality has been an issue of power. Power not in terms of *producing* the city (which seems to be the declination of power in the age of global capitalism), but power in terms of *deciding* the city – constituting and making the relevance of a place. The fact of being in one place and the constituting act of coexistence within a political institution that potentially represents something beyond itself, such as a territory, a culture, an epoch, an *idea,* de facto constitutes the centrality of the city, even (and especially) in the ubiquitous and totalizing realm of urbanization.

At a time when the term *city* is bandied everywhere, reducing its centrality to a purely logistic notion, it is useful to recall the fundamental difference between *civitas* – the origin of the term 'city' – and *urbs* – a term transformed by Idefonso Cerda's popular neologism, *urbanization*, in 1867.[1] *Civitas* is the political institution that signifies the collective will of a community to inhabit and coexist in one place. *Urbs* is the infrastructure that ultimately materially supports this choice.[2] When the city is reduced to mere urbanization – like in the ancient Roman city, in the various forms of urban sprawl, or in so-called 'cities from zero', such as contemporary cities in the Middle East or in China – 'cityness' itself is reduced to a 'Potemkin village' – an urban caricature devoid of any real social or cultural centrality.

In recent world geopolitical history, examples such as public mass demonstrations seem to be investing once more in the idea of centrality as an indispensable form of social and cultural identification. This form cannot be easily replaced by any other organizing or infrastructural system, political or economic framework – not even by the omnipresent scale of globalization and the correspondingly popular notions of urban networks. Nevertheless, and regardless of whether the pervasive nature of the global economy can be evaded, we have entered a cultural phase in which exultant optimism toward the mythologies of globalism, 'genericity' and the free market as 'the end of the city' or 'the end of history' is rapidly waning. Within this vacuum of paradigms, a vacuum at the moment dominated exclusively by dystopian mappings of the present (and a fear of proposing new models) the city must, more than ever, be rediscovered as a strongly identifiable place, a crucial laboratory of urban consciousness and, above all, as a tangible and intelligible physical form. We attempt to address this issue by adopting an urban theme in which centrality assumed a literal and explicit dimension: the Capital City. The Capital City is not only the 'national capital city' or the seat and locus of state power as commonly understood within the nation-state historical paradigm. The Capital City, in a broader sense, is the site of cultural and political capital: a tangible place that, ever more explicitly, renders, materially and monumentally, in one unique and therefore iconic place, what the philosopher Cornelius Castoriadis would have called the *imaginary*.[3]

Urban Rituals
Protesters at the Genoa G8

For Castoriadis the imaginary is not simply the *image of*, but rather the social-historical production of specific forms through which we can speak about something, such as an idea of the world. It is precisely in this sense that cities like Rome, Moscow or Brasilia interest us. Their dramatic political, cultural and urban history far outstrips their national-historical identity. At the same time, their idiosyncratic form, their status as theatres of explicit imaginaries and counter-imaginaries are not easily subsumed in the urban cliché imposed by the universal law of ubiquitous urbanization. It is for this reason that to reconsider these constituent facts of political 'cityness' is not just an act of historical consciousness, but above all a militant act of refusal towards the 'just-mapping' attitude, and a reconstruction of the very concept of the city.

Capital

The Capital City, capital as *caput*, head of the territory it represents, is an urban paradigm that clearly emerged with the advent of the modern state in Europe between the sixteenth and seventeenth centuries. In the Middle Ages, European cities were mostly ruled by local powers and municipalities with a great degree of autonomy from exterior forces and participation by the various social strata that composed them. With the advent of modern states, European cities, within the political paradigm of absolute monarchy, were increasingly deprived of their autonomous political prerogatives and absorbed in the centralized logic implicit in the mechanism of the nation-state.

In this context of political heteronomy, a more Leviathan-like

Event Space
The Vatican Obelisk

and diffused power became necessary to stage the city's representation in one unique place. It is precisely at this moment that some cities became exceptional sites of power: Capital Cities. While Capital Cities emerged within the formation of the nation-state, their fate and evolution was only partially conditioned by this stage of political governance. As direct political expressions of much larger extra-urban territorial units than themselves, such as the nation, they formed the basis of the modern metropolis. Capital Cities are the blueprint of the modern metropolis, systematically assuming the form of the city that exceeds its local political and cultural milieu, becoming a cosmopolitan epicentre.

Indeed, the modern metropolis is first a product of political power concentration and only later an outcome of economic accumulation. This process is parallel to the formation of capitalism itself, the accumulation principle of which would have been impossible without the political armature of the state. After all, the social contract theories of Thomas Hobbes and John Locke predate the economic theories of Adam Smith and David Ricardo. Today, the potential for proximity to a concentration of political and national seats still constitutes the main allure of capital cities as strategic hubs of global economic networks.

Following the initial political logic that formed the exceptionality of Capital Cities as concentrations of extra-urban territorial powers, global capitalism, while decreasing national autonomy, increased the relevance of Capital Cities as strongly identifiable places of political and cultural representation, this time at the service of economic production. In this regard the strategic relevance of Capital Cities is crucial to the counter-forces that contest the powers staged and represented in these sites. After all, demonstrations by constituent powers against constituted powers – from the French Revolution in 1789 to the huge mass demonstrations in Beirut in 2006 against the right-wing government of Fouad el Siniora – always take place in Capital Cities as their proper *theatrical* stage. The materiality and the tangibility of this theatrical stage is used by constituent powers as a potential for a direct link between the political event taking place, visibly and physically, in one unique place and its immediate implications for a much broader and much more complex geopolitical spectrum. This direct link is achieved within the material condition of the collective imaginary – in other words, the fact that 'everything that is presented to us in the social-historical world is inextricably tied to the symbolic'.[4]

Of course, real acts and things such as cities are not in themselves (always) symbols. None of them, however, would be possible outside a symbolic network. This is why Capital Cities are relevant: their exceptionality as geopolitical *loci* of representation helps us break free of mystifications such as the end of geography and various network theories and constantly rediscover the power of the city's physical centrality and its absolute relevance in the constituting of any politics. After all, the city remains a material place and it constitutes an actual site, a concrete ground of action within which and from which political activity takes place and represents itself. Since representation plays a crucial role in what is at stake in Capital Cities – namely the potential for the miniaturized geopolitical identity of a territory in one tangible place – a very crucial contribution to the character and articulation of these cities is the urban form and its immediate manifestation: architecture.

By reading the iconic role for architecture in the development of urban imagination of cities such as Rome, Capital of Christianity, Moscow, Capital of State Communism, and Brasilia, Capital of Latin-American Modernity, we intend to challenge the traditional belief that architecture can only retroactively reflect what the city is about. On the contrary, these examples demonstrate that certain architectural forms have consciously anticipated – in their own singularity of urban facts – contemporary urban scenarios. Indeed, each of these cities exemplifies techniques of urban representation trough the establishment of specific iconic actions, such as destruction and ritual in Rome, radical political subjectivity in Moscow and deliberate exceptionality in Brasilia.

At the level of the representation of the city, this implies that the cognition of the city itself is always implicit in the theories, rhetoric, imaginings and ideologies produced by architectural interventions, even when they are not immediately or not at all realized. Development often follows the imaginings enabled by specific architectural interventions. And these imaginings set the references with respect to which the political, cultural and aesthetic aspects of the city's own reproduction are attuned, consciously or unconsciously.

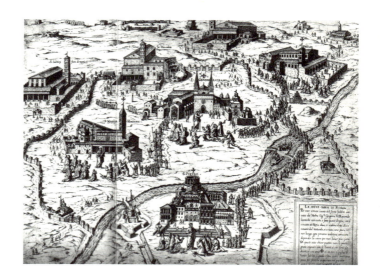

Urban Rituals
Antonio Lafrery, devotional path through Rome's basilicas at the time of Pope Sixtus V, 1585

Destruction and Ritual

While many cities in the Western world long constituted their importance through conquered expansion of their territorial domain, Rome as the Capital City of Christianity inherited the ideological legacy of Ancient Rome and reinvented it as its undisputable charisma. During the course of its history the city underwent dramatic urban crises: a brutal military sack in 1527, population shortage, chronic scarcity of any source of production, as well as systematic corruption. Indeed, Rome was the harshest and cruellest confrontation between a cultural and political charisma, the mythical *caput* of an entire civilization, and the depressing reality of a very poor and provincial city, as many travellers, diplomats and artists discovered *in situ*.

In order to fit the miserable reality of Rome into its pretentious myth, several popes during the course of the sixteenth century – from Julius II to Leo X to Clement VII to Paul III – attempted to alter the city's image with grandiose urban programmes.[5] Only fragments of these programmes were realized. The popes were working under the most impossible constraints: On the one hand a lack of time, since a pope was normally elected at a very advanced age, in order to contain his unlimited power, and on the other the desire of each pope for discontinuity with his predecessor, in order to clearly mark his authorship on the city.

Dramatically far from the images of the ideal city conceived in the Renaissance, Rome in the course of the sixteenth century looked like an eternal building site, in which admired ruins of its ancient past were increasingly confused with the ruins of uncompleted large-scale architectural projects. In Renaissance Rome

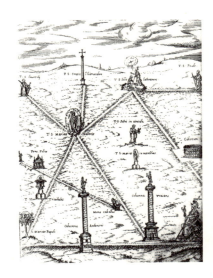

Rome: Tabula Rasa
Antonio Bordini, The road system at the time of Sixtus V, 1588. This map, erroneously assumed by Sigfried Giedion to be Sixtus's 'master plan' for Rome, illustrates the anti-iconic ambitions of the Pope, who wanted to reduce the image of Rome to the system of devotional paths linking the Basilicas.

'power' was exposed at its utmost capacity of imagination, and in its equally utmost melancholic fragility of realization. In this context only one pope and one strategy provided an alternative, to finally make Rome a real Capital: Sixtus V and destruction as an urban creative principle.

Pope Sixtus V's famed strategy to restructure Rome, in the five short years of his papacy (1585-1590), with a series of processional roads connecting existing basilicas and reinforced by the erection of obelisks as visual counterparts to the roads, was anticipated by Sixtus's desire for systematic destruction of the ruins of ancient Rome.[6] It is not by chance that the famous pilgrim map of Rome engraved by Antonio Bordini for the Jubilee of 1585 portrays Rome at the time of Sixtus V as an urban *tabula rasa* marked by the roads and by a few existing monuments, mostly the basilicas.[7] Sixtus saw these as the stepping stones for a radically different geography of the city. For Sixtus the real *capital* of Rome was not the vacuity of its ruins or its monuments but rather the processional circulation of the pilgrims the city attracted during the jubilee, which increased its population tenfold. In his view the real *capital* of Rome was simply a spectacle created by its users.[8]

Radical Subjectivity

Often a change of political regime in a nation demands the change of its Capital City. In 1918, one year after the October Revolution, Moscow became the Capital City of the newly founded USSR, symbolically replacing St. Petersburg, which two centuries earlier, in 1703, had replaced Moscow as the Capital City of Russia. If the Westernized grandeur of St. Petersburg was envisioned by Peter the Great to replace the cultural charisma of Moscow, considered by the tsar as the image of old traditional Russia, Moscow was chosen by the Bolsheviks as the Capital of the USSR in order to shift the centre of power once more to the 'heart' of Russia and away from the West.

The first dramatic decade of the Soviet Union found its most emblematic image in the urban crisis of Moscow during the 1920s. The country's economic crisis and the subsequent forced industrialization resulted in a massive migration of unprecedented dimensions to the city, bringing living conditions down to a dramatic level. Problematic municipal management called for an efficient and integral urban model that, in effect, put an end to the urban experiments of the avant-garde.

It was not an urban planner, but an expert politician, Laazar M. Kaganovich – a very close Stalin collaborator and member of the Politburo – who started actively elaborating proposals for urban planning.[9] In 1930 he became General Secretary of the Communist Party. From this influential position, during the Sixteenth Party Congress, he struck the audience with the decisive persuasive tone with which he convinced the party to adopt a resolution for new directives and open the way to legislation on urban economics in Moscow. However, for Kaganovich, architecture itself had to become a tool to establish ideological directives, and the 'subjectivity' of this political involvement cannot be regarded in purely negative terms.

According to Kaganovich, three issues had to be addressed: first, the socialist transformation of the way of life; second, the reconstruction and reorganization of the existing city; and third, the expansion of the existing city, but without the 'disurbanist' concept of decentralization, preventing the abolishment of the contrast between city and countryside.[10] The original point of this position was that for Kaganovich, cities had to be clearly outlined centralities: they should be neither small entities nor gigantic American-type megalopolises. Under the direction of Viktor L. Semenov, the principal architect of the 1935 Plan, the city was colonized by 'city complexes' that would surround the centre, each with its own economic and administrative autonomy and enclosed in recreational green spaces.[11]

Islands and Lines – Quartalis and Magistralis in the 1935 General Master Plan for Moscow

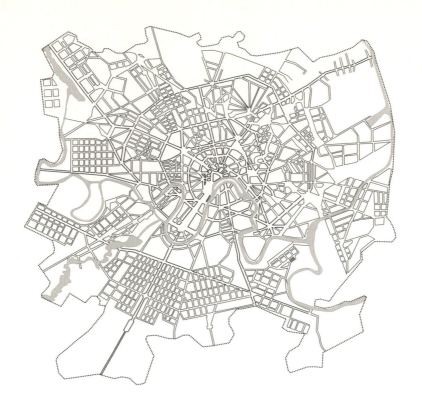

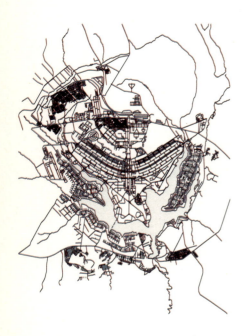

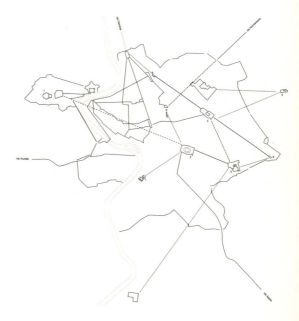

Mobility as Landmark – Ritual circulation in Brasilia

Points and Lines, Urban Minimalism – Sixtus V's Rome

Instead of investing only in landmarks, the core of the building of the new Moscow as the Capital of State Communism was conceived in the construction of the *quartalys:* archetypical housing superblocks with various infrastructural services; each totalled about 15 hectares, basically a small city within the city.[12] *Quartalys* were literally islands distributed in the city to regulate and define an equal density and distribution of services. Complementary to this was a set of large-scale public and administrative buildings as free-standing centres, the new *magistralys* (wide roads), a system of city parks and green corridors, and the creation of an impressive public transport network.

In 1949 the urban form laid out by Semenov was further articulated by an archipelago of seven monumental skyscrapers, the 'Seven Sisters'. The *quartalys*, the metro stations and the Seven Sisters became a veritable urban grammar, which through repetition and formal coherence kept Moscow from becoming merely a flamboyant expression of power and constructed an iconic urban form that has resisted both the decline of the Soviet era and the subsequent invasion of the free market.[13]

Exceptional Case

The construction of Brasilia was a response to a political and conceptual impetus: an attempt to redesign the geography of the country, shifting the position of the centre from its economic and historical location along the east coast, toward the hinterland, in the literal geographic centre of the national territory. The hinterland of Brazil had never been inhabited, and during Portuguese colonization it had been a refuge for slaves who escaped from the coast. For this reason Brasilia had no direct economical or social reason to be founded. Yet, its construction was accompanied by the most daring political programme: the new capital would have to be able to present the 'imaginary' of modern Brazil to its citizens, as the new cultural centrality for the entire country on the verge of breaking, once and for all, with its colonial heritage.

Lucio Costa won the national competition for the master plan of the new capital at the beginning of 1957, and despite the polemics that would accompany the results, this seemed to be the most congruent choice. Following the construction of the Ministry of Culture and Education in Rio in 1936, Costa was appointed head of the Office for the National Historic and Artistic Heritage (SPHAN) and from this position was able to direct a very specific process of thorough reinterpretation of past, present and future.[14] Costa, in those years, produced a new architecture that was the synthesis of modernist, regionalist or neo-colonialist attempts to distil a new language for the Latin-American *res-publica*.[15] The result was the creation of an architectural 'order' at the service of the public domain that had little to do with the European orthodox modern tradition but that would offer a formal vocabulary for the creation of exceptional formal and typological solutions.

In the *Plano Piloto* it was Oscar Niemeyer who largely used this 'order' with great invention, while Costa concentrated on offering a precise palimpsest for the disposition of these monuments. While in Chandigarh, the new Capital City of Punjab, Le Corbusier concentrated on the architecture of the Capitol, leaving the development of the city itself to his collaborators, Costa left the monumental buildings to Niemeyer and focused on the basic civic iconic form of Brasilia: the *Superquadra*, a 300 x 300 m composition of radically simple residential slabs fused by a complex system of open space.

The history of these 50 years of Brasilia reveals, on the one hand, how the deployment of this language accelerated the inhabitants' process of cultural identification with their own city,[16] and on the other, how the legible form of the city – the crossing of the two axes – was able to preserve, despite of the immense growth of the satellite cities within the federal district, a regional model in the form of a latent archipelago. So far this latent archipelago

Brasilia: Building the Zero Degree City
Crossing as the political form

has grown by means of satellite cities devoid of any sense of centrality.

In a project conducted at the Berlage Institute with an international team of ten architects,[17] and presented at this Rotterdam Biennale, we address Brasilia by building on the principle of Costa's project and focus on the present geography of satellite cities in the form of an archipelago of archetypical building and public spaces.[18] With this project we aim to transform the original idea of the *Plano Piloto* into a more self-aware regional model, by imbuing each of the satellite cities with that dignity that marks the difference between an *urbs* and a *civitas* – infrastructure and centrality – and that is, as Costa explained, 'the virtues and attributes appropriate to a real capital city'.[19]

The City Is a Concept!

Today we have to read these examples away from the clichés of totalitarian politics, top-down urban form, and other stereotypical alibis through which we used to edit past vicissitudes of cities in order to feel comfortable in the intellectual and political mediocrity of our present moment. What is interesting and relevant today about the above examples is that they address the city first as a conceptual reality – as an *idea* –to be immediately incarnated in its material constitution. In a world of liberal-democratic imperialism, in which cities are represented in terms of statistics, constructed out of floating and empty landmarks, and inhabited by an ubiquitous periphery left to the despotism of the market economy, we have to rediscover – in new political terms – the city

Public Canopy
'Interior' of Lucio Costa's Superquadra

as a concept, as a space through which to *decide*, and not simply produce, contemporary urbanization. If the political is the decision on the organization of the space among individuals, and the formal is the very materialization of that space, then cities must be seen as political forms: *capital* examples of a conscious, and politically responsible, idea of the world.

1   See Idefonso Cerdà, *Teoría general de la urbanización* (Barcelona: Imp. Española, 1867).
2   Aldo Rossi concluded his book *The Architecture of the City* by asserting the importance of political choices as propelling moment for the evolution of the city. 'The issue of politics concerns the problem of choices. Who chose the image of the city? The answer must be the city itself, but always and only trough its political institutions'. Aldo Rossi, *L'architettura della città* (Padua: Marsilio, 1966).
3 See Cornelius Castoriadis, *The Imaginary Institutions of Society* (Cambridge, MA: The MIT Press, 1998).
4   Ibid., 141.
5   See *Manfredo Tafuri, Ricerca del Rinascimento* (Turin: Einaudi, 1992).
6   See Cesare D'onofrio, *Gli Obelischi di Roma. Storia e Urbanistica di una Citta dall'eta antica al XX secolo* (Rome: Romana Editrice, 1992).
7   See Maurizio Fagiolo, *La Roma di Sisto V* (Rome: Palombi, 1977); Luigi Spezzaferro, *La Roma di Sisto V*, (Rome: Carte Segrete, 1983).
8   This paragraph summarizes a chapter devoted to the urban development of Rome from the time of Donato Bramante to the time of Giovanni Battista Piranesi, developed at length in Pier Vittorio Aureli, *The Possibility of an Absolute Architecture*, forthcoming from MIT Press, Anybooks.
9   See Alessandro De Magistris, 'Landscapes of Social Realism', *Rassegna* no. 79, 1999 (Architecture and Public Administration).
10 See Rolf Jenni, *Learning from Moscow: Planning Principles of the 1935 General Plan for Reconstruction and Its Political Relevance*, unpublished paper developed within the Second Year Programme on the City, conducted by Pier Vittorio Aureli at the Berlage Institute, Rotterdam, academic year 2005-2006.
11 See Viktor Semenov, *Pritsipyy Sovietskvo Grandostrojtel' stava* (Moscow, 1945).
12 See Alexander Saslavskij, *Zilioskno-Kommunalnoje Knosiaistvo SSSR* (Leningrad, 1948).
13 This paragraph summarizes the studio research developed within the Programme on the City, conducted by Pier Vittorio Aureli at the Berlage Institute during the academic year 2005-2006. See *Paradigm Moscow: Redefining the People's Metropolitan Consciousness*, (Rotterdam: Berlage Institute research report no. 9, 2006).
14 See Lucio Costa, *Razoes da nova arquitetura (1934)*, in: Lucio Costa, *Registro de uma vivencia* (Rio de Janeiro, 1995).
15 See the projects for the Park Hotel in Nova Friburgo (1940) and the houses Barao de Saavedra (1940) and Hungria Machado (1940).
16 See Adrián Gorelik, 'Brasilia: Museum of Modernity', *Casabella* 753, March 2007.
17 Second Year Unit, 'Capital Cities – Brasilia: City as Political Form' at the Berlage Institute, Rotterdam, academic year 2006-2007.
18 See *A Project for Brasilia. Archipelago, Border and Landscape* (Rotterdam: Berlage Institute research report no. 14, 2007).
19 See Lucio Costa's Competition Report in *The Architectural Review*, December 1957.

Archipelago Brasilia. Strategic plan for the region of Brasilia

The project proposes a system of centralities developed as the border of each the cities of Brasilia. Project elaborated within the "Research on the City" program at the Berlage Institute. Project Team: Pier Vittorio Aureli, Martino Tattara (Research Directors) Adolfo Despradel Catrain, Elena Gissi, Sahil Abdul Latheef, Miha Pesecs, Lama Sfeir, Melisa Vargas Rivera, Yvette Vasourkova, Juan Bernardo Vera Rueda. Zhong Ping Wu, Shanshan Xue.

Archipelago Brasilia. Garden on the border, community complex on the border of Sobradinho, Brasilia. Plans

View of the gardens on the border. Beauty, 'and by beauty we mean simplicity, largeness, and renewed severity of discipline; we mean a return to form' (Thomas Mann)

Capital versus Capital
Reconsidering the Power of Nation-Building

IND (Inter.National.Design)
Arman Akdogan
Felix Madrazo

Capital City is projected as a designated center within an urban formation whereby political decision takes precedent over market-controlled economic forces.
Pier Vittorio Aureli

Power
When, on 10 December 1997, the President of Kazakhstan Nursultan Abish-uly Nazarbayev announced his intention to move the capital from Almaty (Alma Ata in Soviet times) to Astana, meaning 'capital' (formerly Akmola and Tseloningrad) no one could reverse the decision. 'The move had been ordered by the President and there was no higher authority.'[1]

'The thinking behind this deeply unpopular move was political.'[2] In an age of economic predominance and low-key politicians, the political decision indeed seems to have taken precedence 'over market-controlled economic forces'. It appears, as some critics have pointed out, a purely political move by the Kazakh leader to 'Kazakhize'[3] a region dominated by Russians since the eighteenth century. Some even go as far as to speculate that 'this shift is designed to pre-empt any territorial ambitions from Moscow should an expansionist government come to power in the region'.[4]

But before focusing on political muscle, it is worthwhile to give a brief history of this emerging Central-Asian giant.

History
'Native Kazakhs, a mix of Turkic and Mongol nomadic tribes who migrated into the region in the thirteenth century, were rarely united as a single nation. The area was conquered by Russia in the eighteenth century, and Kazakhstan became a Soviet Republic in 1936. During the 1950s and 1960s agricultural 'Virgin Lands' programme, Soviet citizens were encouraged to help cultivate Kazakhstan's northern pastures. This influx of immigrants (mostly Russians, but also some other deported nationalities) skewed the ethnic mixture and enabled non-Kazakhs to outnumber natives.'[5]

Kazakhstan, the ninth largest country on earth, is approximately the size of Western Europe. Its population, roughly equivalent to that of the Netherlands, occupies an area 65 times larger than Holland. Most of its inhabitants are situated in the southern part of the country, while Kazakhstan's great heart remains empty, with densities averaging less than one person per km^2. The northern steppe is chiefly inhabited by Russians, while the Kazakh people dominate the southern part of the country, including its former capital, Almaty. People of other nationalities – Ukrainians, Germans, Tartars, Uzbeks and Koreans – are also dispersed throughout the territory.

Why the Capital was Moved
When asked the reason behind the president's decision to make Astana the new capital, Chikanayev, Nazarbayev's architectural advisor, admitted that Almaty was heading towards a 'dead end economically'.[6] To liberate it, Nazarbayev chose to free it of its political burden. Another hypothesis was that the creation of the

new capital implied substantial monetary transfer, estimated at around two billion dollars per year for several years to come,[7] and that this was needed in order to diversify the economy[8] while Kazakhstan quickly becomes a net oil export champion[9] (its oil reserves are the largest to be found since the 1967 discovery of Alaska's reserves). Economists are preoccupied with the sudden dependency on oil exports and its implication for the local currency, the Tenge. Worried economists call this negative phenomenon the 'Dutch disease', a term that originated in Holland after the discovery of North Sea gas resources. Dutch Disease describes the sudden process of deindustrialization of a nation's economy that occurs when the discovery of a natural resource raises the value of that nation's currency, making manufactured goods less competitive with other nations, increasing imports and decreasing exports.

'Diversify and survive' seems to be the motto, or as the World Bank states on its website: 'The economy of Kazakhstan is heavily dependent on a few commodities and faces the daunting challenge of diversification.'[10] Because the share of GDP related to oil exports is growing explosively, with a projection of 90 per cent dependency by the year 2030, one could speculate that President Nazarbayev's economic advisors proposed the quick shift of the capital in order to stimulate the economy. This move would have been designed to activate sectors of the economy such as infrastructure, real-estate development and land transformation, the main engines of the city. Economical reasons disguised as political controversy?

Political Coexistence: The Challenge

Capital Cities are discernible not only as capitals of state, but especially as representations of shared ideas of coexistence that form a political space.
Pier Vittorio Aureli

Regardless of past discussions about the 'hidden agenda' of Astana, the newborn capital needs to adapt at full speed from

Astana's economic and administrative centre on the left bank. View looking towards the west, towards the national oil company 'KazMunaiGaz' quarter.

Presidential palace on the left bank

The golden globe of the Bayterek tower, with the hand relief of president Nazarbayev.

The president's golden hand relief points towards the presidential palace and the peace and agreement palace.

its previous status of a small, mostly Russian, cold and quiet town into the international political centre of the new oil superpower of Central Asia. Above all, it must aspire to embrace the symbol of capital city of the recently recognized Kazakh nation. The challenge for Astana is certainly cultural; a massive migration of enthusiastic Kazakhs from the south could easily launch a cultural conflict with the local population composed of 70 per cent Russian, Ukrainian and German people. For example, although construction is underway at full speed, most airlines still hesitate to fly directly there; families of politicians prefer to remain in Almaty for now. Could you read that as resistance? Or will empty buildings finally attract adventurers in search of a better life amid an optimistic capital city that adopts all identities? Can the design of a city allow everyone to be comfortable and be represented properly?

When evaluating the amount of power that the president exercises, one only needs to read the design agenda of the capital and compare it to Brasilia or Chandigarth in order to assess that the architect's big-time role is gone. It seems that the utopian formal visions of politicians like Nazarbayev are leading the way in the creation of cities, while architects quietly remain in the background trying to interpret the politicians personal dreams. For example, world famous Metabolist architect Kisho Kurokawa, who won the competition for the urban master plan of Astana, openly affirms that he designed the capital as if it were a building for a client – the president himself – not for a country or a hypothetical society.[11] Yet could Nazarvayev's ideas of design lead the capital and the young country into a peaceful coexistence of ethnicity, religion, and interests? Could architecture and design – and even symbolism – achieve a level of spatial coexistence between Astana's established inhabitants (mostly Russians, Ukrainians and Germans that were deported or moved here under Stalin and Khrushchev) and the newcomers from Almaty (mostly Kazakhs)? Could a master

Astana Mosque on the left bank, designed by Lebanese architect Charles Hadife.

Construction workers from former Russian countries are resting in front of the National Library and National Archive.

plan help to establish these new relationships successfully?

If peaceful coexistence is the main agenda of a capital for the people of Kazakhstan, how would the physical erasure of existing Soviet urbanism and architecture initiate a healing process? Or would it deepen the differences? Can we call this a metabolic city? How could the Soviet city of Tselinograd (now Astana) 'recognized as one of the most memorable achievements of Soviet Urban Planning',[12] be remembered, preserved, or recycled? Could promoting ethnic identity and specificity enhance the quality of coexistence, as opposed to the generic and neutral Soviet style urbanization characterized by its repetition of modules and universality of man? Or can the creation of a Kazakh capital city on top of a previous Soviet one be a form of 'compensation for past injustices'? And yet, to what extent should the new capital Kazakhize the former Soviet city?

Capital versus Capital
One can assess the uniqueness of the political, economic and architectural developments of Astana by comparing it to the capital left behind in Almaty. Now that Almaty is designated the financial centre of Kazakhstan; its powerful commercial clans will dominate the future development of the city. Almaty also wants to exploit its entertainment status (it was a prime winter sports destination in Soviet times); its model is Las Vegas. If market forces gain power in Almaty, politics should do the same in Astana. But what is an apt urban model for Astana? Rome? Washington? Canberra? Both cities, Astana and Almaty, will be led by, if not opposite, then at least contradictory terms: politics and economy. The amount of difference they project depends on their power sources and diversification.

The Art of Mixing Master Plans
The urban expansion required of Astana is so large that President Nazarbayev has gone into several phases of consultation through local competitions, municipality plans, international competitions

and even direct commissions. All of the proposals have favoured the expansion of the city towards the south bank of the Ishim River. Despite Kazakhs nationalist discourses, all of the proposals, with the exception of Ak Orda (1996), have preserved its previous Soviet layout. This layout is clearly conceived as a linear structure of three bands of land use with a generous approach to recreational areas along the Ishim River.

Between 1996-2001, three significant master plans with different backgrounds were taken into consideration.

Ak Orda – 1996
This national competition for a master plan was conducted by the Ministry of Construction of the Republic of Kazakhstan and Architects Union of Kazakhstan. The proposal by the design and construction company Ak Orda was selected for first prize. President Nazarbayev was not satisfied with the results, however, and recommended inviting international designers for a new competition.

Kurokawa – 1998
As a result of the new competition *International Tender for the Draft of the Master Plan of Development of the New Center of Astana,* Kisho Kurokowa's master plan was selected, out of 40 entries, to be realized. Kurokowa's master plan concepts, which he has been developing since the 1960s, were articulated in Astana as Metabolic City Application and Abstract Symbolism. His plan concurred with the existing linear zoning. In addition to developing his master plan strategies, Kurokawa was politically obliged to bring funds from Japan for his master plan ideas. Luckily he found a solution with grants from Japan. But during that period Kurukowa faced a more severe obstacle: an alternative master plan proposed by the Bin Laden Group, to which the Kazakh government was giving serious consideration.

Saudi Group 'Bin Laden' – 2001
Disregarding the 1998 competition results, a new master plan powered by Arab funds was conceived in close cooperation with

Soviet master plan of 1962 for Tselinograd (Astana)

Master plan by Saudi Bin Ladin Group (2000)

Master plan by Kisho Kurokawa (2001)

Master plan by Ak Orda (1996)
Master plan by Kisho Kurokawa (1998)

the municipality. It was based on actual conditions such as existing roads and ongoing residential development. 'Obviously, this master plan tried to meet the reality of the city rather than to establish a certain concept.'[13] It was also more clear in the monumentality of the city than Kurokawas idea of metabolic change. A green ring boldly encircles the city. The political headquarters included a Washingtonian mall aligned with an axis that pointed to ancient Kazakh settlements.

Kurokawa – 2001

Kurokawa did not give up the project; instead he chose to assimilate the concepts of the 'Bin Laden' group and kept most of its skeleton while adding touches of metabolic discourse here and there. He also emphasized the importance of the symbolic power of clear simple shapes such as domes, pyramids, and so forth, although these have been interpreted with such heavy-handed examples as Norman Foster's pyramid of peace.

The collection of master plans created in Astana's short history of planning reveals the lack of critical power that portrays the battle of architects, politicians and global investors under the umbrella of one man's hand. A Babel of ideas that crossed each other without apparent conflict, that were added up without a common agenda, except that of building a new capital. A diagram of global power?

1 Monica Whitlock reports from Almaty, BBC 6 December 1997.
2 Ibid.
3 Formation of Almolinsk (present Astana), nineteenth century, by Tsubokara Takashi, 2003.
4 Monica Whitlock reports from Almaty, BBC 6 December 1997
5 CIA – World Fact Book, https://www.cia.gov/cia/publications/factbook/geos/kz.html.
6 The Kazakhstan Klondike, Central Asia Power House, Der Spiegel by Christian Neef. November 09, 2006. http://www.spiegel.de/international/spiegel/0,1518,447451,00.html.
7 Ibid.
8 Top world oil exporters, http://www.eia.doe.gov/emeu/cabs/topworldtables1_2.html.
9 World Bank, Kazakhstan, Country profile 2006.
10 'Astana as the New Capital – Masterplan by Japanese architect Kisho Kurokawa', by Ttusbikara Takashi.
11 Tselinograd (Present Astana) - The Construction of a Socialist City By Tsubokura Takashi, December 24, 2003. http://www.astanamp.kepter.kz/sub2.html.
12 The Kazakhstan Klondike, op. cit. (note 6). Up to two million Kazakh people lost their lives when the Soviets 'de Kulaked' the region in the 1920s.
13 Formation of Akmolinsk (present Astana), nineteenth century, by Tsubokara Takashi, 2003.

Cadavre Exquis Lebanese
Channeling the Power of Imagination

WORK Architecture Company
Amale Andraos
Dan Wood

With the end of the 1975-1990 Lebanese Civil War, a public-private consortium called Solidere is formed to rebuild downtown Beirut. Announcing the rebirth of Beirut as a global city, a new visionary master plan is quickly drafted. Squatters are expelled, mines cleared, owners given stocks in exchange for property and buildings deemed significant restored with eerie precision. Symbolic public spaces are rebuilt and new ones are created, signed by celebrity architects. Ground floors become chic cafés while upper floors are left empty – ghostly, overpriced office space waiting for the economic jump start.

Announced as a new deal to revive the economy and to create a renewed, shared social ground and symbolic political centre for the country's multiple populations, the reconstruction of downtown Beirut leads instead to its privatization and Disneyfication. The Solidere plan replaces what was once a bustling mix of people and unedited buildings with a polished and controlled image of its old 1930s self. The centre –deserted throughout the war – is again emptied of real urban life, turned into an artificially reconstructed stage set, ready only for consumption by global media and hordes of tourists and investors. As a capital city, Beirut's centre no longer represents what it claims to include but instead, what it has come to exclude: the middle and poorer classes, who see in downtown's reconceptualization the formation of a country that neither represents them nor is their own.

Ironically, it is only in 2005, with the assassination of Prime Minister Rafik Hariri (the founder of Solidere), and the massive demonstrations from all parties that followed, that downtown Beirut reacquires its status as a symbolic centre. This renewed position is further confirmed by the summer 2006 Israeli-Lebanese war, during which hundreds of thousands of refugees occupy the heart of the city, and by the recent antigovernment demonstrations and permanent occupation of the centre's public spaces. Regaining its relevance, downtown Beirut is again the site of power, political struggle, representation and social compression.

It is here that our project situates itself. With the evident failure of burying difference, conflict, surprise and complexity behind a clean and simplified narrative whose singularity of vision leaves no room for simultaneous multiple stories, we propose to re-create downtown Beirut as a temporal *Cadavre Exquis*. Building on the surrealist tradition of setting up processes that engender situations, rather than reducing the city to yet another instantaneous master plan, we propose a sequential series of possible scenarios, 'epochs' whose final combination constitutes the 'Cadavre Exquis Lebanese', a fictionally re-created complexity willed into being through the power of the imagination.

Tent City
Claiming the tent and not the skyscraper as the true symbol of twenty-first-century modernity, Beirut revives its mythical past as centre for intellectual thought and free debate. Building on the current occupation, a thick infrastructure of tents is deployed across downtown, serving an

array of functions from large auditoriums to intimate coffee shops where East, West, God, Capitalism and the advantages and inconveniences of either democratic or totalitarian rule are debated. Relieved to see its critics, free thinkers and troublemakers leave their home countries for downtown Beirut's refuge, the rest of the world funds and supports the camp in its desperate realization that if debate can not be silenced, it can at least be exiled.

Urban War Coliseum

Faced with its failure as a 'historical tourism' destination and displaced by the UAE as the new economic, cultural and entertainment centre in the region, Beirut develops the 'city of continuous conflict'. Harnessing the world powers' need to fight proxy wars, Beirut sets up an enormous terrain on the abandoned landfill north of downtown – a reinvented coliseum – for the enactment of conflict. Combining its knowledge of real battleground with the latest developments in video games, Beirut sets up a sophisticated environment for simulated urban warfare, surrounded by observation stands. Having given up internal conflicts, the entire country prospers from the income generated by the game.

Metro

As sectarian differences ease, travel – and traffic – between the centre and outlying neighbourhoods increases. The government convinces Beirutis that a metro will end traffic problems, create an open transportation system for all Lebanese, and – perhaps most importantly – serve as a place of refuge when regional tensions inevitably rise. Eight lines weave throughout Beirut, connecting Muslim neighbourhoods with Christian enclaves, the universities and the Palestinian camps; the downtown with the mountains and the airport. The metro achieves a dramatic restructuring of the collective mental image of the city, connecting places, neighbourhoods and zones previously imagined as isolated citadels (worsened by traffic congestion) with a singular network.

Cut-and-fill urbanism

1841

1923

1936

1975 (pre-war)

1990 (postwar)

1992 (solidere)

1996

2006

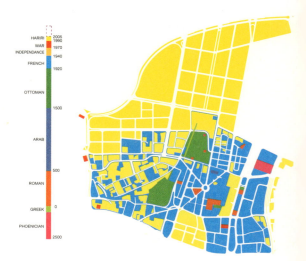

Museum City

Bunkerology

As in times past, Beirutis find themselves shuffling between the above- and below-ground worlds during times of crisis. Now, however, the underground is a collective space, a shared subterranean safety net connecting the city and containing restaurants, classrooms, public spaces, and so forth. As the metro expands to accommodate new programmes, important archaeological remains are unearthed. The stations and excavations eventually join; by default, the metro/bunkers become an immense archaeological museum as well.

Cedar Evolution

Throughout the ages, Lebanese cedar embodied strength, refinement and eternity. Today the famous cedar forest has but a few trees left standing, surrounded by barbed wire. In a renewed attempt to properly represent its varied population, the Lebanese government retires from the war games business and turns to landscape and this most neutral symbol of the nation to cover the coliseum site. Reversing the horizontal landfill sprawling into the water, the city creates an island and builds a new mount at its heart – an experimental cedar nursery. Moving away from the weight of history, the city turns to its green past to finally invest in its future, the environment.

Iconic Programmes

Refocusing on downtown for the final phase of the city's re-emergence, a series of larger-scaled structures are proposed to augment the city's tents. Instead of historic pastiche – tried and rejected with Solidere's failed plan – the new projects are proposed as contemporary celebrations of Lebanese identity, their iconographic quality provided by the buildings' programmes themselves. These 'iconic programmes' include Vertical Souks, Silicon Allee (a plastic surgery centre), a Narguileh-smoking Headquarters, a Lebanese food Tabkhopolis, a national Public School and the Fairuzeum, dedicated to Lebanon's most popular and symbolic singer.

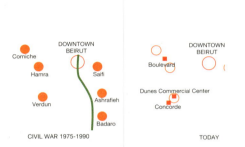

From consolidated centre to multiple, disconnected centres

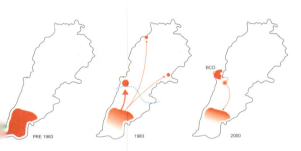

Israeli Aggression/Shiite migration

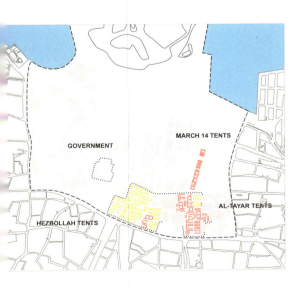

Existing downtown occupation, 2007

Martyrs' Square, downtown Beirut, 1950s
Martyrs' Square/Green Line, 1991

Reconstruction, 1997
Restoration/Privatization

Downtown edited through selective restoration

Solidere's nostalgic vision
Reconstruction/Disneyfication

Downtown tents/protest
14 March 2005: Downtown reclaimed

Capital Cities — Beirut

Aerial view of downtown Beirut, 2003　　　　　　　　　　　　　　　　　　　　　　　　Urban War Coliseum – Tent City

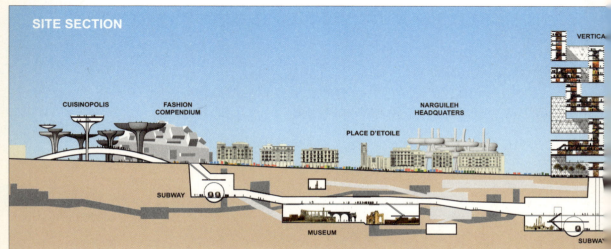

Site section

Cadavre Exquis Lebanese

47 — Capital Cities — Beirut

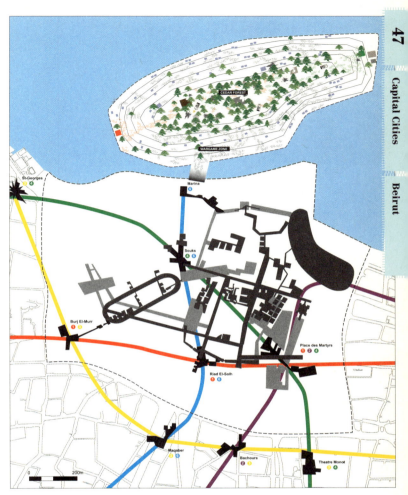

Centerechtomy

As the city grows, a radical solution to the issue of representation is proposed: remove the centre. Moving the boundaries of the 'Downtown Master Plan' to the edges of the country itself, the entire territory is reconceived of as a city to be designed. Significant institutions are dispersed throughout Lebanon, connected by branches of the metro. A series of ecological 'islands' are created for experimental farming, energy production, carbon credits (increasingly valuable) and recreation. What used to be the centre, Beirut, now becomes simply the city-state's model node.

What's more, Lebanon is now an inspiration for the world's increasing number of mega-cities. Difference and complexity coexist with national identity, discussion and debate have replaced armed struggle. The new configuration of the city-state is networked, flexible, and creative. Increased density and urbanization, combined with rural exodus, allow larger and larger patches of nature outside of the networked hubs. Other cities take notice and begin to exploit their differences as sources of strength and inspiration, making connections and celebrating complexity.

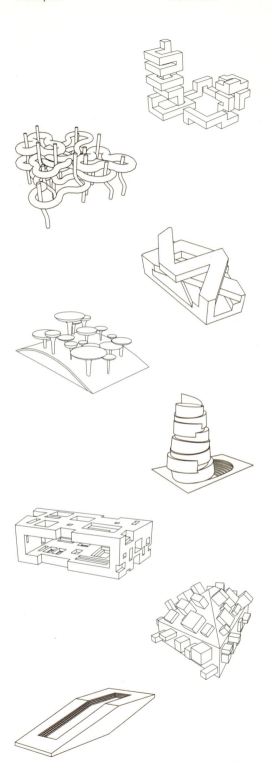

Nargileh Headquaters

Vertical Souks

Cusinopolis

Silicon Allee

Public School

Fairuzeum

Center for Preservation, Research and Exportation of Cedar

Fashion Compendium

Cadavre Exquis Lebanese

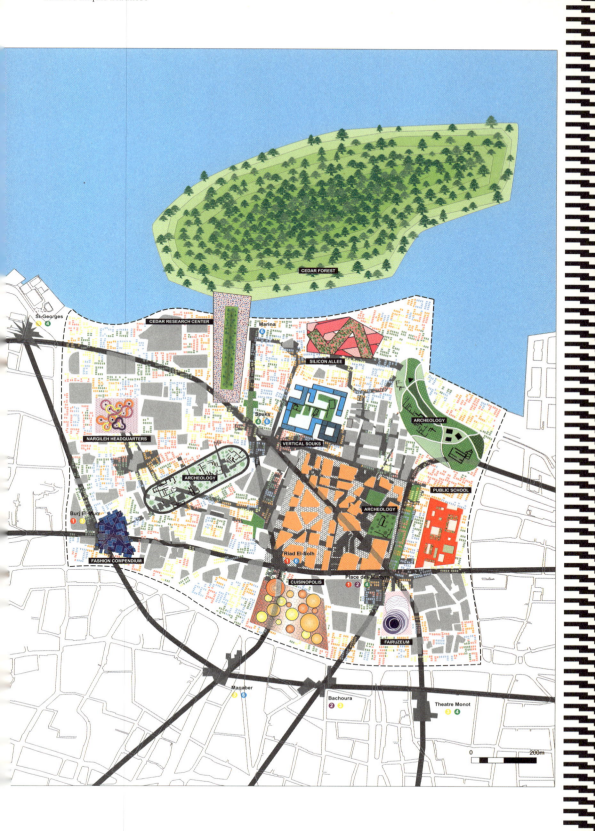

Moscow Prefab

Moscow Prefabricated
Embracing the Power of Mass-Production

Alexander Sverdlov

This project addresses one aspect of Moscow's present situation; namely the city's appearance. Moscow is a booming city in an aesthetic crisis.

Moscow Yesterday and Today

The city as a 'machine of civilization', with its spatio-cultural mechanisms ensuring social cohesion – and of course, democracy – has not become a self-propagating tradition in Russia. If modern cities were created through the development of socioeconomic relationships, whereby economies were the engines of urbanization, Russian cities, and Moscow specifically, were made by political will. Modern Moscow, as we knew it, was a city of monumental Stalinist prospects and endless fields of Khrushev/Brezhnev industrial housing. Moscow did not happen on its own; it was decided. Every level of design, from the greatness of the urban plan to the minuteness of a façade detail, was shaped by a single client and a single architect who were one and the same entity: the state. An exemplary communist city was built – as exemplary, and as communist, as those in power could achieve.

Who is the typical Moscow architect of the late Soviet era? An anonymous person wearing a white protective coat, working in one of the state design offices with more than a thousand others like him. His purpose is to optimize the design of the anonymous housing block (BC-31 it could be called) in order to make it more cost-effective. His colleagues will later insert this optimal housing block into the most optimal urban configuration. That is how the Soviet city will be reproduced.

Who is designing the Moscow of today? As the state design offices are subdivided into numerous studios, because state commissions are just a small part of their portfolio, the private architect enters the arena. After years of anorexia, Russian architectural design has reached the moment of liberty: new housing, offices, and retail require the invention of new forms and plastic language. At the same time, the debate started on how the capital should look. The official (authorities') position is that Moscow suffered tremendously from late Soviet design, and these mistakes should be corrected. That resulted in a campaign against modernist architecture in the city centre. The vocabulary of rectangular silhouettes and repetitive façades was given an anathema, and 'Undoing the Soviet' became a motto for the architects as well as the developers. Instead, new opportunities for architecture should be seen as historical inspiration. The slogan 'new historical centre' was put on the banner. The iconography of the new buildings, rather than its functionality or urban significance, became the main focus of the design . . .

The current transformation of Moscow is very much defined by the new order – capitalism. Private entities define the place, function and shape of new structures. These groups claim the city's most valuable sites and fill them with new matter. Despite attempts by the authorities to maintain coherence of the existing and the newly built, the city has collected a disparate assortment of autistic designs, which, even given the huge size of the city, have transformed Moscow radically.

The aura of the centre, which used to guarantee the city's prominence as a capital, has evaporated. Moscow's centre can no longer serve as a point of cultural reference for the rest of the city, or for the rest of the country.

DSK (Housing Construction Factories)
Stalinist Moscow was a Moscow that projected the ideal image of the city through the new iconography of architecture. It was the city created by strategically monumentalizing elective parts, while the major mass of the city was left in neglect. Khrushchev's Moscow was a Moscow of efficient housing quantity and speed of production. Prefabricated housing factories were there to provide dwellings for everyone, and quickly generated housing mass was a priority.

Today, the periphery of the city is still the domain of prefabricated construction. Of the 5 million m² of annual residential surplus in Moscow, 4.5 million m² is built as prefab housing. Ultimately, the formerly state-owned construction factories are the enterprises building 90 per cent of Moscow today. Holding enormous power and unlimited production possibilities, DSK remain the true masters of the Moscow skyline.

And yet the former pragmatic approach to the design of prefabricated housing no longer exists. The industry, as well as the designers, is mainly concerned with achieving maximum diversity in a building's appearance and configuration... New buildings should have tops that refer to the city, bottoms that address the public space, and an overall configuration that provides a sense of place. All needed for giving compulsory identity to new residential areas.

The periphery of the city is also an area where prefabricated mass housing borders the landscape of dachas (Russian word for second house, used predominantly for leisure). Here the capital anchors itself in the rest of the country and the collision of the large-scale industrial housing with the micro-scale dachas becomes the frontier and the showcase of Moscow. At the same time the two scales

Soviet prefabricated housing: sameness dictated by necessity

Post-Soviet panel catalogue: design for diversification. Buildings require individual character

Prefabricated housing faces the countryside

53 Capital Cities Moscow

The dachas show a culture of intimacy with their material environment, a culture of intelligent leisure in simplified conditions. The industrial housing, remaining more of a forced necessity, has not yet produced a meaningful way of living have never come together in a meaningful way. Is there an opportunity here for some specific urban quality?

Project: 400 Towers for Moscow

This project proposes a design for the overall prefabricated production of the city. It assumes that the representational power of Moscow as the capital will rest on its periphery. Neither the city centre nor the areas claimed by private developers for exclusive projects will be part of this scheme. The project examines the production of housing not as an urban plan, but as an aesthetic model that is self-replicating. Taking the power of mass production as a starting point, the project will embrace the whole greatness of 4.5 million m² of annual housing production.

400 prefabricated towers for Moscow is:
no neighbourhood
no public space
no ground floor
no skyline
no composition
no sentiments
no shame

The 400 towers are located at the edge of the city. Independent of the location, all 400 of them are stretched from south to north for the optimal orientation. The towers are put in the dacha area, yet the towers do not belong to the dacha's urban texture. They are accessible directly by car, which brings the inhabitant straight into the building. Since there is no public space for the towers and the footprint is minimized, the landscape of dachas can retain its soft quality. Moreover, the presence of the towers might even guarantee the preservation of the dacha's environment.

The design of the tower is sanitized from any recent additions:
• All 400 towers are the same
• There is one type of panel used
• There is no ground floor addressing the public space, there is a parking garage instead
• There is no rooftop addressing the skyline of the city, the tower is flat

Moscow skylines

The presence of towers should guarantee the preservation of dacha

Liberated from any illusions, having given up every unnecessary addition, the tower embodies the true essence of prefabrication: endless repetition of one element. There are no sentiments in its architecture. The only architectural design allowed within this scheme is the slight variation of texture and colour of the joints between the panels.

Liberation from the design and from the necessity to create identity opens up possibilities for the new 'whole'. A form of cohabitation, which becomes a new frontier of Moscow . . .

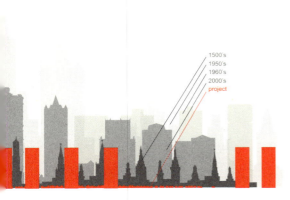

0 towers mark the edge of the city

'The Entrepreneurial City uses architecture not only as a symbol of power, but as the capital of a symbolic economy. From factories to office towers and high-tech campuses, buildings create a framework for economic power – embodying the geographical distance between home and workplace, the social distance between managers and workers, and the moral distance between leading and declining firms.'

Public Architecture and the Social Framework of Power

The theme of Architecture and Power is a dispiriting one, and never more so than today. While invading armies kill buildings as well as people in Africa and the Middle East, fear of terrorist attacks in all regions of the world creates new walls between enemies both real and imagined. Cities that are not directly at war feel as though they are in a permanent campaign for survival – choked by air pollution, fighting for affordable housing, pursuing the elusive prize of economic growth. In richer cities, corporate and public clients are more monolithic than ever, and insist on paying the least money for the most spectacular effect. Design programmes focus on surveillance and social control, and real estate developers pursue those elements of architecture – and those architects – who will create economic value.

No doubt this stark outline reflects a failure of courage among public officials and architects as servants of power, but it also suggests cities under the influence of place-marketing and global competition. Paradoxically, the focus on competing cities hides a general perception that the city as an inspirational idea is dead.

The 'death of the city' in the USA after the Second World War reflected the loss of power of centrality. Factories and wealthy residents had already started to leave cities in the early 1900s, and downtown business districts struggled to maintain both their high level of services and their prestige. Beginning with construction of the national highway system in the 1950s, public investment also shifted to the suburbs. At the same time, new corporate headquarters and modern factories with large shop floors sped jobs and residents out of cities instead of bringing in new resources. Urban renewal programmes financed by the federal government tried to save the city centre by tearing down old districts and replacing them with office and residential towers. But newly built public housing projects became warehouses for the poor and ethnic minorities rather than temporary shelters for stable families.

Cities suffered from growing poverty, crime and – in the urban critic Jane Jacobs' influential work – the bulldozer effect of large-scale building projects that erased neighbourhoods' individual character. Jacobs famously condemned the arrogance of modern architects and city planners who, in her view, had the power to destroy the social vitality of the streets.[1] By contrast, her contemporary, the sociologist Herbert Gans, blamed the *lack* of power of city planners and working class residents. Experts and the poor lacked the access to power real estate developers enjoyed. While city dwellers wondered why their rental apartments were rundown and the streets were not clean, developers made alliances with mayors to tear down their old districts and build more impressive – and more expensive – new ones. Unable to influence public officials and unwilling to believe that they could be displaced, poorer urban residents lost their homes to the highways, office complexes, social housing projects and upscale, high-rise apartment houses that Jacobs despised.[2] Looking back at the conditions Jacobs and Gans describe, we see

US cities confronting a crisis of modernity familiar in Europe from the age of Haussmann. No one knew how to balance capital investment in the built environment, social integration and democratic state power.

During the 1960s and '70s, while suburban shopping centres and office parks boomed, old working class districts in the city, their residents and the factories that supported them were first abandoned and then aestheticized by the selective memory of gentrification. The federal government retreated from financing public housing and criticized city governments for spending too much money on social welfare. At the same time, the city's imminent demise was promoted in popular urban horror films that featured big cities – often New York – menaced by gang warfare and graffiti, where civility was out of place and men and women were powerless to defend their homes.

Since the 1980s – on the other side of gentrification and inner-city revitalization – the 'death of the city' has reflected despair about the combined effects of globalization and electronic communication. The fast pace of social and technological changes has moved social interaction into cyberspace, shifted good jobs overseas and enabled an ever larger population, including new immigrants, to live and work in suburbs. But the death of the city also signifies the abandonment of cultural models that we associate with mid twentieth-century modernism, from social integration through standardized national institutions to public provision of housing, parks and schools. The romantic ideal of the public that inspired architecture in the past century and a half has been exhausted.

The Public City

Great building projects give the impression of moving a coherent public forward into the future. Despite dramatic social cleavages, major cities of the world managed to create and carry out such great projects from the middle of the nineteenth to the middle of the twentieth century. An ideal of serving the public was cast in the infrastructure of water and sewage systems, railroad stations, art museums, underground mass transportation and parks: the city's very skeleton created a frame for the body politic. Certainly these projects were built by privately owned companies, competing with each other and trying to make a profit by any means. They were often aided by corrupt or autocratic public officials and reinforced the upper class's sense of moral superiority. Yet these great building projects fostered an ideology of social inclusion. Over time, and under continuous pressure from critics and reformers, they changed from benefiting private stockholders and reinforcing social class distinctions to public stewardship and ever more public use.[3] Social housing expanded the production of public goods that were directly consumed by the poor. In some cities, municipal governments during the first half of the twentieth century also built public hospitals and universities, providing an alternative modern landscape to skyscrapers, expensive apartment houses and luxury shopping districts that catered to the rich. The Great Depression of the 1930s inspired much of the state's building programme, both to provide immediate support to local populations and to create a base for future development. Foreshadowing future problems, however, the largest cities that built the biggest public projects took the least democratic means under the most autocratic leaders. In New York, Robert Moses built parks, highways and public housing according to a grand vision of modernizing the metropolis and paid no attention to the desires of community residents. In Chicago, the public housing authority deliberately segregated blacks and whites in different areas of the city. Detroit, where white homeowners violently protested plans to build public housing in their neighbourhoods because they feared living side by side with blacks, decided not to build any public housing despite an extreme shortage of affordable homes. But although cities were in many ways divided by social class, religion and – especially in the USA – race, the welfare state implicitly connected architecture to empowerment.[4]

Yet post-war welfare-state programmes benefited whites and suburbanites more than city residents, who were increasingly ethnic minorities.[5] By the end of the 1970s, with traditional industries unable to modernize on their own and many local governments suffering from an image crisis, business executives and public officials reached a new consensus on urban redevelopment. Cities would target investors and visitors – people with money – by rebuilding the centre and making themselves appear attractive. Shopping centres would create financial value from derelict industrial and waterfront land. Culture – the theatres and museums that display a city's unique creative product – would promote mass consumption. While financial firms and the real estate industry played the leading roles in reshaping the city's economy, cultural districts, ethnic tourist zones and artists' lofts presented a clean image of diversity for universal consumption.

This shift in strategic thinking – or really, a shift *to* strategic thinking in a market-oriented sense – led to institutional changes in the ways cities managed the built environment. Local officials allowed developers to propose the projects they wanted to build without imposing their own vision of public needs. Zoning laws were set aside, and officials got into the habit of giving developers financial incentives to build because without such subsidies, developers argued, they could not make a profit. Public entrepreneurs in the state bureaucracy yielded to public-private partnerships with corporate leaders, making official the city's dependence on the presumed power of business to 'get things done'. The Enterprise State encouraged by Prime Minister Margaret Thatcher in Britain and by neoliberal governments in the USA and elsewhere gave rise to an Entrepreneurial City that spread around the world.[6]

The Entrepreneurial City

The Entrepreneurial City uses architecture not only as a symbol of power, but as the capital of a symbolic economy. From factories to office towers and high-tech campuses, buildings create a framework for economic power – embodying the geographical distance between home and workplace, the social distance between managers and workers, and the moral distance between leading and declining firms. The bigger the buildings, the more powerful the economy: Isn't this the lesson of the endless competition to erect ever taller buildings in emerging cities of the world? Not just cities, but entire new financial districts, with the British government raising Docklands against New York as a global financial capital and the Chinese challenging Hong Kong's skyscrapers with Shanghai's Pudong.

Landscape also has material power as a branding tool. A landscape abstracts a city's social identity into a visual logo, in earlier times a tower and now an art museum, or into an urban *terroir* whose name – SoHo, South Bank, Left Bank, LA – suggests intangible qualities of distinction that can be marketed as a corporate headquarters location, a residential neighbourhood, or a tourist destination. But buildings also create 'landscapes capable of symbolic mobilization' that appeal to our deepest emotions. They inspire loyalty, evoke a sense of the sacred and – as the destruction of the Twin Towers of the World Trade Center in New York in 2001 made clear – create an imagined community even by their absence.[7]

It is not surprising that architecture as image has a newfound power, for many prominent buildings in the symbolic economy serve finance, media, food and fashion – industries that manipulate images. Their desired effect in an Entrepreneurial City is to create an image of continual creativity. In the brave new world of 'creative cities', work is play and play creates jobs in retail stores, hotels, restaurants and the arts – the spectacle of mass consumption that supports the service industries. There's a synergy that locks rich and poor, artists and immigrants, together in this landscape. Stockbrokers who use their generous, annual bonuses buy Rolex watches or Chloe handbags at expensive shops, corporate clients who take their attorneys to fancy restaurants and media moguls who entertain at late-hours music clubs all support the artists, new immigrants and older poor who entertain customers, clear the tables and guard the doors.

Everyone in this city is entrepreneurial because they have no choice but to take risks while hoping for future gains. The city government aids the private sector in the hope businesses will create jobs and pay taxes in order to finance public services and the arts and to make cities 'liveable'. Everyone takes the risk of working under conditions of relative insecurity in the hope of earning enough money to pay for a home. At best, landscapes of the entrepreneurial city create an image of glamour, mobility and excitement. At worst, they lead to a dizzying increase in property values and a terrifying increase in homelessness.

The concept that unifies the Entrepreneurial City is marketing. Real-estate developers want to market their buildings, public officials – their city and architects – their professional expertise. The influence of marketing across these groups reflects both the historical expansion of consumer society and the immediate competition for investment and jobs. In a world of standardized products and spaces, competitors need to be *different*. Every city today wants to be as successful as Starbucks, as inescapable as Google and as cool as iPod – each in its own way.

Architecture is expected to play an instrumental role in marketing the city. This works, first, because buildings create a tangible difference that 'adds value' to urban districts. In the past the value of individual buildings reflected their *location*. While the best designers and most expensive materials were reserved for the Gold Coast, the shabbiest treatment was used in the slums. Today however 'celebrity' architects and spectacular designs are used to *position* buildings in a field of competitors and drive up their financial value. So we find new 'luxury' condominiums built on previously worthless land in Harlem and a Richard Meier glass apartment house built on the 'wrong' side of Prospect Park in Brooklyn. Like the Jacuzzi bath and Viking stove, the cultural capital of the architecture translates into a building's market value.[8]

Architecture is also used to position a city against its rivals. Not just a single iconic structure like the Eiffel Tower or the Empire State Building, but an iconic landscape of distinguished architects' signature forms signals a city's market value. If Beijing, Tenerife and Abu Dhabi didn't learn this lesson from nineteenth-century Paris or early-twentieth-century New York, they learned it from the Walt Disney Company, which began in the 1980s to commission prize-winning architects like Robert A. M. Stern, Arata Isozaki and Michael Graves to design a pseudo-urban landscape of corporate offices, themed hotels, 'and even gasoline service stations' at Disney World.[9] Whether the strategic use of architecture refers to corporate branding or individual genius, it strengthens the connection between architecture's image and a city's marketing strategy.

An Entrepreneurial City openly embraces marketing. In New York, this can take the form of lobbying for changes in national laws that affect the city's competitive position compared to London as a global financial capital. Endorsing a report prepared by the private consulting firm McKinsey and Company, Mayor Michael Bloomberg joined Senator Charles Schumer to call on the US Congress to change laws that have made it more expensive and more complicated for corporations to assure the accuracy of their financial information.[10] It can also take the form of creating a more desirable image for New York compared to the smaller cities of New Jersey across the Hudson River where land costs are cheaper and taxes are lower, and where many New York-based financial corporations have opened offices. 'If New York City is a business, it isn't Wal-Mart,' Mayor Bloomberg recently told a meeting of financial executives. 'It's a high-end product, maybe even a luxury product.' This claim signals a strategy imported directly from marketing, with New York trying to leverage the higher cost of doing business there into a niche as a luxury brand. But the mayor is also weighing the comparative advantage of New York's built environment (corporate offices for firms in finance and media, luxury housing, commercial arts facilities, hotels) and its social environment ('just the most efficient place to do business') against its economic limitations (big budgets, high taxes). In either case the implications are clear: Build the city for those who can afford it. Those who can't afford to be there should leave.[11]

Although there are limits to establishing a city as a luxury brand, marketing the city's landscape is becoming more common around the world. Building cultural districts, bidding for the Olympics or other mega-events, and lobbying regional organizations for annual designations as a 'city of culture' restores the glamour if not the power of centrality. Yet it fails to relieve financial pressure. These programmes commit a city to an ambitious building programme, and the trend towards self-financing makes sure that most of the burden rests on the city's shoulders. It's a treadmill: chasing subsidies, investors, tourists and the media compels an Entrepreneurial City to keep up with competitors regardless of past achievements.

Cheaper than cultural districts and mega-events, temporary tourist spectacles offer a provisional landscape that adds financial value to a city's existing resources. Christo and Jeanne-Claude's public art installation 'The Gates' drew tourists to New York's snowy Central Park for two weeks in the middle of the winter in 2005. According to public officials, all the money spent on the event – for travel, food, hotels and souvenirs – added $250 million to the city's economy. Although they are costly, permanent landscapes offer more financial leverage. They usually depend on both public and private funding and create the fixed capital for an unlimited number of spectacular events. Chicago's Millenium Park, a lakeside public green space that opened in 2006 with a sculpture by Anish Kapoor and an outdoor concert pavilion by Frank Gehry, offers three landscapes in one. It enables Mayor Richard M. Daley to promote a populist park with summer festivals for residents, it raises the market value of new residential buildings downtown, and it gives Chicago a marketing image for global competition. 'Millennium Park is much more than just a park,' the website proclaims; 'it is the unprecedented celebration of architecture, sculpture and landscape design that has won acclaim from around the world.'[12]

Yet the developers of many of these spectacular landscapes employ the same designers, whose strong brand identification inevitably weakens cities' efforts at product differentiation. Christo and Jeanne-Claude move from installing 'The Gates' in New York to planning 'Mastaba' in Abu Dhabi. Frank Gehry's plans for Guggenheim Abu Dhabi replicate the same design signature as the Walt Disney Concert Hall in Los Angeles, the Pritzker Pavilion in Millenium Park and Guggenheim Bilbao. For the artists and architects, their signature is a marketable brand. But for the cities that put these brands together in a landscape, the effect is standardization. Describing the effects on Barcelona of the 1992 Olympics and its many building projects, including a collective award from the Royal Institute of British Architects, a very critical David Harvey lists 'more homogenizing multinational commodification . . . later phases of waterfront development [that] look exactly like every other in the western world . . . stupefying congestion of the traffic . . . multinational stores replace local shops, gentrification . . . and Barcelona loses some of its marks of distinction.'[13] Losing distinction makes the treadmill run faster – requiring more architecture, more events and more promotion.

Entrepreneurial Cities all market to the same demographic: people with money. As a result, they become more expensive cities – especially in the centre, where most high-value-added events take place. This trend spreads far beyond London, Paris and New York. When Beijing tears down *hutong,* or traditional residential districts built around courtyards and alleys, their residents cannot find new housing in the centre because the alleys are replaced by expensive, high-rise towers.[14] Shanghai preserves some *shikumen*, small stone houses built in the early 1900s, but converts them to a shopping and entertainment district for the newly rich. While Singapore and Dubai build new cultural districts, housing prices rise. The same logic applies as when establishing a luxury brand: build for the rich and some benefits will trickle down to the poor. It's no wonder this leads to an ever more private city.

Architecture in the Public City

To reinvent the public city, architecture must be reinvented as a public process. This does not only mean that buildings should be open to public use or that designs should be chosen by public competitions. It requires architects to initiate work for a new type of public client – for neighbourhood planning groups, residents' councils, NGOs and non-profit organizations. Together with lawyers and local builders, architects can form a resource base for these public clients to develop mixed-use districts with space for homes as well as for small businesses, stores and workshops – a built environment for residents to develop social capital. This effort requires more than just responding to demands, it requires empowering groups that are excluded from decision making, from voting and even from jobs and housing, to imagine alternative landscapes.

After the World Trade Center in New York was destroyed by a terrorist attack in 2001, architects and designers created just this kind of public. The professionals were frustrated by the rebuilding plans commissioned without public review by the Lower Manhattan Development Corporation, an autocratic committee personally chosen by the governor of New York State and lacking accountability to the public. Together with urban planners, regional planning institutions and urban universities, and promoted by the influential architecture critic of the *New York Times*, the architects and designers organized a number of interconnected ad hoc groups that approached community organizations to set up a series of public meetings to 'imagine New York'. The 'design community' – as they called themselves – operated a decentralized network of councils suggestive of citizen participation in decision making in a tradition that stretches from the Paris Commune of 1870 to the contemporary city of Porto Alegre in Brazil. They solicited opinions on postcards and by e-mail, organized exhibitions and held public meetings to discuss designs. They persuaded New Yorkers to think about the size and shape of buildings, the meaning of their forms and the uses of the Lower Manhattan location. Under pressure from Chinatown's community organizations, they included the East side of Lower Manhattan in their discussions, seeing the district as a whole for the first time in history, and integrating the needs of its constituents – residents, workers, immigrants and financial firms. The design community had never seen itself as united, but in refusing to accept the uninspired decision of an undemocratically chosen group – the LMDC – they made architecture a means of empowerment.

At the World Trade Center site, however, imagination was limited by those who tightly held the instruments of power. A private developer with a lease on the central space – the Twin Towers – would not yield to public ownership. Neither did he accept the site plan developed by Daniel Libeskind that had won public sentiment and, for reasons of flexibility and cost, the governor's approval. When Mayor Bloomberg proposed that the LMDC build fewer offices and more housing, he was ignored. The LMDC agreed to place cultural institutions on the rebuilt site, but those that won places were neither the most famous in the city nor the types of institutions that local residents wanted. The memorial and museum, the most symbolically important parts of the site, were continually challenged by arguments over the way the victims would be represented and constant pressure to reduce costs. Projected costs also forced revisions to Santiago Calatrava's popular plan for a public transportation hub. Because of a battle over political censorship, the museum was abruptly eliminated from the plans. And while the foundation for the skyline marker of the project, the Freedom Tower, was under construction, the structural engineer called for an entirely new design.[15]

The controversies over rebuilding the World Trade Center site show how difficult it is to achieve a public consensus on design. Although architecture crystallized discontent, it could not overcome conflicts of interest between residents and businesses, city and state, and advocates for different groups of victims of the terrorist act and their families. Decisions were more complicated because rebuilding also involved predictions about the market for office space in that district of the city. The design community, however, was able to use architecture as a *process* for achieving consensus. Their appeal to the imagination integrated everyone who cared to participate into a public of New Yorkers.

Perhaps the simplest of architecture's achievements is to enable city residents to put down roots. Yet this too involves architects in initiating process at least as much as it requires design expertise. First and foremost, building for the needs of existing residents requires access to land, water, electricity, sanitation facilities and construction materials. Property developers see these needs through the lens of profit and local officials often help to remove needy residents to clear the ground for developers' projects. But professional alliances with architects and community groups could persuade venture capitalists to finance newly imagined, alternative landscapes as a social investment. Public participation in imagining these projects would free the human capital that venture capitalists talk about when they discuss the need for a creative workforce that can conceive new products and technologies. Imagined landscapes could also create a new built environment for work that suits city dwellers' needs and skills. As demonstration projects, these landscapes would be integrated into central-city redevelopment. No longer waiting for private developers to promise affordable housing and jobs and no longer dependent on meagre state budgets for social housing, the poorest residents would take charge of creating the conditions for their own improvement. This would generate a new synergy between rich and poor, and between artists, migrants and experts, in the urban landscape.

How would architects find the new public clients? The studios that are a part of every architecture school's curriculum could connect professors and their students with community organizations. The same projects that students now develop in class would compete for building funds administered by public agencies and local banks. Prominent architectural firms would initiate *pro bono* work on the model law firms have established. In San Francisco, the not-for-profit organization Public Architecture has already established an initiative for US firms to dedicate one percent of their billable hours to *pro bono* work for community organizations, which can include design, site planning, construction and graphic design. While The One Percent Solution[16] initiative received a grant from the National Endowment for the Arts, work on individual projects is funded by individual firms in cities around the country. In the more traditional non-profit sector, religious institutions and NGOs already sponsor housing development programmes. The task now is to connect these initiatives with permanent sources of funding and create formal recognition for public clients, with the biggest transnational firms leading the way.

Will a public architecture be able to challenge the marketing model? Maybe not, for transnational teams of developers, investors and marketing consultants have been engaging architects to reshape the fabric of cities along entrepreneurial lines for the past 30 years. But we can pose a different model. We can move from the marketing paradigm that sees architecture as an event to a citizenship paradigm that sees architecture as a process. There will be many problems along the way. Public architecture would face a danger of dogmatic populism on the one hand, and visionary elitism on the other. In New York today, the rehabilitation of Robert Moses' reputation comes with a yearning for a single authority – a 'master builder' – who claims to have a vision of the city's future and pushes ahead to build it regardless of social priorities or human costs. But we cannot afford to rely on this approach. Sustaining and improving the natural environment, integrating different social classes and groups, creating the opportunity to put down roots – these are issues of process not vision, and they should be a part of an architect's toolkit.

More than creating aesthetic designs, public architecture would create a new framework for economic and social power. Only by moving away from traditional forms of patronage including those of the welfare state can architecture realize its visionary potential.

1   Jane Jacobs, *The Death and Life of Great American Cities* (New York: Random House, 1961).
2   Herbert F. Gans, *The Urban Villagers: Group and Class in the Life of Italian-Americans* (New York: Free Press, 1962).
3   Roy Rosenzweig and Elizabeth Blackmar, *The Park and the People: A History of Central Park* (Ithaca, NY: Cornell University Press, 1992); Frank Trentmann and Vanessa Taylor, 'From Users to Consumers: Water Politics in Nineteenth-Century London,' in: Frank Trentmann (ed.),*The Making of the Consumer* (Oxford/New York: Berg, 2006), 53-79.
4   Robert A. Caro, *The Power Broker: Robert Moses and the Fall of New York* (New York: Vintage, 1974); Arnold R. Hirsch, *The Making of the Second Ghetto: Race and Housing in Chicago* (New York: Cambridge University Press, 1983); Thomas J. Sugrue, *The Origins of the Urban Crisis: Race and Inequality in Postwar Detroit* (Princeton, NJ: Princeton University Press, 1996). For a great polemic against Robert Moses, see Marshall Berman, 'In the Forest of Symbols: Some Notes on Modernism in New York', in: *All That Is Solid Melts Into Air* (New York: Simon and Schuster, 1982), 287-348 and for the current rehabilitation of his reputation, Hilary Ballon and Kenneth T. Jackson (eds.), *Robert Moses and the Modern City: The Transformation of New York* (New York: Norton, 2007).
5   Lizabeth Cohen, *A Consumers' Republic: The Politics of Mass Consumption in Postwar America* (New York: Knopf, 2003); Ira Katznelson, *When Affirmative Action Was White* (New York: Norton, 2005); Kevin M. Kruse and Thomas J. Sugrue (eds.), *The New Suburban History* (Chicago: University of Chicago Press, 2006).
6   Mark Crinson (ed.), *Urban Memory: History and Amnesia in the Modern City* (London: Routledge, 2005); Sharon Zukin, 'Reading *The Urban Villagers* as a Cultural Document', *City and Community* 6 (2007), 39-48 ; Miriam Greenberg, *Branding New York* (New York: Routledge, forthcoming); David Harvey, *The Condition of Postmodernity* (Oxford and Cambridge, MA: Blackwell, 1989) and 'From Managerialism to Entrepreneurialism: The Transformation in Urban Governance in Late Capitalism', in: *Spaces of Capital: Towards a Critical Geography* (New York: Routledge, 2001), 345-368.
7   Donald McNeill, 'Barcelona as Imagined Community: Pasqual Maragall's Spaces of Engagement', *Transactions of the British Institute of Geographers* 26 (2001), 341; Sharon Zukin, *Landscapes of Power: From Detroit to Disney World* (Berkeley/Los Angeles: University of California Press, 1991); Michael Sorkin and Sharon Zukin (eds.), *After the World Trade Center* (New York: Routledge, 2002).
8   'Redefine your perceptions of a modern classic', says an advertisement for 'Richard Meier on Prospect Park' in the *New York Times* (11 February 2007). 'These iconic residences will set a new precedent in living.' With sales prices of $790,000 to $6 million, these apartments do not suit a neighbourhood whose median household income is only $39,177 (according to 2000 US Census data on www.SocialExplorer.com) – a clear case of architecture being used to gentrify a neighbourhood.
9   http://www.wdwmagic.com/architecture.htm (4 February 2007). At the same time, the Disney Company also contracted famous French chefs Paul Bocuse, Roger Verge and Gaston Lenotre to build a mass-market restaurant for *haute cuisine* in the EPCOT district of Disney World.
10 The law is the Sarbanes-Oxley Act (2002). See McKinsey and Company, 'Sustaining New York's and the US' Global Financial Services Leadership', Bloomberg and Schumer Report, 22 January 2007, http://www.senate.gov/~schumer/SchumerWebsite/pressroom/special_reports/2007/NY_REPORT%20_FINAL.pdf.
11 Diane Cardwell, 'New York Offers Tremendous Value, But Only for Those Companies Able to Capitalize on It', *New York Times*, 8 January 2003.
12 http://www.millenniumpark.org/privaterentals/; also see http://www.nyc.gov/html/thegates/home.html.
13 'The Art of Rent', in: *Spaces of Capital*, op. cit. (note 6), 406.
14 Yan Zhang and Ke Fang, 'Politics of Housing Redevelopment in China: The Rise and Fall of the Ju'er Hutong Programme in Inner-City Beijing', *Journal of Housing and the Built Environment* 18 (2003), 75-87.
15 Guy Nordenson, the well-known structural engineer who worked with architect David Childs of Skidmore Owings and Merrill on the design for the Freedom Tower, blamed the governor's haste to get the building under way before leaving office and beginning a campaign for the Republican nomination for US President, unreasonable security plans and incredibly high costs. 'Freedom From Fear', *New York Times*, 16 February 2007.
16 See https://www.theonepercent.org.

Martijn de Waal

Power Parad

Paradox of the Information Society

In the information age, information is the beginning and the end of everything. Immaterial bits and bytes drive our digital universe – be it atomless mp3 music, electronic stock exchanges, or Second Life town meetings. Even in those parts of the economy still residing in the physical world, it is information – of managerial processes, design or marketing knowledge – that provides the competitive advantage in the production process of goods and services.

However, in the end, even Silicon Valley revolves around physical patterns etched in metalloid elements, running on electric current supplied by coal-, gas- or oil-burning power stations. Many e-commerce transactions actuate delivery trucks running on fossil fuel. And in the end even Cadcam architecture leads to bricks, not clicks. Thus it should be no surprise that in the information age, it is the competition for natural resources that drives much of international economics and geopolitics.

Paradox of Location

In the network society, location doesn't matter. That is why it matters so much. In the information economy, the production process is cut up into interconnected modules that can be geographically dispersed around the world. For instance: research for a new mobile phone is done in Tampere, Finland. Programmers in Hyderabad, India write the software. A factory in Shenzhen, China makes the actual handsets, with parts imported from Taiwan. The marketing strategy is thought up on Madison Avenue, New York. This is a flexible process: each module can be replaced with another – production could be shifted from Shenzhen to Vietnam, for instance, or marketing from the northern to the southern part of Madison Avenue.

At the same time, agglomeration advantages lead to clustering. Producers will seek out logistic hubs. Research and development departments need places that abound with both creative talent and venture capital. Prestige (through architectural landmarks, elite schools and restaurants or the presence of high culture) is important for the establishment of corporate headquarters. So both Thomas Friedman and Richard Florida might be right. As Friedman states, The World is Flat: any place can enter the global competition. However, as Florida claims, the World is Spiked: eventually only a few cities will truly emerge as first-rate Global Cities in which talent, patent registration and financial resources tend to concentrate.

Paradox of the Global Village

Marshall McLuhan seems to be proved right: the media networks of satellite TV and Internet and the logistic networks of low-cost air carriers or Mexican coyotes and Chinese snakeheads have turned the world into a global village. We can plu into any culture, anywhere in the world. As Ulricl Beck has stated: our antennas are now our roots.

However, we might discern two kinds of cosmopolites: 'cosmopolites by choice' and 'cosmopolites by necessity'. The first group deliberately chooses a cosmopolitan lifestyle, albeit one that leads to the emergence of the same designer-chic restaurants in every CBD around the world. The latter group feels they have no choice but to engage in a cosmopolitan lifestyle. For instance when stagnating Third World economies drive the underprivileged into migration to wealthier regions, and set up their Chinatowns, Little Italy's, or Curry Miles and the like around the world, also cosmopolizing their destinations – sometimes willy-nilly – in the act.

Paradox of Individualism

The cultural forces of the 1960s did away with the petty bourgeois era of collectivist norms and forced rituals. We are all individuals now! New technologies of mass customization confirm our sense of uniqueness. In any public space, the iPod plays our own personal soundscape. On the Internet, filtering algorithms present an information landscape adjusted to our personal needs and tastes.

Yet at the same time, the increasing flexibility of the global economy and cosmopolized culture has led to a renewed popularity of collective narratives and group identities. These tendencies even lead to practices of re-territorialization: increasingly, ethnic/economic/lifestyle groups flock together in their own town quarters – sometimes even turning these into urban fortresses.

Although this is not a negative trend per se, it bears the risk of producing an urbanism of non communicating archipelagos – and in its most extreme cases a dialectic of ghettos of exclusivity for the superrich and exclusive ghettos for society's losers.

Paradox of Informality

This, it seems, is the age of informal social relations. This is the age of casual Fridays rather than stiff etiquette; of the bottom-up cut-copy-paste culture of Youtube, Myspace and Blogger replacing a hierarchy of cultural popes and professional gatekeepers controlling procedures of cultural exchange.

However, at the same time, other social relations have become formalized. As Robert Putnam has pointed out, over the last half a century we have replaced the favour bank with Citibank, relying for most personal matters on institutionalized (commercial) services rather than on the informal mercy of our neighbours. Increasingly, unspoken rules of conduct are being made explicit in regulations and codifications. In some developments, homebuyers have to sign agreements determining everything from parking restrictions to which colours their curtains are permitted to be. In Rotterdam, the city council initiated the Rotterdam Code – a set of explicit rules on how to behave in public. We are entering a 'contract society' in which formerly implicit mutual expectations are explicitly being written down and enforced through legal action.

The Corporate City Is the Zone

The corporate city occupies a discrepant territory between two different species of urbanity. It poses for advertisements in the mediagenic urbanism of financial or cultural capitals like New York and Paris while also sheltering in zone variants such as Special Economic (SEZs), Free Trade Zones (FTZs) or Export Processing Zones (EPZs). Heir to ancient pirate enclaves or the freeports of Hanseats and Easterlings, the zone is the perfect legal habitat of the corporation. It is the corporation's legal duty to banish any obstacle to profit, and the zone is the spatial organ of this externalizing – a mechanism of political quarantine designed for corporate protection. The earliest historical urges to incorporate express this desire for freedom and exclusivity. Breeding more promiscuously with other 'parks' or enclave formats, the zone now merges with tourist compounds, knowledge villages, IT campuses, museums and universities that complement the corporate headquarters or offshore facilities. More and more programmes and spatial products thrive in legal lacunae and political quarantine, enjoying the insulation and lubrication of tax exemptions, foreign ownership of property, streamlined customs and deregulation of labour or environmental regulations. Indeed, the zone as corporate enclave is a primary aggregate unit of many new forms of the contemporary global city, offering a 'clean slate', 'one-stop' entry into the economy of a foreign country. Most banish the negotiations that are usually associated with the contingencies of urbanism – negotiations such as those concerning labour, human rights or environment.

In 1934, emulating freeport laws in Hamburg and elsewhere in the late nineteenth century, the USA established Foreign Trade Zone status for port and warehousing areas related to trade. As the zone merged with manufacturing, Export Processing Zones appeared in the late 1950s and '60s. China's Special Economic Zones, allowing for an even broader range of market activity, emerged in the 1970s. Since then special zones of various types have grown exponentially, from a few hundred in the 1980s to well over a thousand today, and special zones handle over a third of the world's trade. Some zones are a few hectares in size; some grow in conurbations that are hundreds of kilometres in size.[1]

Many of the new legal hybrids of zone, oscillating between visibility and invisibility, identity and anonymity, have neither been mapped nor analysed for their disposition – their patency, exclusivity, aggression, resilience or violence.

The Corporate City Calls Itself a City

Often the zone actually calls itself 'city', where 'city' is either a noun describing an urban area or a modifier indicating a place where something is to be found in abundance (a shopping centre might be called 'shopping city', for instance). *HITEC City, Ebene Cybercity, King Abdullah Economic City*, among hundreds of others, take on the title of 'city' as an enthusiastic expression of the zone's evolution beyond being merely a location for warehousing and transhipment. The zone has become a new primordial civilization and a warm pool for a latest cocktail of spatial products (for instance offices, factories, warehouses, calling centres and software production facilities) that move around the world. Many countries in South Asia, China and Africa used export processing zones as a means of announcing their entry into a global market as independent post-colonial contractors of outsourcing and offshoring. For example, with *Ebene Cybercity*, Mauritius, is evolving the EPZ form to include IT with help IT campus developers from India who worked on *HITEC City* in Hyderabad. Dubai has rehearsed the 'park' or zone with almost every imaginable programme beginning with *Dubai Internet City* in 2000, the first IT campus as free trade zone. Calling each new enclave 'city', it has either planned or built *Dubai Health Care City, Dubai Maritime City, Dubai Silicon Oasis, Dubai Knowledge Village, Dubai Techno Park, Dubai Media City, Dubai Outsourcing Zone, Dubai Humanitarian City, Dubai Industrial City* and *Dubai Textile City*.

The Corporate City Is a Double

Duplicity is essential to the corporate city. Theories about the waning nation-state and the waxing transnational realm are the perfect camouflage for a corporate culture that clearly prefers to manipulate *both* state and non-state sovereignty, alternately releasing and laundering their power and identity to create the most advantageous political or economic climate. The zone aspires to lawlessness, but in the legal tradition of exception, it is a mongrel form that adopts looser and more cunning behaviours than those associated with an emergency of state. Commercial interests do not identify a single situation within which exception is appropriate. They move *between* zones, concocting cocktails of legal advantage and amnesty. Just as corporate interests play a number of zone types for advantage they also operate between state and non-state jurisdictions, seeking out relaxed, extra-jurisdictional spaces (SEZs, FTZs, EPZs) while also massaging legislation in the various states they occupy (NAFTA, GATT). The stances of any one nation are therefore often duplicitous or discrepant reflections of divided loyalties between national and international concerns or citizens and shareholders.

Now major cities and national capitals are engineering their own world city *doppelgangers* – their own non-national territory within which to legitimize non-state transactions. The world capital and national capital can shadow each other, alternately exhibiting a regional cultural ethos and a global ambition. Companies like CIDCO and SKIL can now be hired, as they were in *Navi Mumbai*, to deliver an infrastructural legal environment like those in Shenzhen and Pudong. City-states like Hong Kong, Singapore and Dubai, that assume the ethos of free zone for their entire territory, have become world city models for newly minted cities with not only commercial areas, but a full complement of

Cybergateway, HITEC City, Hyderabad (image courtesy Satya Pemmaraju)

programmes. *New Songdo City*, an expansion of the Incheon free trade territories near Seoul, is a complete international city based on the Dubai or Singapore model, designed by KPF. Here, aspiring to the cosmopolitan urbanity of New York, Venice and Sydney, the zone is filled with residential, cultural and educational programmes in addition to commercial programmes. While the emotional streaming videos for any of the smaller 'cities' are often accompanied by tinny fanfares of low production values, the *New Songdo City* video messages are accompanied by new age tunes or heroic strains in the John Williams style – the spectacular theme music of the non-state state.

The Corporate City Is on Vacation

The corporate city considers itself heir to the same privilege and liquidity that petrodollars enjoy. Just as the majority of these funds often remain invisible or unaccounted for, the corporate city should be able to get away and relax. Able to materialize and dematerialize with the caprice of offshore holdings, the newly coined corporate enclaves even assume an ethereal aura and an overlay of fantasy. Operating in a frictionless realm of exemption and merging with other urban formats, the zone also naturally merges with the resort and theme park. Indeed if corporations are often only vessels for liberated money, they can easily be maintained outside of the workweek environment. While corporate headquarters in national capitals and financial capitals portray a glamorous business-like atmosphere, the office park in developing countries has tried to project the image of, not the hotel or club of colonial or Hilton style luxuries, but of a kingdom with unencumbered wealth. IT campuses in India and Malaysia like *Multimedia Supercorridor* sometimes refer to themselves as IT resorts offering lush vegetation and a mixture of small-scale vernacular buildings and mirror-tiled office buildings. To this styling, the various Dubai cities like *Dubai International City* or *Dubai Media City* add themes of Islamic and international architecture. Indeed having re-emerged most powerfully *after* a historical era celebrating national sovereignty as an ultimate, the oil powers of the gulf more easily conflate ancient kingdoms and contemporary empire with perfunctory recognition of national power. *King Abdullah Economic City*, a production of the UAE's Emaar developers on the Red Sea near Jeddah, creates yet another corporate city as world city that now offers cultural, educational, business and residential programmes merged with a resort. Fly-throughs with swelling traditional music render the city as a shimmering golden man-made island filled with multiples of traditional Islamic palace buildings and programmed with leisure space. Even more extreme are those corporate cities that directly merge the corporate city with the offshore island shelter. *Jeju*, for instance, is a quintessential island retreat that has housed, as have many islands, all of those programmes or illicit activities that do not fit into the logics of the continent. Transforming itself from penal colony and strategic military position into a 'free economic city'. Citing Dubai, Singapore and Hong Kong as models, the island 'guarantees the maximum convenience for the free flow of people, goods and capital and for tax free business activities'.[2] A place of ecological purity, casinos, golfer's amnesty and mythomaniacal tradition, this corporate retreat also hosts global sporting events and diplomatic summits. On the island of Kish, off the coast of Iran, *Kish Free Zone* similarly attracts business to the island notorious for its relaxed religious standards. Here, there is not only a loosening of headscarves and a greater opportunity for socializing between men and women, but the standard set of exemptions to which the corporation has grown accustomed. Nearby fantasy hotels like the Dariush Grand Hotel re-create the grandeur of Persian palaces with peristyle halls, gigantic cast stone sphinxes and ornate bas-reliefs depicting ancient scenes.

Function spatial recipes of commerce and business are not only vessels of organizational parameters, but also the medium of the many puffy fairy tales of belief that accompany power.

The Corporate City Is Extrastatecraft

Theories of Total War would speculate that infrastructures and technological developments, even most forms of urbanism, are

Dariush Grand Hotel, Kish Island

first military apparatuses. Yet, often massively capitalized corporate conglomerates create global alliances and transnational infrastructures that avoid war because it is bad for business. Foreign investment is funnelled not only through national treasuries but also through corporate conglomerates. From the US rail conglomerates that employed more people than the US military during the nineteenth century to the consortia that today operate satellite networks and submarine cable, it is private corporations have an elite parastate capacity. Enjoying quasi-diplomatic immunities, corporations may provide to nations the support and expertise for transportation and communication infrastructure or relationships with IMF and the World Bank. Networks of construction companies and infrastructure specialists like Bouyges, Bin Laden, Mitsubishi, Kawasaki or Siemens deliver technologies for high speed rail and skyscraper engineering.

The zone is the parliament for the de facto global governance of corporate headquartering. To the ports around which so many free trade zones, export processing zones and special economic zones crystallize, conglomerates such as PSA, P&O, Hutchison Port Holdings or ECT, like modern counterparts of British or Dutch East India company franchises, deliver transhipment and warehousing technologies. Technology parks around the world grow their own satellite and cable networks with their own headquarters or embassies at the interstices of the network, whole families of corporations stick together in the same legal habitat re-created anywhere in the world and separated by a plane trip or a satellite bounce. Real estate operators like Emaar move between zones to provide the spatial environments and amenities that corporate 'families' recognize as home.

This power must be continually refreshed by the fictions of

Multimedia Super Corridor, Cyberjaya

symbolic capital, often provided by either media messages or architectural imagery. The largest conglomerates appear hat-in-hand in the media wanting the world to get to know them and support their work as they develop alternative energies and more resilient crops that might alleviate poverty. They ask for loyalty – a loyalty beyond brand recognition and closer to a form of patriotism for non-national sovereignty. Architects provide symbolic capital for these self-reinforcing communities in the form of cosmopolitan identities, selective historical traditions, signature skyscrapers or architourism highlights like a Guggenheim. The corporate city often uses business instruments for self-governance in lieu of the tools of a citizenry, but its sometimes also borrows the tools of participatory democracies. *Gazprom City* has asked the world to vote on its architectural monument from among a group of alternatives designed by famous architects. Moreover, for those

Doppelgangers of the state, like *King Abdullah Economic City,* the mixture of corporate and ancient imagery has also become a monument to the state and its 'wise leadership'.

The Corporate City Prefers Non-State Violence

While sometimes engaged as a military contractor, the corporate city benefits most from indirect association with war. Direct association is bad for business.

The gulf widens between the extremes of the Dubai development model and the slums of Lagos or Kinshasa. Yet the corporate city also has a formation within which poverty can be strictly

maintained without the chaos of informal economies. The offshore sweatshops in Saipan or the *maquiladoras* on the thickened border between the USA and Mexico organize a form of labour exploitation that is stable and within the law. The corporate city not only provides a double to the national and financial capital, it has its own double in these offshore enclaves. More discrete and less visible, these backstage formations are not given the 'city' designation. They may be violent, but it is the violence of Bartelby, intractably passive and oblivious to its consequences, it is not involved in war because it says it is not involved in war. In Khartoum, the capital of Sudan, development expertise from Abu Dhabi and Dubai is helping Alsunut Development Company Ltd. to build *Almogran*, which includes 1660 acres of skyscrapers and residential properties. The new corporate city only underlines the extreme discrepancies between oil wealth and poverty due to the exploitation of oil resources in the mostly non-Arab southern Sudan. Indeed, the overt, even hyperbolic, expressions of oil money are among the chief tools for instigating war and violence in the south.

The Corporate City Is an Intentional Community

Given the ethos of 'honour among thieves', the pirate enclave sometimes became an unlikely vessel of democracy when a diverse group of retired or resting brigands tried to live together in, for instance, Salle, on the Northern Coast of Africa. Democracy, however, would never suit the corporate city. It chooses instead that aspect of the pirate enclave that resembles an intentional community with a fixed rule base operating outside of participation. The zone is a vessel set apart from the state and awaiting an overlay of legal parameters. Like Mendel's peas, after many cycles of zone breeding around the world, recessive or unlikely traits begin to appear. The zone as instrument of labour or environmental abuse, can, by way of its political quarantine, be filled with entirely different intentions. *Dubai Humanitarian City*, as an outpost of relief agencies and NGOs, makes a tenant out of the chief critics of zone politics and abuses.[3] Also, since the legal climate for each of these enclaves is designed to advantage, free speech, for instance, is permitted in *Dubai Media City* where the major networks are headquartered. Universities are perhaps the newest corporations to join in the zone habitat. *Qatar Education City* uses the campus/park/zone model to provide a headquarters for the franchise of major universities around the world. Corporate sponsorship makes of the university a kind of incubator of intelligence and manpower for the corporation as well as the region. *King Abdullah Economic City* will follow suit with an education sector. *Saadiyat Island*, a new development in Abu Dhabi, will introduce not only a Guggenheim franchise and a branch of the Louvre, but an outpost of the Sorbonne.

Moreover, it is often the very attempt to maintain massive optimized realms of exemption that lands the corporate city in the cross-hairs of conflict. Shenzhen has become an unlikely cauldron of survival that borrows real-estate survival maneuvers that borrow activist techniques associated with a participatory democracy.[4] The ports and export processing zones of the South China Sea have become the targets of international immigration and security issues that place them in the centre of the national concerns they had hoped to banish.

The Corporate City Launders Identities

Countries just entering the marketplace may use the new zone economy, while also rejecting its incompatibility with state rhetoric or banishing it as a contradiction to the state's purity. The DPRK introduced zones like *Rajin Sonbong* and *Kaesong* to act as cash cows for the state but also remain separate and vilified as a capitalist economy. Kim Dal Hyon (a NK economic reformer) is reported to have said 'Let's consider the Najin-Sonbong area as a pigsty. Build a fence around it, put in karaoke, and capitalists will invest. We need only to collect earnings from the pigs.' Meanwhile vast zone conurbations collect in the *Tumen River Region* between

AllianceTexas

the DPRK and Russia. The Stalinist Dynasty of DPRK understood the way the capitalist economy works so well that they even characterized the Mount Kumgang resort as a 'special tourist zone'. China's SEZs are the world's model of this phenomenon. Their early experiment with four SEZs to quarantine the capitalist market has exploded to produce scores of different zones of various types all across the country. Cross-national growth zones in the South China Sea move products between zones in different jurisdictions to take advantage of different quotas and levels of regulation. In Eastern Europe the zone allows other European corporations to take advantage of less expensive labour from entering EU countries. Similarly, *AllianceTexas*, a classic office park distripark corporate city north of Ft. Worth, renames and redistributes many of the products produced in Mexico under NAFTA agreements so that they can be calibrated to the desired profitability in a US context.

The Corporate City Is Beautiful and Smart; It Has Special Stupidity

The corporate city is a cleaner and smarter version of urbanism. Even those corporate cities that remain largely devoted to logistics, like *Keppel Distripark* in Singapore, win architectural awards for their beauty. *Cyberport* in Hong Kong, developed by Richard Li, heir to the STAR TV corporate dynasty, has developed a city so beautiful that it appears to have jumped directly from the computer screen. The orgmen who tend the self-referential organizations of the corporate city are proud of the fluid, robust,

AllianceTexas

information-rich environments they have created. Their automated warehouses and information *Landschafts* slowly and obsessively sort and stack enormous amounts of information. Yet this information must only be information that is compatible to a common platform. Indeed, an enormous intelligence is deployed to reset or eliminate any errant or extrinsic information. While remaining intact, the hermetic organization develops shrewd auxiliary tactics and strategies to fortify its stupidity and defend against contradiction. Regimes of power at once diversify their sources and contacts while consolidating and closing ranks, extending and tightening their territory. They grow while deleting information. This information paradox – wherein an enormous amount of information is required to remain information poor – is a common tool of power.

The Corporate City Tutors Impure Ethical Struggles

Space, perhaps even more than international law, is often the medium of transnational polity and multiplied sovereignty. Duplicity is the prevailing logic and organizational disposition of this space. The logics of righteousness and the insistence on orthodox political sentiment evaporate in these environments. Most urgent for architecture is not the consolidation of a singular position, but rather the acquisition of an expanded, agile repertoire. Curiosity and ingenuity nourish a position wherein one is too smart to be right. While these unusual levers or toggles may not have the pedigree of political orthodoxy, they may be part of an indirect political ricochet that is instrumental in a cessation of violence, a shift in sentiment or a turn in economic fortunes.

Some backstage knowledge of the bagatelle in exchange, the players in the game and the cards being dealt returns more information about the dirty tools and techniques of extrastatecraft. It may be true that architects are often not at the table when policy decisions are being made. Yet, if most political decisions are made by shills, confidence men and go-betweens, architects are probably already at that table. The corporate city is a discrepant territory within which to rehearse impure ethical struggles and a new species of spatio-political activism.

1   Xiangming Chen, 'The Evolution of Free Economic zones and the Recent Development of Cross-National Growth Zones' *International Journal of Urban and Regional Research*, vol. 19, no. 4 (Cambridge: Blackwell, 1995), 593-621.
2   http://www.jeju.go.kr/
3   http://www.dubaiinternetcity.com; http://www.arabsat.com/Default/About/OurHistory.aspx; http://www.dubaiholding.com/english/index.html
4   *The New York Times*, 18 and 19 December 2006, A1.

Moore's Law Meets Sustainability
The Power of Ecology

INABA
Jeffrey Inaba

Sustainability has become an irreproachable form of power. As a global social phenomenon it has heightened our awareness of the processes of consumption and disposal in cities. It has sensitized us to consider the environmental consequences of every activity in urban space. It has even defined a clear ethics for our professional actions. While it is essential to the survival of the city as we know it, it has not been utilized as a means of power to conceptualize the future city. It has instead been an excuse for otherwise exceptionally poor urban design. Given the unimpeachable status of eco-friendly planning, sustainability also may serve as a platform for imaginative urban thinking far beyond the realm of environmentally conscientious design. 'Moore's Law Meets Sustainability' dramatizes a future moment when sustainability possesses even greater power than today, and serves as an intellectual vehicle for producing new philosophies of urbanization. The story goes something like this . . .

During the first part of the twenty-first century, urbanization was assumed to be a 'resource-intensive' process that consumed great amounts of energy and raw material, and discharged proportional quantities of waste. This cycle of large-scale intake and excretion was accepted as the necessary trade-off for development. Then, accelerated advances in environmental technologies miraculously transformed the urbanization process: it became a form of energy production rather than consumption, a mode of environmental remediation rather than a source of pollution. This change came about through a series of events that shortened the lifespan of buildings and reduced the permanence of cities – both as part of a dynamic, animate cycle to sustain the environment.

In this future moment in time, sustainability is broadly embraced. Corporate investment fuels tremendous creativity in eco-technologies. Three areas of the sustainability sector blossom: (1) alternative energy generation, (2) building systems technology, and (3) land remediation. A period of research and development follows in which the rate of increase in these systems' processing speeds approximate that of Moore's Law.

Moore's Law was the 1990s 'Tech-Boom' observation that the transistor density of integrated circuits doubles every 24 months, resulting in the doubling of a computer's processing power. First an empirical insight, it turned into an industry-wide time-line for companies to create and deliver processors of twice the speed, triggering an extended period during which advances occurred at an exponential rate.

Now that Moore's Law meets sustainability, every 24 months the output of wind and solar energy systems double, the energy consumption of HVAC and mechanical building systems are reduced by 50 per cent, and the remediation time of a brown-field site is halved. In the context of this continually accelerating rate of development, the lifespan of buildings is no longer a function of the durability of its materials. Rather, it is a function of its compliance with exponentially increasing standards for the generation of surplus energy and the reduction of energy consumption. At the end of ten years, a building generates 64 times less surplus energy and consumes 64 times more resources than a new one would. As a result, the building is destroyed, replaced by a new version, and its material is biodegraded through updated technologies of land remediation.

Environmental technologies continue to improve. Buildings provide more energy, impact the environment less, and the lifespan of architecture is reduced to even fewer years to improve the equilibrium of the environment. In this clockwork fiction the systematic 'regeneration' of the city transforms the urbanization process into the management of energy production. Urban design shifts from an activity of densification and expansion, to one of resource harvesting.

Enabled by its high concentration of capital and motivated municipal leadership, Busan, Korea is the first city to implement this urban schema. Its aspiration to be internationally renowned like cities of similar size and resources (Basel, Silicon Valley, Malmo, Kitakyushu, Glasgow, Pittsburgh, etcetera), motivates the local government to develop Busan as a sustainable city. The improvement rates in the efficiency of energy systems, building technology, and land remediation create the incentive to continually rebuild. Busan's leaders decide to replace vast areas on an increasingly accelerated schedule to achieve a richer ecological environment. Other cities adopt the so-named Busan Metabolism to stave off mounting energy and resource costs, and to mitigate the environmental impact of previous urban development.

As the story closes, municipalities throughout Asia and the world realize that the initial implementation of the plan was risky but necessary. It was already certain that the world could not have sustained the successive urbanizations of China and India were planners to follow the twentieth-century logic of development and resource consumption. As Asia urbanized, surpluses of oil and iron ore (the main ingredient in steel) diminished, followed

(Left)
Moore's Law has been no friend to nature. During the late twentieth century, the cities that created the greatest innovations in technology also produced the most toxic urban environments (in the USA they are: Silicon Valley, San Francisco, Boston/Cambridge). Future innovations in technology can reverse this course set by the last century's notion of progress.

(Right)
Can Environmentalism lead to a new philosophy of urbanization?

Inferiority Complex: Like 'Second Cities' around the world, Busan is driven by a desire to compete with its nation's 'first' city (Seoul) by means of its own unique development process. Up until now, Busan's development has been based on port trade. In the future, it can be shaped by ecology.

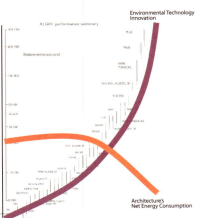

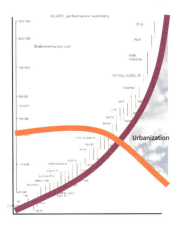

by the worldwide shortage of potable water. By 2050, more cities of one million inhabitants had been constructed during the twenty-first century than during all previous centuries combined. The Busan experiment demonstrated one alternative for planners to meet the resource needs of cities. Like Moore's Law itself, Busan Metabolism became a self-fulfilling prophesy in the environmental technology industry, initiating a humanitarian course correction to the process of urbanization.

Busan Metabolism
2007
20XX

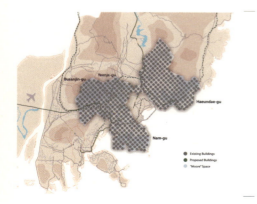

20XX + 5 years

Rather than consume energy, architecture can produce it. When that happens 'obsolete' buildings will be destroyed for the overall sake of the environment. This increased architectural metabolism (faster rate of construction) will result in less density and 'Moore' space.

20XX + 5 years

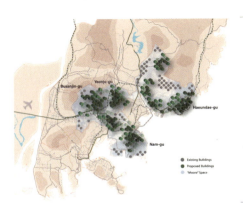

20XX +10 years

20XX +10 years

Sharing: Urban design will become primarily a process of managing energy production. The surplus wind and solar power that buildings generate can be stored in hydrogen cells located in building curtain walls or shared with neighboring structures.

The New City of Luoyang
Negotiating with the Power of Autocracy

Yimin Zhu

Hinterland cities like Luoyang have played a crucial role in the urbanization of China; in fact they compose the major body of contemporary Chinese urban practice. Unlike central metropolises such as Beijing, Shanghai and Shenzhen, the model of late urban expansion of inner cities is more politically oriented than market driven, and operates in diverse contexts. Its approach is derived from a hybrid of rigid control and free market competition. The new city in Luoyang, with its ad hoc pattern of the corporate city, represents one of the few authentic examples of Chinese urbanization.

City of Luoyang: From Communism to Consumerism

Located in the middle of China, some 700 km southwest of Beijing, Luoyang is China's most ancient capital city. Founded 4,000 years ago, the city has historically been the capital of more than nine Chinese dynasties. Its original planning is considered to be the paradigm for ancient Chinese cities.

After the Communist Revolution in 1949, Luoyang, like most hinterland cities, underwent a process of urban explosion and industrialization; 46 per cent of the new urban areas built in the 1950s were industrial zones.

The major urban expansion started in late 1970s – the beginning of the 'reformation era'. Luoyang's population jumped from 540,000 to 1,000,000 between 1980 and 2000. Industry was declining and the labour market was being reshuffled. By the 1990s, Luoyang's culture and economy had been transformed from industry to consumerism.

The New City on the South Bank of the Main River: Miniature Great Leap Forward

In 2003, the local authorities launched a new master plan, with the aim to construct a new city across the river, to the south of the existing city, within a few years. According to the master plan, the new city's land area is 71.3 km^2, half of that of the existing city; its total population is 500,000. The main functions of the new city are residential, commercial and public services, education and technology. It consists of six zones, with a total investment of 17 billion euros.

At the end of 2006, a total floor area of 3.7 million m^2 had been constructed; 174 high-rise buildings were under construction (65 finished); 2.52 billion euro had been invested in the project. The project was promoted and executed by Mr Sun Shanwu, then the general secretary of the Communist Party committee of Luoyang.

Context 1: Two-Tiered System – 'Socialism with Chinese Characteristics'

In the late 1970s, the Communist Party of China launched its economic reformation plan. It pursued a transformation of the economic system to avoid financial bankruptcy, while maintaining ideological purity and political power. The new agenda lead to the introduction of a 'two-tiered track system', combining communist sovereignty with elements of a capitalist free market. The strategy was proclaimed by the party leader as a search for 'socialism with Chinese characteristics'. This duality caused ideological confusion among party leaders of all levels and produced a widening gap between political legitimacy and practical feasibility – the means to fulfil its social and economical promises to all people for better living conditions.

Context 2: The Corporate Power Structure

In 1992, Deng Xiaoping called for a further development of reformation and suggested to lay aside ideological disputes.

Under his guidance, the Communist Party reached an agreement that the economy should be the primary concern of its political agenda.

The new policy led to the establishment of a free market system in almost all industries. It instantly stimulated the growth of the economy. Along with the steady and rapid growth of the economy and the urban population, most cities expanded dramatically in the late 1990s.

Market economy demands emancipation from totalitarian control. It challenges the legitimacy and privilege of the party and runs the risk of social instability and chaos. To guarantee the integrity of the society and ensure the success of economic reformation, the Communist Party advocates and insists on the autocracy of its power and strengthens the role of political control of the local government.

The boundary between political power and economic activities is blurred. The relationship between Communist Party authority and commercial activities is similar to that of a corporation and its own business. The power structure of the Communist Party is identical to that of a corporation.

Context 3: The City-Making Movement and 'Face Projects'

The new agenda of the Communist Party simultaneously introduced an alternative political criterion. Instead of the ideological correctness of the past communist era, the increased growth rate of the local economy became the sole measure of political success. The GDP index became the crucial issue.

Both political and economic circumstances propel the national 'city making movement'. Old cities are rebuilt, renovated, densified. New cities are planned and constructed overnight. The city is taken as the container for increasing investment and enterprises. For party leaders, the hidden agenda is that the city can simultaneously be a step for political promotion.

The GDP is still an abstract standard; a new city image is a crucial and concrete proof of economic development. The suc-

Location of Luoyang on the map of China
Luoyang is an inland city established more than 4000 years ago, some 700 km to the southwest of Beijing.

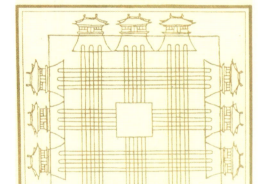

City map of Luoyang in the Zhou dynasty – the urban prototype for Chinese cities

City map of Luoyang in the Tang dynasty

Luoyang city map, 1954

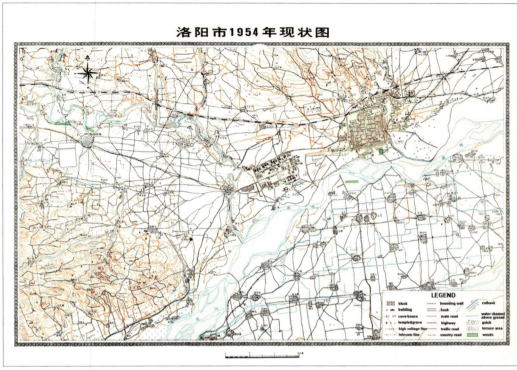

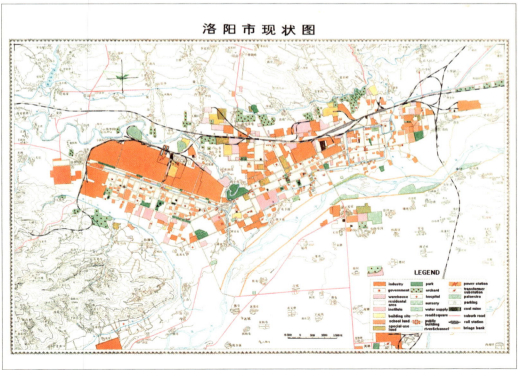

Luoyang city map, 1980

Impression of the new city of Luoyang, 2006
Existing rural area in the preserved zone
of the Sui-Tang dynasty city relic

View of Sui-Tang dynasty city relic park

Luoyang master plan
The New City on the South Bank of the Main River:
Miniature Great Leap Forward

ousing development along the river in the new city
r Sun Shanwu at the construction site of the new city

In the year 2003, the local authorities launched a new master plan, aimed at constructing a new city to the south of the existing city on the other side of the river within years.

Total area: 71.3 km²
Central area: 11.2 km²
University town + sports centre: 8.5 km²
Technology zone: 13.9 km²
Protected district of Tang dynasty city relic: 22 km²
Commercial and trade zone: 10.8 km²
Linear park along the river: 4.9 km²
Total investment needed: 17 billion euros
Population: 500,000
Green space coverage: 40 %

cessful images of Shenzhen and Shanghai became the models, followed by many hinterland cities. In response to these images, new projects for other cities are planned and built, not in accordance with market needs, but for the sake of getting noticed. These image overhauls are known as 'face projects' – Chinese versions of the 'Potemkin Corridor'. The new city of Luoyang is a 'face project'.

Strategy and Intervention: Project as Negotiation Tool

For financial reasons, it is difficult for hinterland cities to copy the successful models of China's central metropolises; therefore autocracy is negotiable. A feasible alternative vision of future development is indispensable; this vision is the most efficient and useful tool for negotiating with the bureaucracy and autocracy of the corporate structure.

According to the new city plan, the waterfront, as the most important city image, will be the focus of the next phase of urban development: at least 100 towers will be completed along the river bank by the end of 2007. To quote the slogan of the government: 'make another Lujiazui (the most spectacular waterfront of Pudong District, Shanghai) in Luoyang!' An alternative vision for this area will be proposed, along with a housing pattern for a different way of living in the city.

The project conveys a historical perspective and cultural consciousness, both of which have been broken by the present urban strategy and erased from the planning agenda of the new city of Luoyang. In addition to the current speed-driven strategy that aligns with the market hegemony and manipulation, a new practical dimension will be integrated into a true quality of urban space via the introduction of the new vision.

Main urban spatial axis
A. Industrial zone built in the 1950s
B. Sui-Tang Dynasty relic preserved zone
C. The main river of the city of Luoyang
1. Cemetery of the communist party victims in the war against the nationalist regime before 1949
2. Central railway station
3. Municipal square
4. Stadium
5. Television tower
6. New municipal building and artificial lake
7. Location of high speed railway station and regional transportation hub

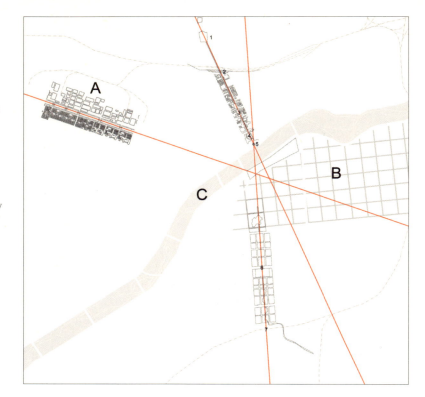

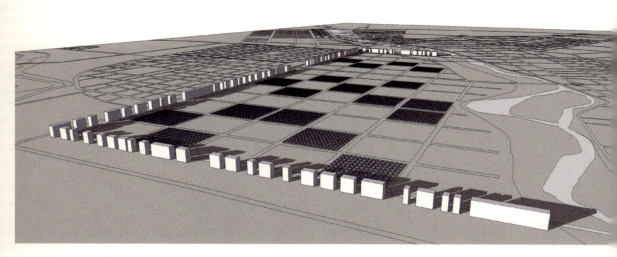

Perspective of the project, view from east to west. Linear high-rise zone and low-rise housing (near front)

The conceptual plan of the project for the new waterfront aims to introduce a new quality of public and living spaces along the river, while questioning the existing isolated habitation pattern and the a-historical skyscraper model.
A. Sui-Tang dynasty relic
B. Linear high-rise zone along the edge of the preserved zone of the Sui-Tang dynasty relic
C. Public spaces and installations on the river
D. New housing blocks along the river

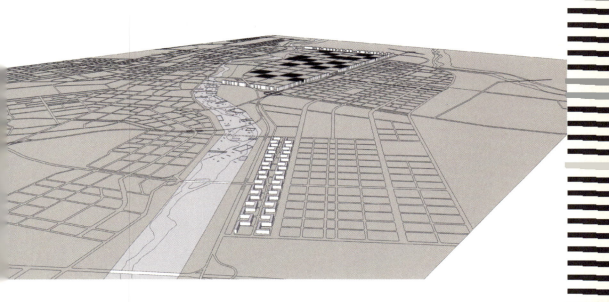

Perspective of the project, view from the southwest

Garden State Back City

Garden State/Backyard City
Within the Power of Corporate New Jersey

Princeton University Center for Architecture, Urbanism and Infrastructure
Team Leaders
Rafi Segal
Els Verbakel

New Jersey is a twenty-first-century *CityState:* although geographically defined as a state, it has become one continuous city. New Jersey is the densest state in the USA (reaching over 1,000 people per square mile), yet it has no major cities within its borders. In its advanced state of dispersal, New Jersey offers an urban model for the future as cities all over the world succumb to sprawl and de-densification. This project, *Garden State/Backyard City* defines this model and establishes working concepts by which to both understand and operate within it.

Corporate power plays a significant role in defining and creating this *CityState*. At the same time, New Jersey's particular settlement patterns condition the very possibilities of corporate expansion. New Jersey's location, geography, size, and roles within the region – both past and present – have led to the development of certain corporate spaces, typologies, and networks that could not have developed in more traditionally dense metropolitan areas. The seeds of corporate power are not to be found, as one might expect, in the heart of the metropolis; instead, they lie in New York City's backyard: the peripheral, apparently suburban setting of New Jersey. Through networks of flow and distribution, corporate power has instigated and determined the urbanization of the seemingly non-urban.

Historically, New Jersey has been defined by agriculture, industry, and its suburbs, differentiated only by their exit numbers on the NJ Turnpike. Its location within the region as a crossroads between other states and cities (equidistant from the urban centres of Manhattan and Philadelphia), its transportation infrastructure, and its proximity to major ports turned the state into a regional industrial hub. The subsequent migration of office spaces from the dense city centres to their outskirts eventually spurred the development of the office campus, or the research park – often a new type of office headquarters implanted in an idyllic setting. Due to its infrastructure, established communities and land availability, New Jersey became a breeding ground for such enclaves of corporate power. As a type of dispersed urbanism, this corporate enclave has been exported to other parts of the world, contributing to the evolution of the special economic zones which emerge under very different political-economic regimes.

Alongside programmes of office and research, New Jersey's residents, with the highest income per capita in the USA, fuelled the expansion and development of new typologies of retail and entertainment. The urban fragments deposited into this backyard city on the one hand, and the 'Garden State' suburban expansion of desirable neighbourhoods on the other, gradually met, juxtaposed, and combined to produce a new form of urbanism: a twenty-first-century *CityState*.

The examination and analysis of this urban model reveals its components: expansive density, socio-demographic diversity, decentralization (fragmentation) of government; political power and space, high frequency and proximity of distribution and mobility, ecological and multi-scalar public space. New Jersey has

A method for urban hybrids of the future city-state.

REVERSED CENTRALITIES

JUXTAPOSITIONS OF
EXTREME SCALES

PARALLEL NETWORKS

HAZARDS / HAVENS

The spatial products of New Jersey; objects, buildings, cities, and landscapes, are collected, categorized and dissected into separate architectural elements.
These elements – New Jersey's urban traits – are then combined and mixed to breed new offsprings for a future New Jersey *CityState*.
This project proposes a tool for urban speculation and experimentation, whereby the architect generates new urban

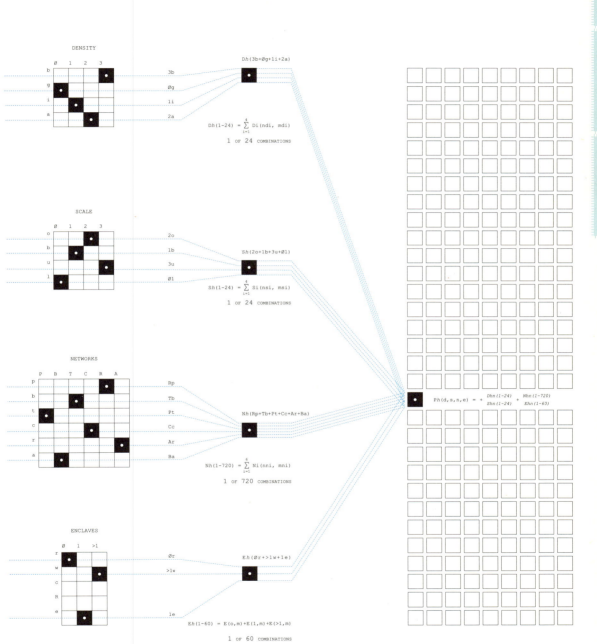

entities (programs and forms) using units and elements of corporate power and expansion. As New Jersey outgrew its suburban nature, transforming into a new dispersed urban condition, its typical physical features – the generic products created by corporate power, have now become the genes for urban hybrids of a 21st century *CityState*.

GROUP CATALOGS

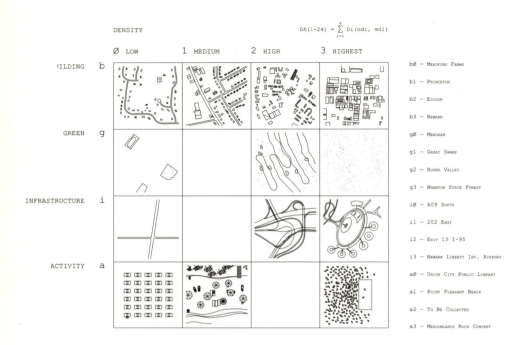

DENSITY $Dh(1\text{-}24) = \sum_{i=1}^{4} Di(ndi, mdi)$

		0 LOW	1 MEDIUM	2 HIGH	3 HIGHEST	
BUILDING	b					b0 — Meadford Farms b1 — Princeton b2 — Edison b3 — Newark
GREEN	g					g0 — Mendham g1 — Great Swamp g2 — Round Valley g3 — Wharton State Forest
INFRASTRUCTURE	i					i0 — 609 South i1 — 202 East i2 — Exit 13 I-95 i3 — Newark Liberty Int. Airport
ACTIVITY	a					a0 — Union City Public Library a1 — Point Pleasant Beach a2 — To Be Collected a3 — Meadowlands Rock Concert

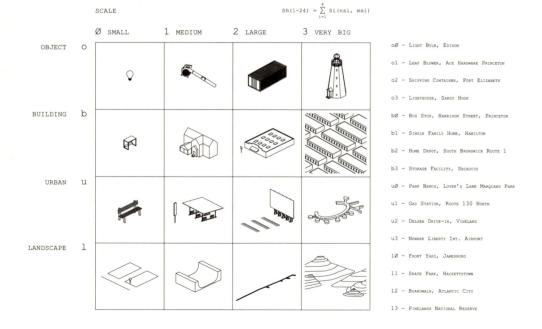

SCALE $Sh(1\text{-}24) = \sum_{i=1}^{4} Si(nsi, msi)$

		0 SMALL	1 MEDIUM	2 LARGE	3 VERY BIG	
OBJECT	o					o0 — Light Bulb, Edison o1 — Leaf Blower, Ace Hardware Princeton o2 — Shipping Container, Port Elizabeth o3 — Lighthouse, Sandy Hook
BUILDING	b					b0 — Bus Stop, Harrison Street, Princeton b1 — Single Family Home, Hamilton b2 — Home Depot, South Brunswick Route 1 b3 — Storage Facility, Secaucus
URBAN	u					u0 — Park Bench, Lover's Lane Marquand Park u1 — Gas Station, Route 130 North u2 — Delsea Drive-In, Vineland u3 — Newark Liberty Int. Airport
LANDSCAPE	l					l0 — Front Yard, Jamesburg l1 — Skate Park, Hackettstown l2 — Boardwalk, Atlantic City l3 — Pinelands National Reserve

NETWORKS $Nh(1-720) = \sum_{i=1}^{6} Ni(nni, mni)$

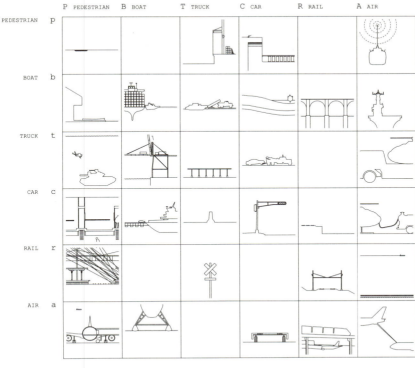

ENCLAVES $Eh(1-60) = E(o,m) + E(1,m) + E(>1,m)$

pP — Sidewalk, Hopewell
pB — Ellis Island Ferry, Liberty Park
pT — McMaster Carr Loading Dock, Princeton
pC — Forest Elementary School, Montgomery
pR — To Be Completed
pA — Lakeland Aircraft Modelers, Erial
bP — Hanson Park Canoe Club, Cranford
bB — The Narrows Waterway
bT — Trash Skimmer, Passaic River
bC — Holland Tunnel, Hudson River
bR — Raritan River, New Brunswick
bA — Seaplane Base, Jersey City
tP — Axel Carlson Reef, Near Manasquan Inlet
tB — Port Elizabeth, Elizabeth
tT — Exit 10, 295 South
tC — New Jersey Towing, West Orange
tR — To Be Completed
tA — Helicopter NJ, Medford
cP — Toll Booth, NJ Turnpike
cB — Public Landing, Hoboken
cT — Jersey Barrier, NJ Turnpike
cC — Intersection, Trenton
cR — Alexander Road, Princeton
cA — Helicopter, Atlantic City Airport
rP — Train Station, Princeton Junction
rB — To Be Completed
rT — Railway Signal, North Elizabeth
rC — To Be Completed
rR — Train Station, Metuchen
rA — Above Exit 14, NJ Turnpike
aP — Gate 27, Newark Liberty Int. Airport
aB — NY Ship Building Corporation, Camden
aT — Hess Corporation, Trenton
aC — Coast Guard Station, Atlantic City
aR — Air Shuttle, Newark Liberty Int. Airport
aA — McGuire Air Force Base, Wrightstown

r0 — South Woods State Prison, Bridgeton
r1 — Levittown, Willingboro
r>1 — "Little Lima" Peruvian Enclave, Paterson
w0 — Fort Dix Army Base, Burlington County
w1 — Bristol-Myers Squibb, Princeton Township
w>1 — Office Building, To Be Collected
c0 — Internet Retailer
c1 — Alexander Hamilton Rest Area, NJ Turnpike
c>1 — Cherry Hill Mall, Burlington County
R0 — Church of the Hills, Farhills
R1 — Trump Plaza Hotel & Casino, Atlantic City
R>1 — Hidden Acres Campground, Cape May
e0 — Marshlands, Kearny
e1 — Eagle Point Oil Refinery, Westville
e>1 — Cape May

GROUP COMBINATIONS

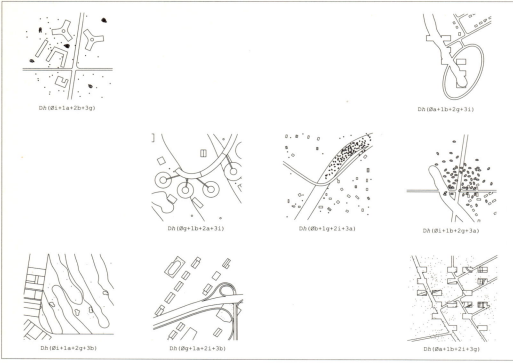

Dh(Øi+1a+2b+3g) Dh(Øa+1b+2g+3i)
Dh(Øg+1b+2a+3i) Dh(Øb+1g+2i+3a) Dh(Øi+1b+2g+3a)
Dh(Øi+1a+2g+3b) Dh(Øg+1a+2i+3b) Dh(Øa+1b+2i+3g)

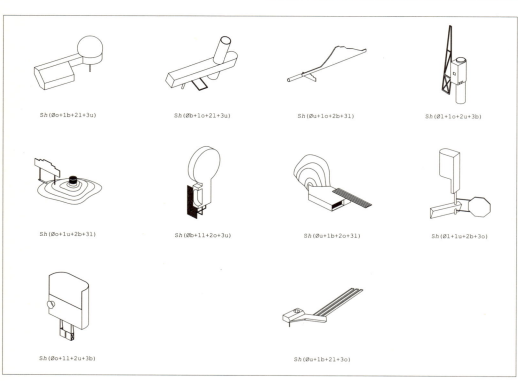

Sh(Øo+1b+2l+3u) Sh(Øb+1o+2l+3u) Sh(Øu+1o+2b+3l) Sh(Øl+1o+2u+3b)
Sh(Øo+1u+2b+3l) Sh(Øb+1l+2o+3u) Sh(Øu+1b+2o+3l) Sh(Øl+1u+2b+3o)
Sh(Øo+1l+2u+3b) Sh(Øu+1b+2l+3o)

109 Corporate Cities New Jersey

Nh(Pr+Bc+Tb+Cp+Rt+Aa)

Nh(Pa+Br+Tb+Cp+Rt+Ac)

Nh(Pc+Br+Tb+Cp+Ra+At)

Nh(Pc+Bb+Ta+Cp+Rr+At)

Nh(Pa+Bb+Tp+Cc+Rr+At)

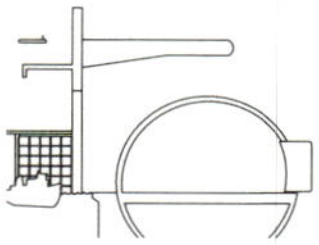

Nh(Pa+Bt+Tp+Cc+Rb+Ar)

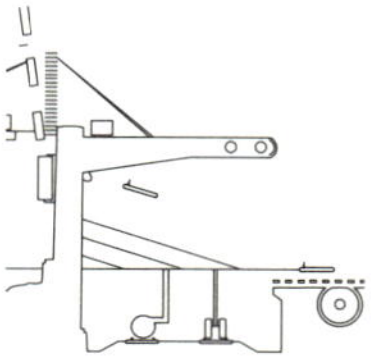

Nh(Pa+Bc+Tb+Ct+Rp+Ar)

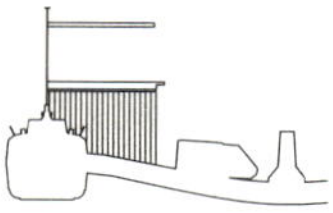

Nh(Pc+Ba+Tt+Cr+Rb+Ap)

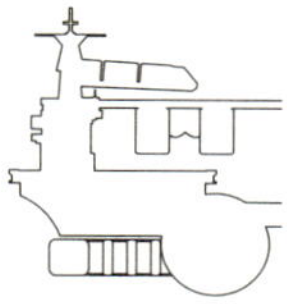

Nh(Pr+Bc+Ta+Cb+Rp+At)

Nh(Pp+Br+Tb+Ct+Ra+Ac)

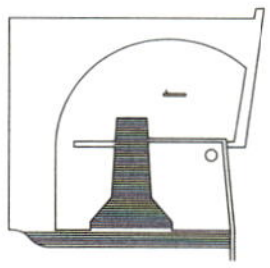

Nh(Pc+Bb+Tp+Ct+Ra+Ar)

Eh(Ør+1c+>1R)

Eh(Ør+1w+>1e)

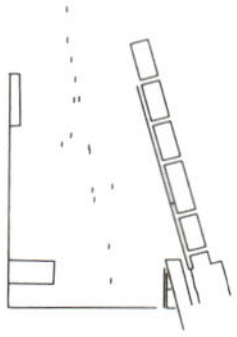

Eh(Ør+1w+>1R)

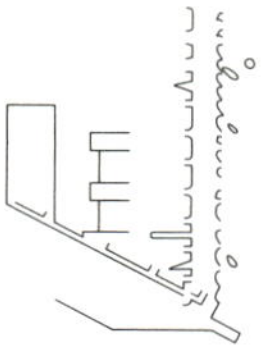

Eh(Ør+1w+>1c)

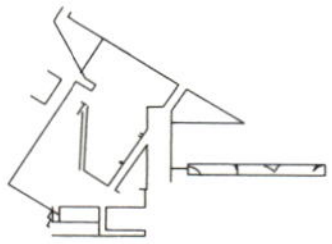

Eh(Øw+1e+>1r)

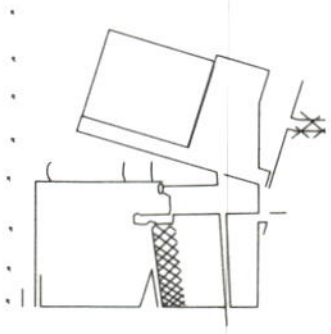

Eh(Øw+1R+>1e)

Eh(ØR+1c+>1e)

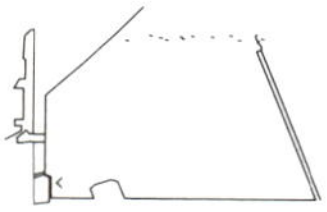

Eh(Øw+1e+>1R)

Eh(Øw+1c+>1R)

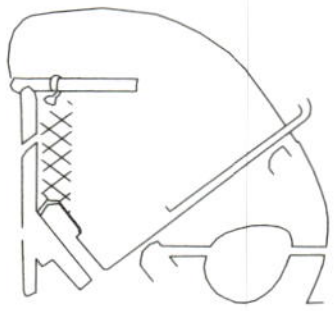

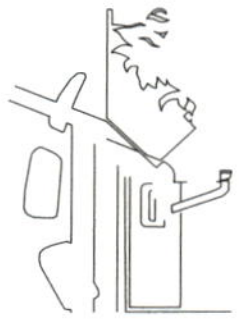

Eh(Ør+1c+>1R)

Eh(ØR+1c+>1r)

Eh(ØR+1r+>1c)

thus produced new notions of urban space stretching beyond the urbanism of the traditional dense city.

These components, produced largely by forces of corporate power, have been made manifest in a set of spatial mechanisms characterizing this *CityState*. Four mechanisms will be distilled and addressed in this project: reversed centralities, parallel networks/shortcuts, juxtaposition of extreme scales, and enclaves of hazards and havens.

- Reversed Centralities: The common understanding of the growth of traditional dense cities is of an outward radiation from a central core. New Jersey presents a reversed development pattern, from the outside in.

- Parallel Networks/Shortcuts: New Jersey's commuters, distribution of goods (and waste), and local communities each constitute linear systems running the length of the state; shortcuts cutting across these systems become powerful sites of urban exchange.

- Extreme Juxtaposition: Enormous storage structures and single family houses coexist without precedent, each belonging to different systems of influence and reach. The attraction and repulsion between these distinct scales constitutes an unstable built fabric.

- Havens and Hazards: The twenty-first-century *CityState* is built on enclaves of havens and hazards. Each enclave (corporate, domestic and commercial) possesses varying degrees of accessibility, safety, and danger.

This project does not propose specific buildings or plans, but provides a tool for the formation of New Jersey as an urban model. This tool is used to read, interpret, and intervene. Our first step is to analyse, dissecting phenomena by certain parameters; then we synthesize, recombining these phenomena in order to explore other possible forms, programmes, and spaces that can be part of New Jersey's urbanism.

III CROSS-GROUP COMBINATIONS

Dh (Øi+1a+2b+3g)
Sh (Øb+1l+2o+3u)
Nh (Pa+Bc+Tb+Ct+Rp+Ar)
Eh (Ør+1w+>1c)

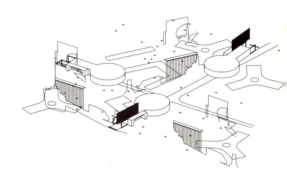

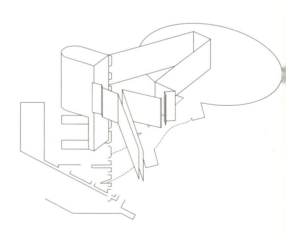

Dh (Øa+1b+2g+3i)
Sh (Ø1+1u+2b+3o)
Nh (Pr+Bc+Tb+Cp+Rt+Aa)
Eh (Ør+1w+>1R)

This tool organizes components of the city according to the four mechanisms of the *CityState* in the form of a matrix. By taking apart the different components of each mechanism and closely investigating its internal spatial logics, this tool provides ways of characterizing the urban qualities of this new *CityState*. By recombining these components, the existing urbanisms can be revisited, augmented, questioned and transformed to fertilize a future architecture and urbanism.

The tool encompasses the engagement with and orchestration of the spatial mechanisms of the built and non-built that reach beyond buildings, thereby redefining the limits and scope of the architectural operation. It allows its user – the architect – to intervene in the process of de-coding and re-coding several different elements of the environment, thereby promoting participation in the political and economic powers that brought them about. The architect's role has thus expanded from designing space to processing the environment of this CityState to come.

```
Dh(Øa+1b+2i+3g)
Sh(Øo+1b+21+3u)
Nh(Pa+Br+Tb+Cp+Rt+Ac)
Eh(ØR+1c+>1r)
```

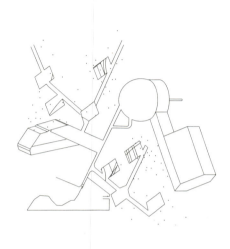

```
Dh(Øb+1a+2g+3i)
Sh(Øo+1u+2b+31)
Nh(Pc+Bb+Tp+Ct+Ra+Ar)
Eh(ØR+1r+>1c)
```

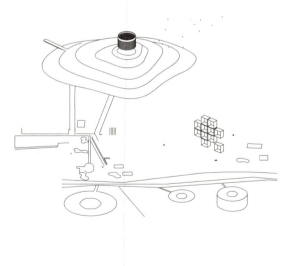

In Pro
Disco

In Praise of Discontinuity
or 'La Leçon de Rome'

Gabriele Mastrigli

'It is within the conceptual density of the European city, the effect of the experimental and often devastating succession of strategies – in Rome as in Paris, Berlin and Rotterdam – that the architectural project becomes, in fact, a critical instrument that can be used to formulate an opinion about the city itself and proactively question its current and past conditions.'

In Praise of Discontinuity

Since the 1960s, European cities have been subject to profound transformations: the compact and continuous city has evolved into an urban form dominated by fragmentation and dispersion. While in many European regions territorial processes of densification have been continuous and politically sustained, they have proven themselves to be inefficient in producing an urban condition that meets expectations. The result, at the dawn of the third millennium, is that they are now accepted as inevitable 'mutations' of the Western city, at the mercy of the unpredictable forces that are extraneous to

the traditional domains of architecture and urban planning. Today, notwithstanding the fact that we are witness to impressive processes of urbanization and concentration – no longer exclusively in Asia, but also in the Middle East and in Africa – a reflection on the future of the world-metropolis is still being played out in the European city, considered as being representative of a more emblematic and advanced condition, if not an implicit model, of dispersion and its relative problems.[1]

The characteristic of *discontinuity* that marks the urban form of the European city now appears to be a phenomenon that is much more complex and over-determined than urbanization and concentration; it is a phenomenon that escapes the prefigurations of design and leads to the fear of the dissolution of the city, generating the main obsessions of urban planning and architecture during the last 20 years: *filling the gaps*, welding and reconnecting parts of the city, as if they were pieces of a body that is no longer seen as unitary, but that we are not willing to abandon to its own nature. Discontinuity thus becomes nothing more than the banal metaphor of an idea of the city as a *patchwork*, a mosaic of identities that are increasingly more global and generic and which constitute a *continuum* of differences that have already been resolved in the presumed homogeneity of urban space and its flows.

In reality discontinuity is a much more structured condition of the European metropolis and it must be recognized in the tension between two opposing ideas of the city: on the one hand the concept of urbanization as *infrastructure*, a system of territorial organization and control based on the performance of a certain number of activities; on the other hand the idea of the city as a *centre*, a system for the representation of political, social and religious values that justify and orient these activities. This tension between the two souls of the European city that, during the modern era, progressively dissolved into the respective and ever more self-referential domains of urban planning (the increasingly abstract system of rules) and architecture (the obsessive and autistic accumulation of exceptions), has always constituted

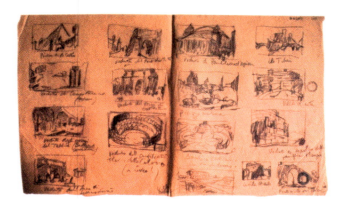

Taddeo di Bartolo, Roma, 1414 (Fresco, Siena, Palazzo Comunale.

Charles-Edouard Jeanneret, Sketches of famous monuments in Rome, including the Pyramid of Cestius, the Pantheon, the Colosseum, after Piranesi, *Vedute di Roma*, in the Bibliotèque Nationale, Paris, 1915. FLC [272]. (Image from: Stanislaus von Moos and Arthur Ruegg (eds.), *Le Corbusier before Le Corbusier*, New Haven: Yale University Press, 2002, 188.)

the richest and most original patrimony of the European city, whose peculiarity can, in the end, be traced back to *Rome*. Since the dawn of the system-Europe the essentially organizational-functional nature of urban planning, structured around large mobility networks and the military grid is opposed, in fact, to the singular characteristics of Rome itself, its condition as the political-symbolic centre of an empire, without being strictly a model of urbanization – an idea so strong that it was re-appropriated during Christianity, the Renaissance and, in more recent times, for the political foundation of modern Europe and, obviously, the era of cultural tourism. If the typical Roman city is produced, so to say, by the precepts of urban planning, Rome is, instead, the *locus* within which this role falls directly upon architecture that, materializing the successive symbolic aspects of the city, continually questions and redefines, using its own instruments, the very nature of its urban structure.[2] What Rome has offered over the centuries, to Europe and the Western world, feeding the most radical architectural visions for urban projects in the modern and even the postmodern era, is the exemplary nature of the city. Rome, contrary to the typical Roman city, was never witness to a phase of growth resulting from the application of universal concepts. Thus, more than a model, it represents an *example*, in the sense of a 'species' that consists of a sole individual and which can only be *politically reproduced* and never transposed into an omnivorous 'general programme': its force is 'the authority of the prototype and not the regulation of the command' – the force of representing a different idea of the city.³

One

Among the numerous references to ancient and modern history that populate the pages of *Vers une Architecture*, Rome is the only example to which Le Corbusier dedicates specific attention. Unlike the temples of Greece, the

mosques of Turkey and the grain silos of the USA, the works of architecture that the young Jeanneret observes in Rome are read as a function of their context, as belonging to a discourse about the *city*.

It is well known that Le Corbusier's first idea for what would later become the *Voyage d'Orient* was the idea of a visit exclusively to Rome, where he wished to admire, above all, the architecture of Bramante.⁴ Upon his arrival in the Eternal City in 1911, Le Corbusier was fascinated by the existence of the monuments of classicism within the articulated urban *corpus*. However, it was when he returned to Rome some ten years later that he began the preparation of an essay on the city, filled with systematic, if auto-didactic studies, of the culture of classical architecture in relation to the city. In particular, he spent the entire summer of 1915 in the Bibliothèque Nationale in Paris consulting treatises and producing numerous annotations and sketches, some of which were dedicated to Piranesi's *Vedute di Roma*, from which he extracted the monuments of classicism that stand out in virtue of the essential nature of their form, set against the backdrop of a Rome that was half buried in the 'natural' decadence of its era. In this way Le Corbusier transforms the *Vedute* into a catalogue of abstract architectural solutions, which are almost the same as those found in the opening to the chapter 'La Leçon de Rome' in *Vers une Architecture*:[5] the Pantheon, the Pyramid of Caius Cestius, the Arch of Constantine, the Coliseum, as well as the works of Michelangelo and even those of Byzantine Rome (S. Maria in Cosmedin). Framed up close, devoid of any context, often presented as if they had arrived intact in the present, these examples are finally recognized as the forms that constitute the sense of Roman architecture and the 'materials' for the construction of the modern city. For Le Corbusier, 'Roman' was akin to 'unity of operation, a clear aim in view, classification of the various parts', in substance *strategy, methodology* and *typology*: by 'clear aim in view' (strategy) he recognizes in ancient Rome the awareness of architecture as an instrument for the creation of a political programme; the 'unity of opera-

Le Corbusier, 'Architecture I, La Leçon de Rome', from *Vers une Architecture*, Paris: Crès, 1923, 119.

Le Corbusier, 'La Leçon de Rome, the Pyramid of Cestius', from *Vers une Architecture*, Paris: Crés, 1923, 124.

Le Corbusier, 'La Leçon de Rome, the Colosseum and the Arch of Constantine', from *Vers une Architecture*, Paris: Crès, 1923, 125.

Le Corbusier, 'La Leçon de Rome', Sketches after Pirro Ligorio, Antiquae Urbis Imago, from *Vers une Architecture*, Paris: Crès, 1923, 128.

tion' (methodology) makes reference to the techniques of construction and the structural solutions, admiring their efficiency and essentiality; finally his idea of the 'classification of the various parts' (typology) advances the hypothesis that Roman architecture produced – in particular in Rome – a catalogue of examples that are capable of constituting not only a simple repertoire of ready-made solutions, but also the structure that is simultaneously the *grammar* and *syntax* of the city.[6]

Nonetheless, the cupola of the Pantheon or Michelangelo's apses at St Peter's are not evoked as a petition for the geometric principles related to an ideal truth or beauty, but are emblematic of the search for a density of meaning in form that, according Le Corbusier, can restore dignity to architecture *on its own*. The monuments are not only elementary solids, but rather take advantage of geometry to intensify their relationship with the city – perhaps even contrasting it – through an efficient synthesis of form and function.[7] The triumphal arch, like the dome of the Pantheon and the amphitheatrical structure of the Coliseum are not the celebration of geometric perfection as much as the identification of a *language* for architecture that is appropriate to the scale of the city. To the homogeneous fabric of baroque Rome, celebrated in the grey *poché* of the Nolli Plan and still dominant in the Rome of Victor Emmanuel I, Le Corbusier opposes the image of a *discontinuous* Rome, the product of a combination of abstract forms that represent order, articulation (*modénature*) and scale, 'the ultimate case for a notion of architecture in which emotion is conveyed through the direct impact of form, without the mediation of a narrative'.[8]

The structure of this Rome is synthesized in the image of the *Antique Urbis Imago* by Pirro Ligorio from 1561, a detail of which Le Corbusier redraws in the closing chapter of 'La Leçon de Rome'[9] Ligorio's *Imago* is not simply one of the numerous reproductions of the ancient city and its monuments, as much as the birth of a desire to reproduce classical Rome based on scientific and critical data, with a global investigation of archaeological

«

Le Corbusier, Sketches of Place Vendome, the courtyard of the Louvre, the Place de la Concorde in Paris, in *Le Corbusier, Oeuvre Complète*, 1938-1946, 154.

Le Corbusier, Sketches for the 1929 conference in Buenos Aires, published in *Précisions*, Crès, Paris, 1930, 173.

data, historical sources and compositional invention that is simultaneously focused on the past, the present and the future. By representing this piece of Ligorio's *Imago*, in which large public buildings are even more isolated, Le Corbusier implicitly represents the idea that is made evident in his *Plan Voisin*, the plan for the transformation of the centre of Paris developed beginning in 1925: the urban nucleus grows through monumental elements that constitute both the *image* of the city and the points of reference for its urban structure; these elements belong to the history of the city and, what is more, constitute the necessary starting point for the new city.[10] By declaring that 'we have a legacy of objects we admire, whose dimensions and presence are an unfailing source of joy: the Place Vendome, the courtyard of the Louvre, the Place de la Concorde', Le Corbusier demonstrates how, in substance, the *Plan Voisin* is not a proposal for a generic tabula rasa, but rather a highly sophisticated approach towards the city through a careful evaluation and selection of its relevant elements.[11]

Two

The attention that Le Corbusier focused on Paris can thus be considered similar to Piranesi's interest in Rome: an interest that can already be appreciated in the *Vedute*, but which becomes explicit in the *Campo Marzio* drawings from 1762, where the frontispiece by the Venetian engraver features his own version of the *Imago urbis* from the Imperial Age.¹² The image of Rome that appears in the famous *Ichnographia* – in which the vestiges of the past appear to be projected into a timeless zone where the language of architecture exceeds the concrete space of the city so much so that it replaces it – cannot be understood, nonetheless, if not in light of his preparatory drawings. In fact, it is in the *Scenographia* and the *Topographia* that Piranesi clarifies the presuppositions – and implicitly announces the objectives – of the entire campaign of reconstructing the city. Where in the *Scenographia*

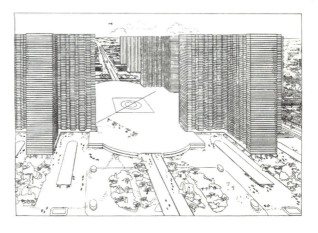

Le Corbusier, 'Plan Voisin' de Paris, 1925, from *Oeuvre Complète, 1910-1929*, 109.

»

Piranesi, *Il Campo Marzio dell'Antica Roma*, Frontespiece, 1762

»

Piranesi, *Il Campo Marzio dell'Antica Roma*, Ichnographiam Campi Martii antiquae urbis, 1762

»

Piranesi, *Il Campo Marzio dell'Antica Roma*, Topographia Campi Martii, 1762

the 'future' of architecture in Rome is prepared for through the meticulous removal of its present, leaving the few existing ruins of its Imperial past in their place, reduced to an *ante literam* tabula rasa, in the *Topographia* he describes the other elements that orient the urban structure of the new city: the Aurelian and Vatican Walls, the most important road networks (the Via Salaria, Via Flaminia and Via Giulia) and, above all, the Tiber River, at the time one of the most important infrastructures in the city. As can be clearly seen in the final reconstruction of the *Ichnographia*, the river, for Piranesi, is not only the main (and in some ways the only) element that renders Rome recognizable, but above all the spinal column for the growth of the city on the banks opposite the Campo Marzio: the Campo Vaticano, which Piranesi imagines as the home of the most monumental of the complex 'inventions' of his Rome, the *Area Martis*, not by chance shown in the frontispiece of the work. By moving the axis of the city towards the north-east and hypothesizing the Campo Vaticano as the home of the most important port structure in

Rome, Piranesi thus makes the river more than a simple piece of topography, turning it into the principle infrastructure in his reinvented city and, finally, the context with which architecture establishes a very close contact.

While defining the heart of the *Plan Voisin*, Le Corbusier could not avoid evoking Piranesi's urban strategy: the axis of his new Paris is, in fact, its infrastructural system and its centre is the large central station surrounded by four skyscrapers whose composition evidently recalls the structure of the complex of the *Area Martis* shown in the frontispiece of the Campo Marzio. The pieces of classical architecture, studied and verified by Le Corbusier in terms of their formal grammar are recomposed, deriving a rather syntactical structure from their historical structure: the quadrilobate shape of the platform of the station, the circular element at the centre of the airport runway, the two canopies/symmetrical circles of the principle axis and, above all, the choice of the point of view do not simply reproduce elementary spatial structures, but extrapolate the general principles of composition

that are to be extended and verified at the scale of the city. In the same way the internal structure of the station is based on another crucial reference to Rome: the Michelangelesque plan of the Basilica of St Peter's, to which Le Corbusier had dedicated a lengthy and passionate defence in the chapter devoted to this Florentine master. More than the four cruciform skyscrapers that directly recall the columns of the Basilica, for Le Corbusier the decisive choice is that of enclosing the station in a single form reminiscent of the Michelangelesque drum, 'a single mass, unique and entire' whose mouldings organize and manage the entire architectural programme.[13] What Le Corbusier derives from his Roman references is thus a formal apparatus to be used to confront the programmatic requirements imposed by the new scale of the modern city. 'We are important, great and worthy of the past. We will do better. This is my credo . . . We will thus leave behind coliseums, baths, an acropolis and mosques.' the young Jeanneret wrote to his friend William Ritter in 1911.[14] Recognizing the great works of architecture of the past, for Le Corbusier as for Piranesi, thus meant identifying them as *examples*: elements that, once actualized, are capable of confronting the city and constructing a new idea of urban structure, thus organizing a real space of projection of the city itself into a future that is worthy of its architecture, but above all of its history.

Three

Piranesi's harsh judgment of mid eighteenth-century Rome, analogous to that of Le Corbusier's view of Paris at the beginning of the 1920s is not so far off from the criticism made by OMA about the historicist positions that characterized debate about the European city during the 1980s. If Piranesi attacked baroque Rome for displaying the ancient without understanding the sprit of its 'magnificence' and Le Corbusier condemned the 'surgical

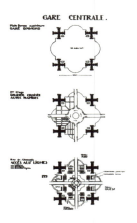

Le Corbusier, La Leçon de Rome, Sketches of the Michelangelo's project for Basilica of St. Peter's, from *Vers une Architecture*, Paris: Crès, 1923, 137.

Le Corbusier, 'Plan Voisin' de Paris, central Station, 1925, from *Urbanisme*, Paris: Crès, 1925.

Ètienne Dupérac, St Peter, Michelangelo's project in posthumous editing, around 1560, ground plan, Staatliche Museen Preußischer Kulturbesitz – Kupferstichkabinett, Berlin.

interventions' that destroyed the centre of Paris without offering urban-planning solutions that were suitable to the needs of the modern city (and worthy of the ancient one), in the same manner the attitude adopted by OMA with regards to the European city is based on the attempt to reinsert it – even violently – into the framework of a tangible modernity, exhuming, one by one, precisely those examples that had been forgotten or banished by postmodern historicism. Projects such as the addition to the Dutch Parliament in The Hague (1978), the social housing project along the Koch-Friedrichstrasse in Berlin (1980), the Boompjes residential building in Rotterdam (1980-1982) and the City Hall in The Hague (1986) are all 'polemical demonstrations' aimed at testing not so much the possibility of the coexistence of an architecture that makes use of a modern language in the heart of historical European centres, as much as the efficiency of an urban planning strategy founded on *discontinuity*; or better yet, a strategy that makes use of architecture to act selectively, without any claim of global harmony, but with the explicit mandate to 'turn the tensions and contradictions – that tear the historical city apart – into a new quality'.[15]

Thus the project for the Business Park in Lille, France, conceived of by OMA at the end of the 1980s, emblematically concludes a decade of projects that are all based on testing the potential of modern architecture in apparently impossible contexts in historical European cities. This gesture, so titanic as to brush the limits of failure, points at demonstrating the necessity of deviation – a 'quantum leap' – from one idea of the city to another, elaborating, in broad terms, the same themes found in Le Corbusier's *Plan Voisin*: the infrastructural strip, the dialectic with the historical centre, the identification of a scale of architecture that is appropriate to the new scale of the city.

As a result the project for Lille, as a confrontation between new architecture and the historical city *at the same scale* and without the mediation of auxiliary regulating systems, marks the critical point of arrival in an

approach begun in 1972 with the *Exodus* project. This linear megastructure, which operates not in a generic urban condition, but in the centre of London, with two parallel walls that section the urban fabric and the arms that extend in a radial manner towards the periphery, does nothing other than reiterate the centrality of the architectural gesture as much as that of its context, the city, to the point that it deliberately celebrates it.[16] From the London of Exodus to the Berlin of the Wall, passing through Amsterdam, Rotterdam and even New York, 'utopian Europe' reunites 'all the desirable elements that exist scattered through the Old World',[17] it is the heart of the 'European metropolis', its expectations and its protagonists that constitute, for OMA, the backdrop against which to imagine 'the most provocative settings for the experiment that is modern life'.[18] Not by chance the first 20 years of OMA's activity are, mainly, a systematic survey of the potential and 'terrifying beauty of the twentieth century', revealed to its maximum level in Europe. It is this survey that leads to the epic tale of the office's history that is told in *S,M,L,XL* and which concludes in theorizing the Bigness, 'the maximum architecture can do', the last bastion of an architecture that radically competes with the city, aiming to *be* the city itself.[19]

In opposition to the impressionist and picturesque tradition that, before as now, sees Rome as the quintessence of the decadent beauty of the past and, more in general, the European city as the virtual site of the spectacularization of History through the fetishist consumption of its icons, Piranesi's project for Rome, Le Corbusier's designs for Paris and OMA's approach to the European metropolis all reveal – notwithstanding their different historical and ideological contexts – the principle of *discontinuity* as the value to be used in understanding the fundamental role that architecture plays in relation to the city, rediscovering it as a concrete and immediate element.

It is within the conceptual density of the European city, the effect of the experimental and often devastating succession of strategies – in Rome as in Paris, Berlin and Rotterdam – that the architectural project becomes, in

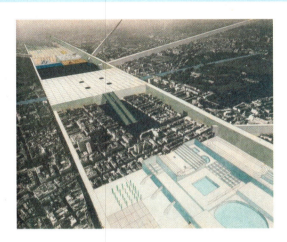

OMA, Apartment Building and Observation Tower Boompjes, Rotterdam, 1979-1982

OMA, Euralille: Centre International d'Affairs, Lille, France, 1989. First sketch of the project (from OMA, Rem Koolhaas, *Six Projets*, (ed. Patrice Goulet), Paris: IFA – Edition Carte Segrete, 1990, 53).

Rem Koolhaas, Elia Zenghelis with Madelon Vriesendorp and Zoe Zenghelis, *Exodus or the Voluntary Prisoners of Architecture*, 1972 (from Martin van Schaik and Otakar *Máčel* (ed.), *Exit Utopia. Architectural Provocations 1956-76*, Delft – Munich: IHAAU-TU – Prestel, 2005, 238).

fact, a critical instrument that can be used to formulate an opinion about the city itself and proactively question its current and past conditions. When the project confronts the city (and not simply operates *within* it), that is when it reconsiders its comprehensive meaning through the mechanisms of selection, revision and construction of the elements of which it is composed, architecture reacquires its condition of existing on its own. From here architecture can experiment with its real mandate with regards to the city: confirming its existence, reiterating its centrality, in ultimate terms, creating the conditions such that the city is capable of realizing what Le Corbusier, referring to Paris in the *Plan Voisin*, called the 'gesture of its history': 'Continuer!'.[20]

1   Cf. Bernardo Secchi, *La Città del ventesimo secolo* (Rome-Bari: Laterza, 2005).
2   Rome is known to be the only 'non-Roman' city: it is the sole example that is not based on the structure of the cardus and decumanus. Furthermore, notwithstanding the fact that during ancient times its size was that of a modern metropolis, Rome has never had a master plan that truly defined or changed its physiognomy until the end of the nineteenth-century. Cf. Léon Homo, *Roma imperiale e l'urbanesimo dell'antichità* (Mursia, 1976).
3   The meaning of 'example', in this broader social-political sense refers to the description by Paolo Virno in *Mondanità. L'idea di 'mondo' tra esperienza sensibile e sfera pubblica* (Rome: Manifestolibri, 1994), 106.
4   See Francesco Passanti and Stanislaus von Moos, 'Rome', in: Stanislaus von Moos and Arthur Ruegg (eds.), *Le Corbusier before Le Corbusier* (New Haven: Yale University Press, 2002), 188-193.
5   'La Leçon de Rome', 'L'illusion des plans' and 'La Sixtine de Michel-Ange' were the three articles on Rome written by Le Corbusier upon his return to Paris and published in *L'Esprit Nouveau* (no. 14, 1922). The first two were later chosen to create the core of *Vers une Architecture*: the section entitled 'Architecture'. See Le Corbusier, *Vers une Architecture* (Paris: Crés, 1923), English translation: *Towards a New Architecture* (Dover/New York: publisher, 1986), 149 ff.
6   Ibid., 158.
7   See Francesco Passanti, 'Architecture: Proportions, Classicism and Other Issues', in: *Le Corbusier before Le Corbusier*, op. cit. (note 4), 88.
8   See Passanti/von Moos, 'Rome', op. cit. (note 4), 188-193.
9   Le Corbusier, *Vers une architecture*, op. cit. (note 5), 159.
10   See the sketches for the 1929 conference in Buenos Aires, published in Le Corbusier, *Précisions* (Paris: Crès, 1930), 173.
11   *Le Corbusier, Oeuvre Complète, 1938-1946*, (Basel: Birkhäuser, 2006), 154.
12   Cf. Mario Bevilacqua (ed.), *Nolli, Vasi, Piranesi. Immagine di Roma Antica e Moderna* (Rome: Artemide, 2005); Mario Bevilacqua and Mario Gori Sassoli (eds.), *La Roma di Piranesi. La città del Settecento nelle Grandi Vedute* (Rome: Artemide, 2006); Luigi Ficacci, *Piranesi. The Complete Etchings* (Cologne: Taschen, 2001).
13   Le Corbusier, *Vers une architecture*, op. cit. (note 5), 170.
14   Cf. Giuliano Gresleri, *Le Corbusier. Viaggio in Oriente* (Marsilio, 1984), 401.
15   Rem Koolhaas, 'Sixteen years of OMA', *A+U*, 1988, 17.
16   It should be noted that of the eleven quadrants that make up the Exodus 'strip', the central one is dedicated to the conservation of the fabric of Nash's London (seen as a 'predecessor of the ruthless plan'), 'as a remainder of the past and as useful housing for migrant visitors and new arrivals.'
17   Rem Koolhaas, *Delirious New York. A Retroactive Manifesto for Manhattan* New York/London: Oxford University Press/Academy Editions, 1978), 11.
18   Koolhaas, *A+U*, op. cit. (note 15), 80.
19   See Patrice Goulet (ed.), *OMA, 6 Projets* (Paris: IFA-Edition Carte Segrete, 1990); and 'Bigness', in OMA, Rem Koolhaas and Bruce Mau, *S,M,L,XL* (New York/London/Rotterdam: The Monacelli Press/010 Publishers, 1995), 495 ff.
20   Le Corbusier, *Précisions*, op. cit. (note 10), 196.

Martijn de Waal

Power Urban

Ersatz Urbanism

The design of cities that look like cities, but on close inspection lack important parts of urban culture. Often these designs focus on one or two specific functions of a city and cater to one or two specific groups using and living in the city, but deliberately leave out the public spaces for interaction or confrontation between groups. Their borders are often hard borders rather than soft ones, which isolate rather than connect the design with the city at large. Its identity is not a continuous historic process of negotiating between groups, but top-down supplied by the designers, often through thematization. Public spaces are often mimicked – like the piazzas in shopping malls – but are not true public spaces. Their use is often highly formalized and regulated.

Backyard Urbanism

The centrifugal forces that happen to move the city into your backyard, rather than concentrating its main functions in the (historical) city centre. It is usually not visionary planning or utopian urbanism that produces this city, but rather plain practicalities. The backyard city is an 'emergent' form that arises from functional decisions taken by actors such as developers, city officials and retailers. Their amassed decisions concerning agglomeration advantages, profit maximization and market demands creates the chequered, sprawling, polycentric, edge-city big-box landscape of supercentres, parking lots, office plazas and post-suburban housing estates.

Backstage Urbanism

Even fibre-optic cables and iPods are produced somewhere from something,
not to mention all the other luxury and everyday items that the digital economy allows its participants to acquire. Thus, even in the information age, manufacturing matters, and many Third World countries compete to turn the cities into giant manufacturing backstages, often offering companies willing to relocate special deals on land acquisition or exemptions from environmental or labour laws.

Petrolist Urbanism

With the expanding economies of among others India and China, demand for natural resources and prices for crude oil are booming. It is these petrodollars looking for investment opportunity, global esteem or legitimacy of power that finance the rising skylines from Astana to Caracas and from Moscow to Khartoum, entering some of these formerly marginal cities in the international recognition race of global cities.

Civic Urbanism

The use of the concept of 'urbanization' often implies that it is an inevitable process forced upon us by abstract and intangible powers, its outcome unavoidable. The idea of 'the city' and 'civic urbanism' claim its opposite: it is indeed still possible to plan the city serving its political community of citizens and their needs and identities, rather than hand them over to the

...sms

...whims of the neoliberal global economy. One point ...discussion remains: how to establish the needs ...f a community? Does it still entail working from ...rand Theories, and 'building for mankind'? Or ...hould Market Research lead to a more modest ...uilding for man'?

...CV Urbanism

...he design of cities as a way for bureaucrats ...build their résumés. Ambitious plans are ...unched solely for the career advancement of ...ty officials. This often leads to megalomaniacal ...onumental projects supposed to boast the aura ...the city and its leaders who whish to show off ...eir vigour. That the millions of dollars invested ...re often wasted is usually only discovered after ...e official has been promoted to a higher position ...meplace else, leaving its former community ...ith a hubris reflecting skyline of concrete ...rcasses and empty mirror-glassed towers.

...oftware Urbanism

...he revitalizing of a city and its cityness by ...terventions in social relations – the software ...the city – rather than in its infrastructure ...dwellings and piazzas. When public space ...es not automatically lead to encounter and ...change, special programmes – be it street ...rbecues or community art projects – are set ...to foster recognition and respect between ...tizens. Sometimes these social measures ...e accompanied by minor adjustments to the ...ysical hardware as well, for instance the ...tablishment of a community or youth centre.

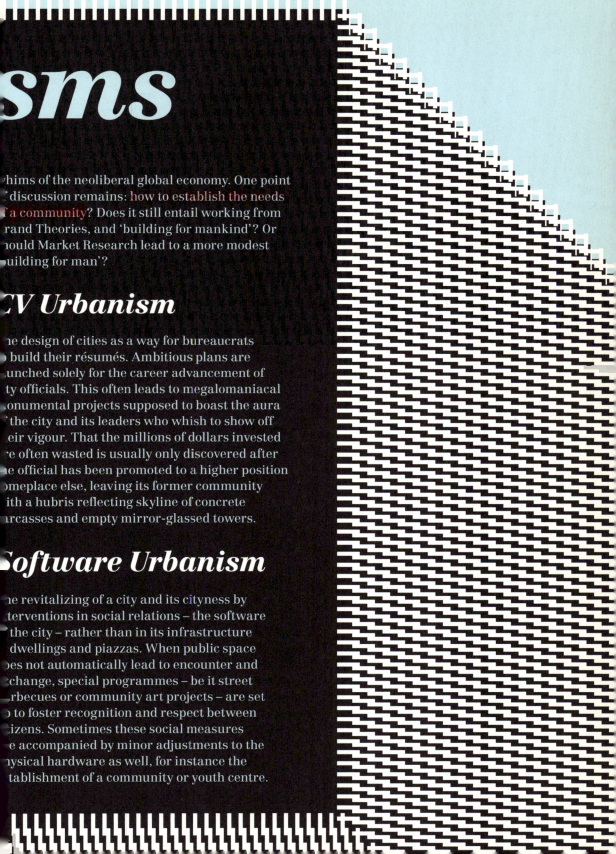

The

of

Spe

The Power of Spectacle[1]

John Urry

Introduction

It sometimes seems as if all the world is on the move. It is predicted that by 2010 there will be at least 1 billion legal international arrivals each year (compared with 25 million in 1950); there are 4 million air passengers each day; at any one time 360,000 passengers are in flight above the USA, equivalent to a substantial city in the sky; and there were 552 million cars in 1998 with a projected 730 million in 2020, equivalent to one for every 8.6 people across the world. Today world citizens move 23 billion kilometres a year; by 2050 it is predicted that that figure will have increased fourfold. And almost all mobilities entail movement between places and there is something about places that are complicit within that movement. Places draw or repel particular residents and visitors.

I am particularly concerned here with the power of spectacle within place, that for various reasons people find something about that place as the reason for moving, for being 'drawn' there. What is it that makes one want to see that spectacle for oneself, to be immersed in it, to feel its affective register? What makes it a spectacle? When Freud finally got to Athens in his forties he found that the Acropolis he had known about from his childhood took his breath away. He could not believe that this spectacle really existed and he was really there in its overwhelming presence. Many other visitors to places often find it hard to believe that they are in the presence of that spectacular city of their dreams.

A Brief History

This 'spectacle-ization' of place stems from the general shift in the culture of Western societies from that of 'land' to that of 'landscape'. Land is a physical, tangible resource to be ploughed, sown, grazed and built upon, a place of functional work. Land is bought and sold, inherited and left to children. But such sites of labour (of agriculture, mining and manufacturing) gradually turn into sites of visual consumption. With landscape an intangible resource of appearance develops in Western Europe from the eighteenth century onwards, part of the emergence of a specialized visual sense separate from the other senses. Treatises on travel shifted to travel as eyewitness observation. Travel came to be justified through connoisseurship, 'the well trained eye'. Areas of wild, barren nature, such as the English Lake District or the Alps, that had been sources of terror and fear became transformed into places of spectacle. With the gradual replacement of land by landscape, Wordsworth's poem *The Brother,* written in 1800, signifies the beginning of modernity when people stop simply belonging to a culture and increasingly begin to tour it as indeed Wordsworth himself does (the poem begins with 'THESE Tourists, heaven preserve us!')

Although there had been places of religious spectacle reached through pilgrimage, the first modern towns of spectacle were spas providing medical and leisure services for wealthy sick people (such as Wiesbaden, Vichy, Baden-Baden, Harrogate, Budapest, Bath). These spa towns were socially select places where a newly-formed cosmopolitan elite gathered across Europe, able to travel by train and where there was a growing circuit of travel and meetings. These spas enabled the European wealthy to meet each other in new places of spectacle with elaborate baths and neighbouring grand hotels.

Almost certainly the first major modern city of spectacle was the rebuilt Paris during the Second Empire. This resulted from Haussmann's construction of the grand boulevards that enabled people for the first time to see well into the distance, their eyes being seduced by the sights located at the end of each boulevard, and they could envisage where they were going to and where they had come from. Paris became a uniquely enticing spectacle with the Eiffel tower as a distinct new kind of tourist spectacle. Simultaneously, new technologies of spectacle begin to be produced and circulated, including postcards, guidebooks, arcades, cafés, dioramas, mirrors, plate-glass windows, photographs and models of famous spectacles.

Around the same time the 1851 Great Exhibition was held at London's Crystal Palace. This was arguably the first-ever national tourist spectacle with 6 million visits being made to it although the total population was only 18 million. In the second half of the nineteenth century similar mega-events of nationhood took place in capital cities across Europe with attendances sometimes reaching 30 million or so. In Australia a Centennial International Exhibition was held in Melbourne in 1888 and two-thirds of the Australian population attended. Indeed, much late-nineteenth-century travel involved visiting spectacles of nation, with the building of national museums, concert halls, theatres and galleries within nationally significant towns and cities.

In the twentieth century the power of spectacle was to be seen in large capital cities, seaside resorts, historic towns and theme parks – especially the many Disneylands. In the next section it is suggested that the late twentieth century has seen a major new shift in the power and significance of spectacle cities.

Global Recognition

What now seems important is the development of a global stage upon which towns and cities are placed and seek 'recognition'.

Machu Picchu, Peru

Almost all places are now 'toured' and the pleasures of place derive from the emotions involved in 'consuming' places. This produces the emotion of motion, of bodies, images, information, moving over, under and across the globe and reflexively monitoring places in terms of abstract characteristics, through people developing as connoisseurs of place. Each place is subject to a relentless competition as they are on the march, seeking to improve their ranking in a ruthless 'spectacle-stakes'.

Thus it seems that 'spectacle-ization' is necessary in order for places to enter the global order, to somehow be 'recognized' as being on the 'global stage'. Such cities can only be taken seriously in the new world dis/order if they are partly at least places of distinct spectacle, through events, museums, ancient remains, festivals, galleries, meetings, sports events and iconic teams, shops, universities, and especially new or refurbished iconic buildings.

Guggenheim, Bilbao

A new arts centre in a refurbished Havana building

Johannesburg hotel pool

Refurbished Gum shopping Centre, Moscow

These provide the context for the 'right experience'.

Thus places are economically, politically and culturally produced through the multiple mobilities of people, of tourists, migrants, design professionals, asylum seekers, business and professional travellers, students and other young people 'travelling the world', but also of capital, designs, objects, signs and information moving across borders. There are many overlaps between 'tourism' and other kinds of business, professional and migratory movement. In attracting these flows (apart from the flows of terrorists and refugees), places are 'performing' on this global stage. Especially significant is the spectacle-ization necessary in order for places to enter the global order, to somehow be 'recognized' – as with what had been East Berlin after the bringing down of the Berlin Wall in 1989.

Some places come to be known as global icons, wonders of

the world, places that can take the breath away, worth dying to see, to linger in, that make one 'cosmopolitan' because one has been there for oneself. Touring the world is how the world is in a way performed, people are connoisseurs and collectors of places (especially aided by guides, web sites, TV programmes and so on). This connoisseurship can apply to all sorts of places, those with good beaches, clubs, views, walks, mountains, unique history, surf, music scene, historic remains, food, drug scene, landmark buildings, gay scene, party atmosphere and so on. Locals can also be part of the attraction of place, such as straight-talking New Yorkers, good-talking Dubliners or chic Parisians. Collecting particular kinds of spectacle is a marker of social status.

In this global competition existing or new buildings are crucial, they can make a place worth dying to see either as a visitor or as somewhere to buy another 'home' in, to 'see Venice and die'.

The Taj signifies the 'exotic orient', the new Guggenheim stands for the rebirth of Bilbao, Machu Picchu is taken to signify Inca heritage, the Eiffel Tower is Paris and so on.

New landmark hotels, new airport termini, new beaches in city centres (Paris, Brisbane), new islands built out at sea (Palm Island, Dubai), memorable office blocks and galleries designed by celebrity architects are some of the newer global spectacles with the 'whole world' now watching. While other spectacles can also be crucial, including heritage buildings, fashionable clubs, places to acquire and display the bronzed tan, globally recognized beaches, waterside restaurants, contemporary art galleries in refurbished buildings (as in Havana), cocktail bars, fashionable shops (as in Moscow), regional high quality food, exhibitions and performances by globally branded artists, architects, musicians, elegant hotel pools (as in Johannesburg) and so on.

This global competition between places presupposes 'place reflexivity', a set of disciplines, procedures and criteria that enable more or less each town and city in the world to monitor, evaluate and develop its potential spectacle within the emerging patterns of global travel. This reflexivity is concerned with identifying a particular place's location within the contours of geography, history and culture that swirl the globe, and in particular identifying what are that place's actual and potential material and semiotic resources. Many consultancy, design and architectural practices have developed and are interlinked with local, national and international states, companies, voluntary associations, universities and NGOs. This reflexivity enables towns and cities to monitor, modify and maximize their positioning within the turbulent global order, especially through allowing new buildings or redeveloping those already there as spectacle. Such procedures 'invent',

design, produce, market and circulate spectacles, especially through global TV and the Internet, even when these are housed within 'old' buildings and streets. These processes of place-design apply not only to places of the 'West' but also increasingly to those of the 'East'.

Such reflexive process also operates through attracting 'global spectacles' of mega-events such as the Olympics, World Cups, Expos and many festivals that are held in such 'global' cities. One exemplary example of this was the spectacle of the 1992 Olympics Games that catapulted Barcelona onto the global stage and into the heart of 'global tourism'. The staging of such events presupposes extensive time-specific travel to the various events that make up what we could begin to call the global calendar. Only certain cities are deemed appropriately spectacular to host such events. Barcelona had interestingly not been one of those cities a few years before it hosted the games; it had been a rundown industrial city, a backwater during the Franco years.

We can thus suggest that places are not fixed and given. They can be 'on the move', moving closer to or further away from various centres of power that populate the world. Each city is in competition for recognition, a version of the politics of recognition and how that recognition of place can ebb and flow. World Heritage status is one distinct way of bringing about this recognition. The refurbished heritage or a spectacular environment is thus centrally implicated in an often spectacular movement of place. Other factors moving places about concern changing technologies of movement, such as new roads, high speed trains, airport expansions and so on.

The transformation of many cities into places of spectacle is one of the most distinctive features of the contemporary world.

Parc de la Villette, Paris

Finland Station, St Petersburg

Hiroshima memorial, Japan

And this is especially striking when this 'spectacle-ization' takes place, not in a place of spectacle like Athens (as visited by Freud), but in places which were the very antithesis of spectacle, places that repulsed the eye and probably the other senses. And for those living in such places this transformation from ugly duckling to beautiful swan can be unbelievable and sometimes a matter of contestation and regret at the kinds of buildings, work and social practices that have been lost. Many former industrial cities that are turned into post industrial centres often evoke such negative reactions. These have been marked in Glasgow ever since its surprising designation as the European City of Culture in 1990.

However, what are also crucial are the sets of performances that can and should occur within such spectacle cities. Places depend upon both hosts' and visitors' performances. The former include the nature and skills of local service delivery, the degrees of friendliness and welcome, the skills of designing and refurbishing spectacle and the array of appropriate enterprises. The later include flâneurie, photographing, running, shopping, swimming, sunbathing, talking, reminiscing, reading, playing or listening to music, surfing, eating, partying, drinking, collecting, climbing and so on. These two sets of performances need to come together to ensure the realization of that place, a realization which is a contingent achievement.

Sometimes places of spectacle can be full of bitter disappointment, frustration and despair for visitors since visitors' performances cannot be realized or there are highly contested. The spectacle is not what it seems, performances cannot be realized. People's fantasies of a place compared with what performances it affords are a constant trope in tourist tales. The spectacle is 'cracked' we might say, as evocatively captured in the film *The Beach*.

Informal settlement, Soweto

Moreover, as fast as places are produced as spectacle, so they are consumed, wasted, used up as they are 'toured'. Travel practices can thus move on and leave behind places that are no longer spectacular because one era's spectacle is often mundane in the next era. The once spectacular Maremagnum in Barcelona has become less fashionable since its opening in 1995. In such a 'touring' world therefore, places come and places go, some places speed up and others slow down or die. One place of spectacle in the early years of spa towns was Harrogate but part of it is now waiting to die since its heritage has lost its allure.

People may try to escape from where there is a 'drudgery of place', of being inexorably tied there and where time is fixed and unchanging. Such places remain heavy with time and are left behind in the 'slow lane', as with many old-style beach resorts in northern Europe and America that were spectacular in the late nineteenth and early twentieth centuries. Atlantic City in New Jersey is an example where the spectacle has faded, but through casinos and gambling new kinds of spectacle are developed.

Contrasting Spectacles

There is much variation in these struggles around power and spectacle. What kinds of places reveal and problematize these struggles? And what transformations materialize in such places of spectacle especially through the re-imagining of place and heritage?

First, most common are those places that have dramatically gone from run down de-industrialized cities to new post-industrial spectacle. Manchester, the first great industrial city and

Partial refurbishment in Havana

colloquially known as Cottonopolis, dramatically shows this with many former industrial buildings and sites of backbreaking industry now transformed into post-industrial leisure and pleasure uses (as in the canal and railway area of Castlefields[2]). Le Parc de la Villette in Paris shows a similar pattern with the science park being located in a former meat market and slaughterhouse.

Second, there are many places with historic cores that stem from and signify a previous industry or political project. A contemporary example of such a city is St Petersburg that demonstrated its break with its Soviet past and the name Leningrad by renaming itself. Part of its historic core consists of Soviet-period buildings and hence there is much conflict over preserving that particular past. There is much controversy over whether these 'Communist' spectacles should be erased or celebrated.

Further, there are places that because of geopolitical processes have no real choice but to seek to 'enter' the global order since that would seem the only alternative. In the case of Havana in Cuban that had its ties with the Russian Federation broken in 1991, it has developed a wide-ranging UNESCO-ization of its derelict historical core (designated in 1982[3]). Our research will demonstrate how the rebuilding and re-imagining of Havana is transforming a centre of massive dereliction into what has been termed 'tourist apartheid', as shown in the illustration of two refurbished buildings straddling one still occupied by multiple poor families.

Other places too are subject to the power of 'world heritage', such as the cities of Austria – though Innsbruck has 'escaped' such a power by comparison with Salzburg (designated in 1996).

Then there are places that attract without any kind of visual spectacle. But it is possible that there is a different kind of spec-

Nelson Mandela's former prison, Robben Island, off Capetown

tacle-ization, of one or more of the non-visual senses, with 'buildings and brochures' especially deployed to illuminate smell (the odours of Grimsby), taste (Lyon) or sound (Memphis). There are thus many different ways of being a spectacle and some will be unpopular with 'locals'.

There are also other places of suffering that are apparently without spectacle, that no one could have imagined being drawn to, such as Soweto (South Western Townships, near Johannesburg) which has invented spectacles of national achievement and pride central to the memories of the anti-apartheid movement and the birth of the modern South African nation. Here tourists are actors in new kinds of commemorative practice, being witness to the new nation – although much of Soweto has no spectacles to draw the eye even if it is one of South Africa's major visitor destinations.

Then there are even large cities that seem to have lost their powers apart from those of tourism. As with Rome the astonishing ruins seem overwhelmed by the performances and practices of tourist spectacle that are transforming their public spaces into 'dead spectacles'.

Finally, another set of places in the modern world are various 'dark spectacles'. There are many examples of where death, disease and suffering are turned into tourist spectacle. These major destinations worldwide include: slave plantations, northern Ireland where there are 'troubles tours', Ground Zero in New York, Hiroshima, and Robben Island in South Africa (a UNESCO World Heritage Site), and Auschwitz-Birkenau (also a UNESCO World Heritage Site since 1979).

These are places of imprisonment or death that have come to be represented and visited in very large numbers as new kinds of 'dark spectacles', where in part tourists are key to the processes of remembering the dead or the tortured.

Conclusion

Global recognition is thus highly contingent; it cannot be fixed and is not a given, but is uncertain and unpredictable within the swirling vortex of 'global travel'. Many places can suddenly find that they are places of desire, of unexpected spectacle as with these sites of dark tourism. Within such spectacle-struggles cities move closer or further away from global centres.

Places we have thus seen are not fixed and unchanging but depend upon the performances within them, by 'hosts' and especially by various kinds of 'guests'. The former include the nature and skills of local service delivery, the degrees of friendliness and welcome, the skills of designing and refurbishing spectacle and the array of appropriate enterprises. The latter we noted include flâneurie, photographing, running, shopping, swimming, sunbathing, talking, reminiscing, reading, playing or listening to music, surfing, eating, partying, drinking, collecting, climbing and so on. These two sets of performances need to come together to ensure the realization of that place, a realization which is a contingent achievement very much depending upon design. In a global era tourism tends to rapid change as places come and go. The challenge for design professionals is to produce places that stabilize spectacle and prevent the churning of visitor demand.

Whatever the latest spectacles dreamt up by architects and urban planners, what in the end matters are the performances by residents and visitors that occur within and around them. Here and there we might say good places and worthwhile performances do get made and they sometimes get made it seems despite the spectacles. This is the challenge for design.

1   Many thanks to Tom Urry for comments and suggestions and for his help with the images for the associated PowerPoint presentation. Thanks also to Alex Arellano, Javier Caletrio and Amy Urry for their images.

2   See http://www.manchester2002-uk.com/castlefield/castlefield1.html.

3   See http://whc.unesco.org/en/list/204.

The F
of UN
Worl
Herit

The POWER of UNESCO World Heritage
Macchiavelling the Power of World Heritage

bad architects group
Ursula Faix
Paul Burgstaller

Fake Views

A close look at postcards of Innsbruck reveals that most are montages. The mountains have been adjusted to a desirable angle, equipping the city with a more spectacular backdrop; unsightly views have been erased and replaced – sometimes even with portions of outdated photographs. These fake postcards have become deep-seated idealized images of the city. Many contribute significantly to tourists' expectations of the city, providing a sort of preconditioned visual experience. In cities like Innsbruck, tourism's bond to the preconditioned image of the city is sometimes much stronger than its connection to the 'physical city' – raising the question of whether it is the real or the manifested image of a city that should be preserved. How far can we go in changing the substance of a city before it is noticed?

Personal Heritage

According to the latest research, our brains have the ability to store all data acquired during our lifetimes, although in the long term, we only consciously retain what has an 'emotional tag' on it.[1] Over time, good and bad memories become condensed and idealized montages that relate to other experiences. World Heritage Sites work in a manner similar to the emotional tags in the human brain that contribute to personal heritage: they retain memories, each of which has an emotional tag.

Since 'memory attaches itself to sites'[2] and every building has a 'metaphorical side',[3] sites and buildings are always related to human memory. The difference between personal and cultural heritage, however, lies in the power figure declaring what qualifies as 'cultural heritage', and is therefore worthy of preservation. Is cultural heritage the lowest common denominator of personal heritage?

The POWER of Listing

In the case of the UNESCO cultural World Heritage, it is the UNESCO World Heritage Committee,[4] consisting of 18 to 21 persons, with its advisory bodies,[5] that has the power to decide which properties[6] of the applying state parties will receive the international recognition of being included on the UNESCO World Heritage List.

New UNESCO World Heritage inscriptions are announced publicly each year after the UNESCO World Heritage Committee meeting. After a two-year application and evaluation process, to finally earn a position on the list is an emotional event for an applying state party. This publication leads to increased media attention, and potentially the attraction of tourists, however remote the property may be.

Alternatively, a property can be relegated to UNESCO's *Red List*[7] due to, for instance, a large urban development or a dilapidated neighbourhood. Although placement on the Red List has no legal consequences per se, it humiliates a city, generating the sort of public debate that politicians fear. The Red List is thus a significant instrument of power for the UNESCO World Heritage Committee. But, could it also be used as a tool? Could a city deliberately provoke, in order to be 'punished' with a position on the Red List, and thereby attract more tourists? If Innsbruck had World Heritage status, would its new projects – 'Hungerburgbahn'[8] and 'Kaufhaus Tyrol'[9] – put it on the Red List?

The POWER of Blurriness

If a UNESCO World Heritage city plans a large urban development, the intention is for the project to be approved by the UNESCO World Heritage Committee and its advisory bodies. The project is judged not for its architectural qualities, but for its potential interference with the city's cultural heritage. For this evaluation, images or renderings are consulted.

Although each UNESCO World Heritage property has a defined 'core' and 'buffer zones', architectural developments outside these zones are evaluated in cases where they obstruct the views of a site, reducing the UNESCO heritage city to frozen images from certain viewpoints, mostly defined by ancient idealized paintings[10] or (fake) postcards.

Interestingly enough, the UNESCO World Heritage zone system is a scheme usually used for peacekeeping actions[11] in war zones. In contrast, preservation zones issued by the municipality in cities like Innsbruck are defined by clear lines or borders. A building is either inside or outside the zone. Is it possible to rethink the borrowed territorial zoning tool by developing a different tool?

UNESCO Business

It is not money that makes the UNESCO World Heritage Committee powerful (its annual budget of four million US dollars is vanishing), but the fact that UNESCO World Heritage is an idealistic label with the tourism industry as its closest parasitic ally. The mix of international recognition and economic value for an applying state party makes fundraising for the company UNESCO World Heritage unnecessary. With more applying state parties than can be processed per year, the UNESCO World Heritage Committee is booked for the coming five decades.

The Power of Withdrawal

One problem concerning the protection of UNESCO World Heritage cities is that every architectural development is forced

Typical postcard of Innsbruck

Typical postcard of Innsbruck

Typical postcard of Innsbruck and analysis of the mountain outline with the main sites 'Seegrube' and 'Hafelekar'

Photograph (bad architects group) from the same viewpoint as on the postcard. The analysis shows that the mountain backdrop has been reworked (copied and moved) to idealize the view of Innsbruck

Typical postcard of Innsbruck and analysis of the mountain outline with the main sites 'Seegrube' and 'Hafelekar'

Photograph (bad architects group) from the same viewpoint as on the postcard. The analysis shows that the mountain backdrop has been reworked (copied and moved) to idealize the view of Innsbruck

Proposed project for the 'Komet Tower' in Vienna. The UNESCO World Heritage Committee requested a 50 per cent decrease in height, although the project is outside the 'Schönbrunn' buffer zone. The montage shows the tower higher than it would appear.

The UNESCO buffer zones are much more undefined and blurry than zones issued by a state preservation authority.

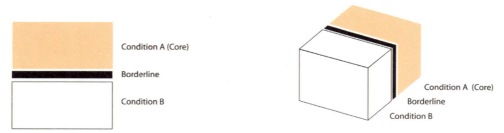

SOG Borderlines

The UNESCO World Heritage City. All urban areas listed on the UNESCO World Hertiage List assembled according to their geographical location."

Proposed project of the 'Kastner & Öhler' department store extension (arch: Nieto Sobejano Arquitectos). The UNESCO World Heritage Committee requested a 30 per cent reduction in volume.

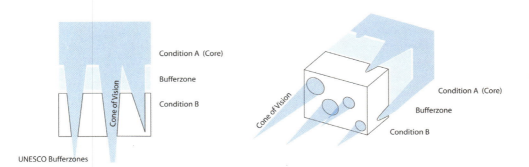

UNESCO Bufferzones

Condition A (Core)
Bufferzone
Condition B

Cone of Vision

Condition A (Core)
Bufferzone
Condition B

into a role subordinate to the manifested image of that city. Another is that no solutions have been found for cities that have been abandoned by their residents, because UNESCO's restrictions restrained their ability to grow with the actual needs of the population. A third problem is the negative impact of tourism in once remote towns. The Vienna Memorandum[12] was an important step in finding an adequate solution, especially for 'living heritages', but has shown no impact on ICOMOS' decisions. Imagine cities like Vienna or Graz, no longer able to stand the pressure of World Heritage, seeing withdrawal as the only way out. Would the withdrawal suddenly provoke a swap of hierarchies and weaken the power of the UNESCO World Heritage Committee?

HeritageRank

Like emotional tags in the human memory, heritage is a fact that we need to deal with. Is it possible to preserve a dynamic process like a city? Could the virtual side of heritage, which has been neglected in the cultural heritage debate so far, unleash the potential to introduce a different logic to the implementation of heritage? What can we inherit from devices like Google Earth, You Tube and Second Life in order to develop urban planning?

Returning to the fake postcards of Innsbruck, we could see them not only as fake images producing the manifested image of the city, but also as the linking of fore- and background, or of two highly ranked images of the city. The postcards introduce the virtual aspect of memories to 'cityness'. Our project replaces the outdated zoning tool with a newly developed ranking tool in order to better respond to the needs of city dynamics. It uses the power of the Architecture Biennale to launch the Innsbruck-based prototype of HeritageRank, a dynamic notion of heritage.

1   The human brain stores all information using 'emotional tags' to prevent excessive strain on the brain and enable it to cope with daily business. Recent studies showed that 'autistic savants', who have a distortion of this 'filter' can remember everything, regardless of emotions attached to it, but have difficulty managing day to day life.
2   Michael J. Dear, *The Postmodern Urban Condition* (Malden, MA: Blackwell Publishing, 2000), 252: 'Memory attaches itself to sites, whereas history attaches itself to events.'
3   Ibid., 251: 'Monuments are not just spaces of the body, subjectivity and language, but are also grids of meaning and power . . . where for example chairs become thrones, buildings become monuments, and so on.'
4   The UNESCO World Heritage Committee consists of 21 member state parties. The term of office is six years. (UNESCO Basic Texts of the 1972 World Heritage Convention, I.I.E.19, 37)
5   Advisory bodies of the UNESCO World Heritage Committee: ICOMOS, UICN, ICCROM and DOCOMOMO, TICCIA, IFLA.
6   A property is an entity of the UNESCO World Cultural Heritage List and can be monuments, groups of buildings or sites (UNESCO Basic Texts of the 1972 World Heritage Convention, II.A.45, Article 1, 45)
7   UNESCO World Heritage properties on the so called 'Red List' are properties in danger.
8   This project is a fast cable-car connection directly from the old centre to the mountains, allowing only one-day tourists to see both. The architect of this project is Zaha Hadid.
9   This project is a shopping centre in the old centre. One of its main façades in the Maria Theresienstrasse is very much discussed.
10   Canaletto (1697-1768) is an Italian painter, famous for his paintings of urban settings in Venice.
11   In order to calm disputes over a borderline, the UN issues a buffer zone, which leaves room for interpretation, rather than a strict borderline.
12   The Vienna Memorandum was adopted by the International Conference 'World Heritage and Contemporary Architecture – Managing the historic Urban Landscape', held in 2005 in Vienna, Austria.

New Culture of Heritage, Logos

WORLD HERITAGE ™

powered by Google
World Heritage

Google™ Heritage

Preserve Yourself

Reintr
the Cit
in Hau

Reintroducing the City in Havana
Challenging the Powers of Spectacle

a-u-r-a
Marisol Rivas Vélazquez
Christian Schmutz
FÜNDC BV
César García
Paz Martín

A key power in the production of today's cities is their transformation into places of visual consumption – their *spectacle-ization*.[1] This efficient and complex system camouflages an uncontrolled economical offensive by producing, (re)inventing, and/or attaching artificial meaning to specific places.

This artificial meaning or *MeanINC*[2] is a device that reconceptualizes the history of buildings or places through a process of amplification or elimination of the built environment. MeanInc has become the Trojan Horse of tourism. It suggests the fragile promise of recognition – the link between places that aspire to fame and a global world of political and corporate interests. It produces a stereotype, and with it an alienation that compresses the imaginary projections of the foreign and tourist initiatives with the everyday reality of the local, resulting in the city's 'ascension' into myth.

Several cities in the modern capitalist world, as well as in the remains of the socialist era, have undergone the process of Spectacle-ization, but none have done it like Havana, which in the space of six decades has gone from *spectacle-ization* to *de-spectacle-ization* to *re-spectacle-ization* while keeping the same building substance.

Batista: The Spectacle-ization of Havana

During the 1950s, Havana – the 'little princess of the sea' – was loaded with the flashy vision of a bourgeois capital for the American tourists, a spectacle of excess. The vision gave birth to the MeanInc architecture of hotels, casinos and nightclubs. Josep Llouis Sert's Plan Piloto (1955-1958) summarizes the desires of this time: endless views to the sea and a monumental urban celebration dressed in a modern casual code.

Revolution: De-Spectacle as a Pragmatic Doctrine

In 1959, when revolution took over Havana, the contrast between the spectacular capital and the impoverished countryside became more evident. From this point on, greater efforts were devoted to the social and economic development of the countryside. Havana was no longer seen as the 'little princess'. A strict migration policy controlling the distribution of the population on the island gave way to a relevant change: the city lost its importance, becoming equal to – if not less than – the rest of the country.

The revolution refused to create any physical manifestation of itself through architecture; self-construction and utopias were replaced by repetition and prefabrication. The buildings of excess were filled with practicality.

It was in this process of amputating MeanInc that the values of the city and architecture were extirpated as well.

Special Period:[3] Re-Spectacle-ization of Havana

After the collapse of the Eastern bloc, tourism seemed the only viable option for alleviating the economic crisis that Cuba was facing. Under the guidance of Dr Eusebio Leal, and with full support of Fidel Castro, the City Historian's Office introduced new urban policies making possible the (re)construction and restoration of the historical centre of Havana and other buildings and quarters.[4]

In 1982, with Old Havana's designation as a World Heritage site, MeanInc was officially reintroduced into the inner texture of the city, and architecture became one of the most important elements in the reconstruction of this overpopulated and decadent city centre. The strategy used for the reconstruction of Old Havana is nothing new. What is striking is the implementation of a capitalistic model: Habaguanex,[5] a very profitable company for tourism run by the City Historian's Office, finances building reconstruction in cooperation with European governments, along with other socialist projects designed by internationally renowned architects.

The reintroduction of Spectacle has led Havana to a dualistic system: two currencies, two societies, a two-tiered economy. This system fosters a state of apartheid in a city where the Power of Spectacle (tourism) and *Domestic Manoeuvres* meet.

Spectacle-ization is opposed in Havana by the magic realism[6] of the everyday. This everyday (hi)story is written by Domestic Manoeuvres, an informal but resolute power that builds the city on the by-products of Spectacle. Domestic Manoeuvres are pragmatic strategies executed by Havana citizens to increase their incomes and cope with building and ownership regulations. Practices like housing interchange, *cuarterias* (old subdivided houses) and *barbacoas* (informal mezzanines, etcetera) represent alternative ways to activate the urban structure while ignoring MeanInc. Although these manoeuvres are not direct responses to the re-spectacle-ization of Havana, their consequences seem to stir the local and international debate regarding potential areas for renovation in the city.

Tourism is simultaneously a cultural product and a producer of culture.[7] It is complex and collective construction by tourists, entrepreneurs and planners. The following three interventions challenge the *powers* at play by constraining and canalizing their effects.

Primary location of Spectacle
The zoomed frames represent places where MeanINC is present, whereas the dotted frames are those where MeanINC will soon be introduced.

Billboard in the streets of Havana

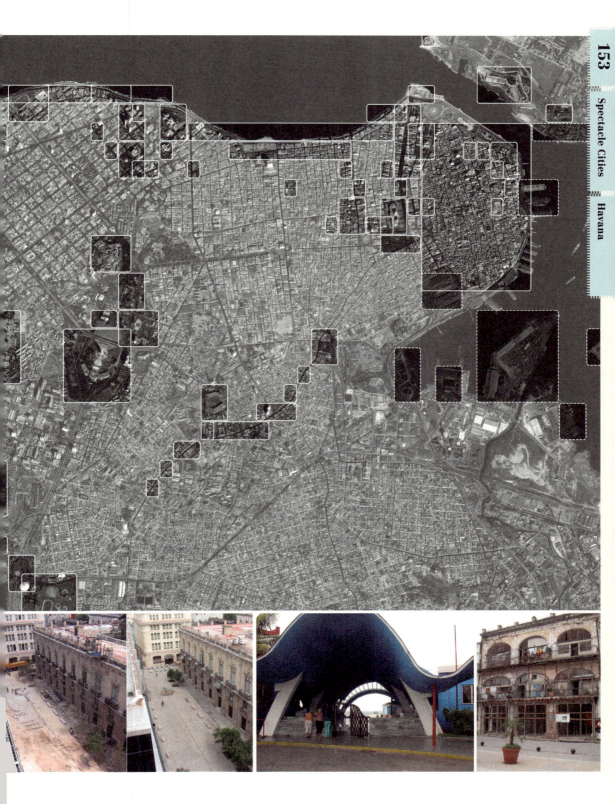

Street in Old Havana, before restoration (2006) and after (2007)

El Club Nautico, 1957

Barbacoa at Plaza Vieja in Old Havana

153 Spectacle Cities Havana

Hall of Spectacle-ization in Havana
Hall of Fame MeanINC from the Forestier master plan to a modernistic architecture and the Plan Sert

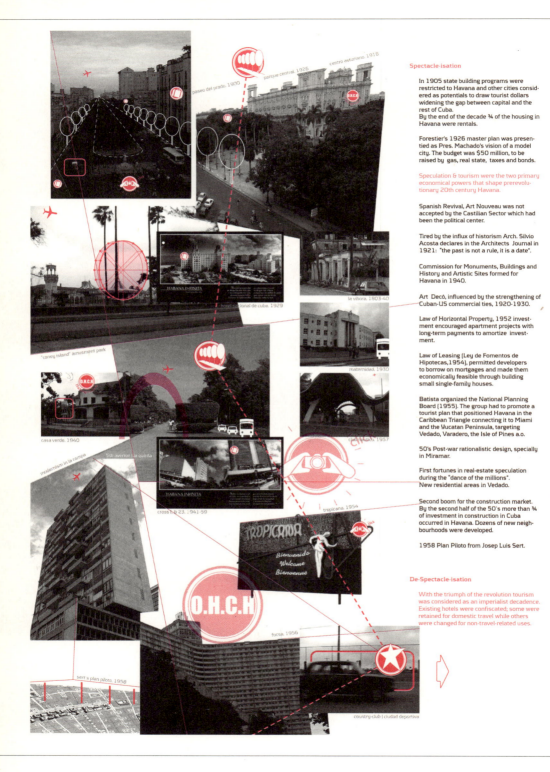

Spectacle-isation

In 1905 state building programs were restricted to Havana and other cities considered as potentials to draw tourist dollars widening the gap between capital and the rest of Cuba.
By the end of the decade ¾ of the housing in Havana were rentals.

Forestier's 1926 master plan was presented as Pres. Machado's vision of a model city. The budget was $50 million, to be raised by gas, real state, taxes and bonds.

Speculation & tourism were the two primary economical powers that shape prerevolutionary 20th century Havana.

Spanish Revival, Art Nouveau was not accepted by the Castilian Sector which had been the political center.

Tired by the influx of historism Arch. Silvio Acosta declares in the Architects Journal in 1921: "the past is not a rule, it is a date".

Commission for Monuments, Buildings and History and Artistic Sites formed for Havana in 1940.

Art Decó, influenced by the strengthening of Cuban-US commercial ties, 1920-1930.

Law of Horizontal Property, 1952 investment encouraged apartment projects with long-term payments to amortize investment.

Law of Leasing (Ley de Fomentos de Hipotecas, 1954), permitted developers to borrow on mortgages and made them economically feasible through building small single-family houses.

Batista organized the National Planning Board (1955). The group had to promote a tourist plan that positioned Havana in the Caribbean Triangle connecting it to Miami and the Yucatan Peninsula, targeting Vedado, Varadero, the Isle of Pines a.o.

50's Post-war rationalistic design, specially in Miramar.

First fortunes in real-estate speculation during the "dance of the millions".
New residential areas in Vedado.

Second boom for the construction market. By the second half of the 50's more than ¾ of investment in construction in Cuba occurred in Havana. Dozens of new neighbourhoods were developed.

1958 Plan Piloto from Josep Luis Sert.

De-Spectacle-isation

With the triumph of the revolution tourism was considered as an imperialist decadence. Existing hotels were confiscated; some were retained for domestic travel while others were changed for non-travel-related uses.

Hall of Spectacle-ization in Havana
Hall of Fame MeanINC after the Special Period and the reintroduction of tourism in Havana

De-Spectacle-isation

... elimination of a "polyvalent" design & **superficial symbolism** that reflected class differences in favour of a search for an **architecture with a social responsibility**.

School of arts complex, a project aiming to present "revolution-romantic" aspects.

The State assumed the construction of housing, promoting in 1965 the construction of **100,000 new tenements per year.**

First **Microbrigades** established in 1971.

Revolution means to build.

USSR donated a **fabrication plan** in order to produce prefab houses followed by the **shortage** of steel and wood.

Construction of hotels for cuban workers.

Foreign tourism was re-introduced in the 70s through trading blocks of hotel rooms (Cuban off-season) to Eastern bloc countries, Spain & Canada in return for oil & machines.

Creation of travel companies to serve exiles short visits to the island.

Old Havana as national monument 1978.

In 1990 the state declared the "*Special period in Peacetime*" inaugurating austerity measures.

Re-Spectacle-isation

Introduction of the **CUC** (Cuban Convertible Peso) in the early 90s that installed a parallel currency sytem to control foreign exchange in Cuba.

In 1984 Cuba attracted fewer than 200,000 foreign visitors; in ten years the average annual figure of the Batista years was tripled.

Old Havana and its surroundings is listed in 1982 as *World heritage N°27* by UNESCO.

Best Practices 2000 awarded by UNESCO Habitat.

Mise en scene of Havana to tourists trough a huge model of Old Havana.

Projects on track by OHCH: Chinese Quarter, Casa Verde and Art School Complex

Postcards of Havana reintroducing the "Colonial Style" as major heritage of Havana.

Controversial Fence sorrounding the fountain in Plaza Vieja.

Habaguanex publications promoting the cultural heritage of Havana.

Concept of Havana 2007

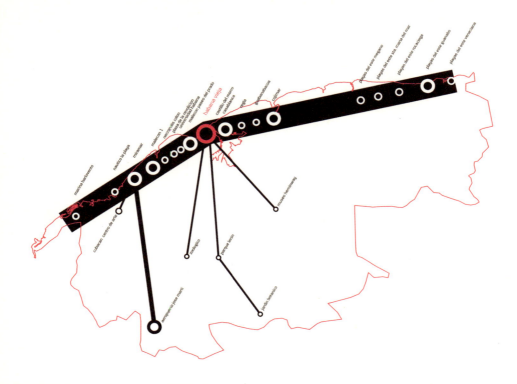

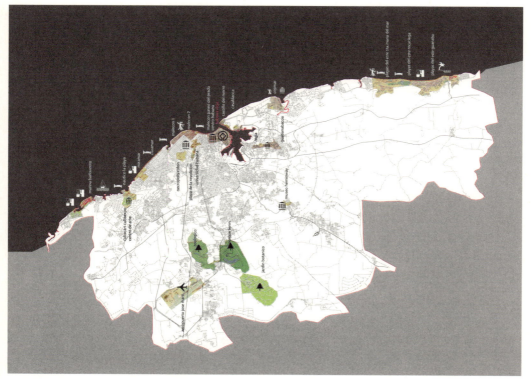

Plan of Havana 2007

Concept of Havana 2015

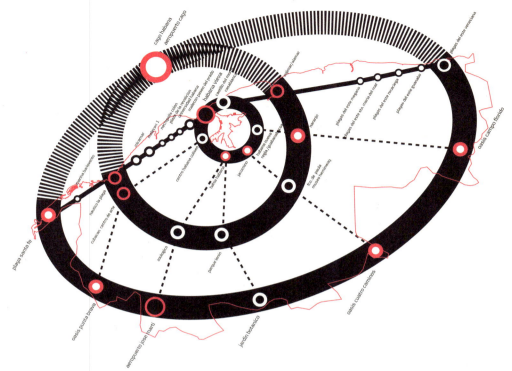

157 Spectacle Cities Havana

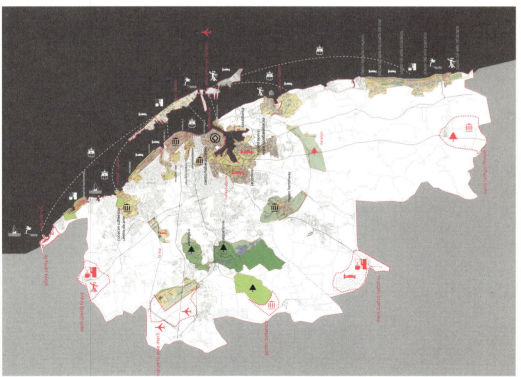

Plan of Havana 2015

Concept of Havana 2025

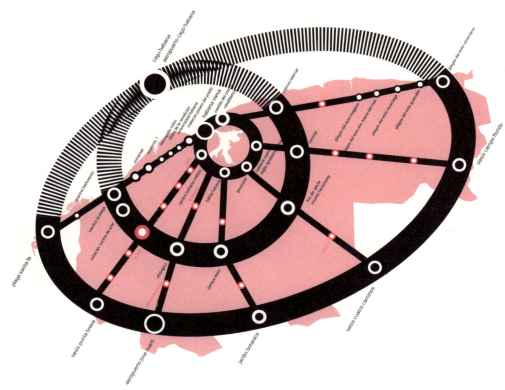

Plan of Havana 2025

1. Archipelagos of Condensed MeanInc – Scanning MeanInc in Havana

They already exist; several places and buildings where the city has been packaged for tourists. As others are added to the list, a catalogue of MeanInc architecture and places will be compiled. The archipelagos will function as attractors in order to develop other authentic and apparently unimportant areas, where Dr Leal's 'successful' formula could be implemented. These Archipelagos will radically fulfil tourists' expectations, as promised by the tourist industry.

2. Spectacle's Island – Havana Key

To relieve the growing pressure of tourism on the city, especially on the bay, a prototype island for tourists is created as a preventative measure. The island is a parallel system of social and building order located in the sea; it is detached from Havana, but visible from every point. At night, the lights of the *Havana Key* Island can be seen from the Malecón across the sea. This artificial environment will also function as a breakwater, protecting the authentic city from the sea.

3. Architecture as Sustainable Infrastructure or Reintroducing the City

Havana demands architecture of action that, like a sustainable infrastructure, is capable of delivering development free from imposed meaning without sacrificing beauty and the city itself. Between the archipelagos of MeanINC, buffer zones are created. The buffer area is the city itself; a space of urban consciousness, and, above all, a constructible and intelligible political form. These areas, MeanInc-free, deliver to inhabitants the opportunity to continue building their city, their identity and maybe their revolution.

The interventions are a critical reappraisal of the possibilities of the city as concept. Each one is an incursion into the powers that have, are and will be shaping Havana; an attempt to anticipate its future in the hope that as the city is further absorbed by the global tourist machine, it will continue to develop a *meaning* of its own.

---

1   See John Urry's text 'The Power of the Spectacle' earlier in this book
2   As the engine to foster tourism, spectacle-ization requires the embedding or even re-embedding of stereotypes.
3   After the collapse of the Soviet Union, Cuba took limited free market-oriented measures to alleviate the economical crises. These measures included allowing some self-employment, the legalization of the use of the dollar in business, and principally the encouragement of tourism. Cuba has tripled its market share of Caribbean tourism in the last decade. In 2003, 1.9 million tourists visited Cuba generating revenue of $2.1 billion.
4   'Several important projects are being implemented and consolidated in different parts of the capital, among them: Havana's Chinatown, the old business squares of the historical centre, the traditional Malecón and Obispo Street and the Prado promenade, In addition Habaguanex is now carrying out the construction of a gallery for boutique shops at the Santo Domingo Building' extract from Habaguanex's dossier text.
5   Habaguanex runs more then 527 exclusive hotel rooms, several bars and restaurants, three real estate companies, a travel agency and taxis in the historical centre generating, in 2004, a revenue of $77 million.
6   Magic realism is an analogy to a literature genre that collapses time in order to create a setting in which the present repeats or resembles the past, inverts cause and effect, incorporates folklore and presents events from multiple standpoints, often shifting between characters' viewpoints and internal narration on shared relationships or memories.
7   Brian McLaren and D. Medina Lasansky (eds.), *Arquitectura y Turismo* (Barcelona: Gustavo Gili, 2006).

Roman Holiday
Exploiting the Power of Tourism

baukuh
with
Romolo Ottaviani
Martin Sobota
collaborators
Beatrice De Carli
Ettore Donadoni
photos
Francesco Jodice
Giovanna Silva

1. In 2005, more than eight million tourists visited Rome. Tourism means consumption of the major monuments, congestion in the centre, and the transformation of the baroque city into a monofunctional shopping district. Roman citizens tolerate the evils of tourism because of the economic benefits it brings. Yet tourism can be more than a nuisance: it presents an opportunity to reorganize the city in a way that will benefit both visitors and residents.

2. Pope Sixtus V (1585-1590) and Domenico Fontana were able to imagine a project for Rome stemming from the needs of contemporary religious tourism. They used a very basic concept: establishing connections among the seven major churches. These links would clarify the structure of the city and reactivate the richness of the Roman ruins inside of a new ideological frame. The success of the extremely empiric, thrifty and fast enterprise of Sixtus and Domenico is the practical demonstration that tourism does not necessarily destroy the city; on the contrary, tourism can produce the city.

3. There are three main attractions in Rome: the Vatican, the shopping district distributed throughout the baroque city, and the Roman ruins. The Vatican was reorganized for Jubilee 2000; the baroque city evolves through the actions of its many inhabitants; the Roman ruins remain more or less unchanged since the fascist interventions. The realization of the new C metro line, passing below the Fora, offers a concrete opportunity to rethink the entire area.

4. The area from Piazza Venezia to the Coliseum is slowly developing into an informal, self-organized theme park. Provisional solutions spontaneously grow in response to the touristic demand: kiosks market drinks and souvenirs, gladiators enliven family photos, multimedia productions show *Brutus Plotting to Kill Caesar – in your language*.

5. Compared to Disney's *Magic Kingdom,* Rome's central archaeological area – from the Fora to Caracalla baths – is five times larger, four times less attractive in terms of visitors, and 20 times less profitable.

Yet Rome is not a theme park, and profit is not the only reason to keep the Rome business going. Ruins are more complicated to keep than cardboard castles; property is split among multiple owners, both private and public. Management is correspondingly intricate: various administrations are involved in heritage protection, events promotion, gardening and safety. Customers are different as well.

6. Contrary to a theme park or a museum, Rome has no clear border: as one moves outward from the centre, the tourist attractions gradually diminish; they do not disappear abruptly. In the *campagna* there are plenty of minor buildings, amazing landscapes, lovely coasts.

Rome is not Venice; it is not delimited by an 8-km² island. Rome is not the *Magic Kingdom*. To think of Rome as such is both cynical and unrealistic. In Rome, the business of tourism can grow to involve a broader territory. The reorganization of the touristic city enacts the reorganization of the entire post-bureaucratic city.

Model of Imperial Rome
Circus Maximus — Trajan's Forum

7. In a global market of cities competing as providers of space, facilities, environment, it is not difficult to recognize Rome's qualities. As the only global city already complete in its collection of spaces, Rome only needs to rediscover its metropolitan assets.

Rome needs no major changes to its public spaces or its architecture collection; it can avoid the blind search for masterpieces that occupies the painful last chapter in the history of post-industrial cities. Rome as a *spectacle city* is nothing new; its identity as a *spectacle city* was already re-established after the return of the Popes from Avignon.

Spaces in Rome are ready for contemporary uses. What still needs work in Rome is infrastructure, not only as sheer network – roads, tunnels, cables – but as a grammar of the urban experience, as a code that enables one to understand the city in all of its richness.

8. Rome is made of projects. Rome has been a project and a re-foundation from the beginning. Romulus had a project for Rome; it was an urban and an international one; and it was a re-foundation. He chose to build the city on the Palatine hill, transforming the very heart of the previous settlement. Remus, on the contrary, proposed to start a new city on the deserted site of the Aventinus hill, and his project failed because it was not metropolitan.

All of the projects that followed were, again, re-foundations; it was repeatedly the sheer amazement with the city of the past that inspired visions of the new city. The main business of Alberti and Bramante was to show to their clients the impressive beauty of the ancient city.

Rome is made of universal projects, one on top of the other. And being, from the beginning, a universal project translated into urban space (Rome is a civilization project that is mainly encoded into laws and urban artefacts, a civilization project whose main tool is the city), it is a universal project in the form of a stage.

Acquedotti park
Forum of Augustus

ew of the Via Sacra, from the Arch of Titus to Campidoglio hill

farella park
Appia Antica

The stage is there. The problem is: a stage for what? A stage to rent for signing treatises, just as a Palladian villa is rented for a wedding party?

9. Rome, as a ready-made global platform for metropolitan events, only needs to discover which event to locate in its various spots in order to reactivate them.
The ancient city has demonstrated its suitability for contemporary events. The Jubilee 2000, the strikes and manifestations against the Iraqi war, the celebrations for the World Cup 2006, have all inhabited the ancient city, revealing territories that are surprisingly aligned with contemporary rituals. The contemporary multitude used the immense, indeterminate, yet precise and contained space of the Circus Maximus to identify itself as a political body. As pure space, by now completely deprived of any meaning, the Circus allows its occupants absolute freedom. As a room with precise dimensions and with no intentions, the Circus embraces events without suggesting any stable definition for the mutating contemporary multitude, simply allowing half a million people to recognize each other inside of a large hole in the ground with a glorious, somehow exotic, Roman name.

The events that invade the contemporary city in increasing numbers require spaces to be enacted: *public* spaces, but different from the nineteenth-century and modernist ones. Rome provides them: spaces for individuals and for the multitude, colossal and indeterminate, abstract and popular. Imperial Roman spaces provide the most suitable environments for contemporary metropolitan events. A network connecting the central zones with infrastructure, and with larger areas at a strategic distance from the centre, defines Rome as a landscape ready for happenings, ranging from everyday meetings to impressive mass manifestations. Rome becomes a global supplier of space; tourism is absorbed into new nomadic metropolitan patterns.

Rome is the contemporary public space; Shanghai is lacking.

Appia Antica archaeological park, from km 0 to km 3.5
(black and grey: existing situation / blue: project)

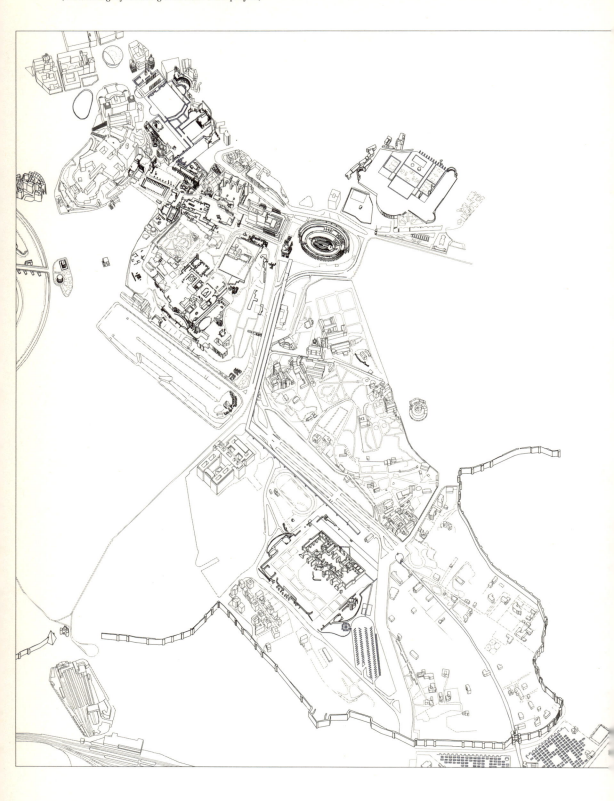

Appia Antica archaeological park, from km 3 to km 6
(black and grey: existing situation / blue: project)

10. There is nothing to build in Rome. Architects must be humble. The city only needs a framework by which to understand what is already there (and this may accidentally require a bit of architecture). It is only necessary to build the infrastructure that enables the existing spaces to perform within their global context. After all, Rome's most influential architects during the last couple of centuries were painters and writers – Piranesi, Goethe, Stendhal – who produced the software through which to understand the ancient city. Now the infrastructure with which to decode the ancient city must be built for the contemporary multitude.

11. Roman relics must find their place within a culture that is becoming increasingly visual. Ruins should be exposed; spaces should be evident. If ruins do not produce spatial experiences, they are lost for an increasing majority of (not necessarily uneducated) visitors. And without an initial spatial experience of the ruins, no further intellectual experience is possible. There can be no understanding of what goes unnoticed.

The archaeological park has to be spectacular enough to attract the masses; it has to be straightforward without compromising its richness; it has to allow the coexistence of organized, fast, plebeian visits and refined, slow, random promenades. It has to communicate with both Goethe and Goethe's maid, and to accommodate visits of two years or two days.

12. To restore clarity to the Roman spaces, the most important step is to reintroduce the crowds for which they were conceived. Mass tourism, in this respect, could be a tool with which to re-establish the urban organization of the ancient city. The opening of the Via Sacra in the Roman Forum gave back clarity to the organization of the Forum by reactivating an easy and logical path and establishing the proper hierarchy between a main road and the related spaces. Tourism can be the unexpected promoter of urbanity, colonizing the ruins and thereby expanding the collection of spaces at the citizens' disposal.

The museum/transfer at the Coliseum

The Trajan Forum after the demolition of Via dei Fori Imperiali

The museum/transfer at the Caracalla baths

The 'passeggiate romane' inside of the museum/transfer. Like in a time machine the ancient city reappears, providing visitors with the basic knowledge necessary to decode the contemporary ruins.

The new metro station at piazza Venezia allows a general reorganization of the traffic fluxes. By transforming the uncertain setting of the square, the new metro station rediscovers the alien beauty of the Vittorio Emanuele monument.

New nomadic citizens are accommodated next to the Aurelian walls during their busy roman holidays.

Francesco Jodice, 'Roma A.D. 2007'

13. The reactivation of the ruins is a rediscovery of the urban potential of the ancient plan. In order to perform, the city needs a pavement on which to move without excessive preoccupations (according to Raymond Hood's formula: *the plan is of primary importance, because on the floor are performed all the activities of the human occupants.*)

Ruins can be part of the contemporary city only if the pavement of the contemporary city is at the level of the Roman city. Gestures have to happen in the Roman scene. The present (fascist) organization of the Fora only allows one to pass by the buildings and look without entering. Ancient buildings are pure background. Everything is distant, flat, impossible to touch. The city is empty; citizens do not deserve the city.

14. In a 1994 advertisement of the Barilla company, some of the main Italian public spaces appear to have been invaded by large corn fields. The Barilla commercial describes a *lite* city, one that is able to couple history and quality of life, moderate urbanity and pastoral isolation, nature and spectacle.

It is easy to dismiss Barilla urbanism as cheap, populist and philistine, yet the Barilla campaign not only recognizes desires that are part of the contemporary city, but also discovers tools for its transformation. Surrendering to nature seems to be the last resource of urbanity; green matter, the ultimate tool with which to build the city.

Green matter can make ruins understandable and usable. Green matter is tolerant and precise, robust and comfortable. It can evolve, allowing spaces to be experienced and allowing archaeological areas to mutate according to changing interpretation paradigms. Green matter defines a group of recognizable activities for the places where it appears and immediately provides a name – *park* – for whatever it touches. Green matter protects architecture with its intimate moral legitimization. It gives the system a touch of realistic unrealism: the ancient city is gone, and the first reason not to rebuild

it, is not to erase the fact that Rome was really there.

15. Be more confident. The contemporary city must be nothing less than the best possible city. Reject the obsession with layering both as desire for protagonism (the stupid idea: we have to invent something just because we are here) and as complete lack of responsibility (the cowardly idea: nothing in the history of the city is worth a decision). Think of the city in terms of spaces and rediscover their differences. Remove the nineteenth-century cellars in the middle of Trajan's Forum because they compromise the space of the Forum; remove them because Imperial *spaces* are better, not because Imperial *times* were better. Architecture is a judgement of urban resources, a commitment not to waste. A project is just something for the city to gain or to lose in terms of space. Excavations in the Imperial Fora will be sheer gain, yet excavations in the Circus Maximus will be pure loss for the city. To excavate in the Fora will add an extraordinary system of spaces to the city. To excavate in the Circus Maximus will eliminate from the city a performing urban tool, leaving an entire category of events without a place in which to happen. Solve problems the Roman way: be confident. Use the tremendous openness of architecture to find a possibility for the coexistence of tourism, heritage and the contemporary city. Rely on a given, shared architectural knowledge. Beauty can be easy. Erase traces. When asked to restore Diocletian baths and to transform the building into a church, Michelangelo decided not to do anything. He simply determined where to put the door, and thus how to move within the Roman spaces. Then he suggested painting the vaults white. Erase traces. The city does not need authors.

Archi

in the

Globa

'To advance territorial modification as the basis of a new cultural discipline is to accord a compensatory status not only to the art of landscape as it has been traditionally understood but also to built-form formulated as if it were a landscape in itself or, alternatively, an object so integrated into the ground as to be inseparable from the surrounding topography.'

Architecture in the Age of Globalization

The globalization of capital is, of course, somewhat spurious. Yet it is an important ideological innovation. The capitalist system undergoes a kind of mutation to its essential form, the culmination of which would be the complete (notional) capitalization of nature in which there no longer remains any domain external to capital. This is tantamount to the assumption that an external nature does not exist. The image is no longer Marx's (or the classical economists') of human beings acting on external nature to produce value. Rather, the image is of the diverse elements of nature (including human nature) themselves codified as capital. Nature is capital, or, rather, nature is conceived in the image of capital. The logic of the system is thus the subsumption of all the elements of nature-considered-as-capital to the finality of capital's expanded reproduction.

Theoretical difficulties immediately arise as a result of the fact that this is a largely imaginary functional integration. The rhetoric stresses harmonization and optimization; the reality is disorder and conflict. As Baudrillard remarks, 'Everything is potentially functional and nothing is in fact'. Two sources of contradiction are inherent in the process of the capitalization of nature, which furnish our justifications for proposing a shift from an industrial to an ecological Marxist perspective on production, on the 'eventual' and 'inevitable' collapse of capitalism, and thence on the conditions for some sort of socialism. The first is the fact that the planet is materially finite, a situation that creates biophysical limits to the accumulation process. The second, which is synergetic with the first, is the fact that capital does not and cannot control the reproduction and modification of the 'natural' conditions of production in the same way it purports to regulate industrial commodity production.

Martin O'Connor
Is Capitalism Sustainable? 1994

The diverse phenomena that accompany globalization are closely associated with the ever-escalating rate of telematic communication and the constant increase in transcontinental air travel. As a consequence, the practice of architecture today is as global as it is local, as we may judge from the international celebrity architects that are increasingly active all over the world directly responding to the flow of capital investment. Our current susceptibility to spectacular imagery is such that today the worldwide reputation of an architect is as much due to his or her iconographic flair as it is to their organizational and or technical ability. This worldwide phenomenon has been termed the Bilbao effect – so coined for the way in which, throughout the 1990s, provincial cities vied with each another to have a building designed by the celebrated American architect Frank Gehry, largely as a result of the mediatic acclaim accorded to his sensational Guggenheim Museum realized in Bilbao in 1995. During the decade that succeeded this spectacular triumph, the scope of the celebrity architect widened immeasurably, with signature architects travelling all over the globe in order to supervise the erection of iconic structures, thousands of miles apart, in totally different cultural and political contexts. This is particularly evident in Beijing today, where diverse architectural stars rival each other with the projection of one spectacular building after another, from Paul Andreu's National Grand Theatre of China, with its three auditoria housed under a single titanium dome (2006) to Jacques Herzog and Pierre de Meuron's over-structured Beijing National Stadium, currently under construction for the 2008 Olympic Games.

For its equally gargantuan size, structural audacity and perverse shape, it would be difficult to imagine a more spectacular structure than Rem Koolhaas's 70-floor Chinese Television Headquarters (CCTV) in Beijing, with its inclined, trapezoidal profile crowned by a 70 m cantilever, some 230 m in the air. Such technological ostentation recalls the audacity of the Eiffel Tower, along with El Lissitzky's Wolkenbugel proposal of 1924, by which the CCTV seems to have been inspired. However, totally removed from the axiality of both Eiffel's tower and Lissitzky's 'anti-skyscraper', the imbalanced asymmetrical structure and arbitrary siting of Koolhaas's television megastructure precludes it from having any urbanistic or symbolic significance, except for its gargantuan representation of manipulative mediatic power. When complete and fully operative it will house a working population of 10,000 engaged in the programming of some 250 channels streaming out to a billion people a day.

Skyscrapers of a much greater height are equally symptomatic of our 'society of spectacle' in which cities compete with each other for the dubious honour of realizing the world's tallest building. As of now Dubai, although hardly a city, is the leading contender with its 160-floor Burj Tower designed by Skidmore, Owings and Merrill. While such extravagances seem to become increasingly irresistible in capital cities throughout the developed world, witness the Gasprom skyscraper projected for St Petersburg 2006, global megalopoli are ever more inundated with impoverished people, particularly in the Third World, where cities continue to densify their already congested infrastructures, so that Mexico City now stands at 22 million; Beijing, Bombay, São Paolo and Tehran at around 20 million each; Jakarta at 17 million, Bogota at 7 million and Caracas at 5 million. To these statistics we may add the alarming predication that within the next 15 years, 300 million rural Chinese will migrate into new or existing cities within the Republic of China. A transfiguration on such a scale will only exacerbate the fact that Asian cities are among the most polluted in the world with the air quality in Beijing being six times more polluted than that of the average European capital.

With equally wasteful consequences as far as gasoline consumption is concerned, cities in the USA such as Houston (5,350,000), Atlanta (5,050,000) and Phoenix (3,850,000) continue to lose population in their centres while constantly expanding their suburban hinterland with little or no provision for public transport. The negative socioecological nature of such settlement patterns is only too familiar, apart from the fact that, in the USA alone, well over 3 million acres of open land are lost each year to suburbanization. This goes along with the fact that the current pattern of government subsidy in the USA is skewed four to one in favour of auto routes rather than rail or bus transit.

Despite of this dystopic prospect of an ever-expanding 'motopia' we have to acknowledge the positive impact of increased mediatic communication in general, since this seems to have had the effect of raising the general level of current architectural production. Thus although urban sprawl remains as entropic as ever, the one-off architectural work is possibly, on balance, of a higher quality now than it was some 20 years ago. Today, architects increasingly seem to assess their work against a constantly elevating global standard of technical and cultural sophistication. The vagaries of fashion notwithstanding, this upgrading is as prevalent on the periphery as in the centre and occurs as much in local, small-scale works as in the global activity at an international scale.

Topography

Two seminal publications dating from the mid 1960s and early 1970s announce the emergence of *topography* and *sustainability* as the two environmental meta-discourses of our time; together they will exercise a pervasive influence not only on landscape and urban design, but also on the field of architecture in general. The two texts in question, Vittorio Gregotti's *Il territorio di architettura*, of 1966, and Ian McHarg's *Design with Nature*, of 1971, emphasize in different ways the significant integration of man-made form with the earth's surface. Complementing Semper's emphasis on the primitive hut, Gregotti sees the marking of ground as a primordial act, undertaken in order to establish a man-made *cosmos* in the face of the *chaos* of nature and he emphasizes the fabrication of *territory* as a strategy by which to establish a public place-form in the face of the new nature brought into being by the emergence of the urbanized region. He first demonstrated this thesis in his designs for the University of Calabria, built as a linear megastructure across a large swathe of agricultural land, in Cosenza in Southern Italy in 1973. Eschewing architectonic intervention, McHarg's research focused more on the need for a comprehensive approach to the biosphere in order to facilitate and maintain the mutual interdependence of regional ecosystems across a wide front. In retrospect, both approaches were attempts to mediate the effect of the continual expansion of megalopoli throughout the world. Today they may still be regarded as viable strategies with which to resist the reduction of the man-made world to a limitless diffusion of ill-related, free-standing objects, as alienated from the needs of man as from the processes of nature.

To advance territorial modification as the basis of a new cultural discipline is to accord a compensatory status not only to the art of landscape as it has been traditionally understood but also to built-form formulated as if it were a landscape in itself or, alternatively, an object so integrated into the ground as to be inseparable from the surrounding topography. It is just such a reconception of the scope of landscape that currently favours the emergence of the new sub-discipline, *landscape urbanism*, conceived as a mode of intervention having a totally different strategic aim from the now largely discredited practice of master-planning. As the landscape architect James Corner was to put it in 2003: *In recent years we have witnessed an important shift: every location has begun to be regarded as a landscape, either natural or artificial, and has ceased to be a neutral backdrop, more or less decidedly sculptural, for architectural objects. With this change in point of view, the landscape becomes the subject of possible transformations; no longer inert, it can be designed, made artificial. The landscape has become the primary interest, the focal point of architects.*

It is within such a widening prospect that landscape architects have been able to assert their ability not only to conceive of projects that are relevant at both an urban and a regional scale but also their parallel capacity to have such broadly conceived proposals brought to realization within relatively short periods of time. The American landscape architect Peter Walker was able to demonstrate this in an exemplary way in his 800 acre layout for the IBM Campus in Solana, West Texas (1992) realized in collaboration with the architects Romaldo Giurgola, Ricardo Legoretta and Barton Myers. Walker characterized the reparatory scope of his intervention in the following terms: *When we found the site, it was not a particularly rich meadow. It had been grazed very heavily and over half the topsoil had been lost. There were a few handsome trees that stood up to the grazing and somehow survived . . . To repair the rest of it, we took the topsoil off every single road, building, or parking lot site, stockpiled it and put it on the meadow, thereby doubling the amount of topsoil.*

Walker pursued an equally large-scale topographic transformation in his Marina Linear Park, San Diego (1988), designed with Martha Schwartz, wherein the right of way of an existing light rail system was converted into an exotic sub-tropical park. Comparable infrastructural landscape interventions have been standard policy in France over the past two decades wherein one third of the state budget allocated to either regional high-speed transit or local light rail is given over to the design of landscape settings that are capable of integrating the new infrastructure into the pre-existing topography. Michel Desvigne and Christine Dalnoky's implantation of a new TGV station outside Avignon in 1995 is typical in this regard, as are numerous other works executed by them in relation to public transit. In Avignon, plane trees were employed to reinforce the linear extent of the station while the adjacent parking lots were shaded by rows of lime trees selected for their resemblance to the orchards of the surrounding apple-growing region, thereby integrating the station into the character of the pre-existing landscape.

Despite the evident success of both the American Parkway and German *Autobahn* in the 1930s, the universal expansion of auto routes over the last half century has not always been accompanied by environmental design of a comparable quality. An exception to this in Europe were the concrete viaducts and tunnel entrances that the Swiss architect Rino Tami designed for the Ticinese auto route extending from the San Gottardo tunnel in the Alps to the Italian frontier at Chiasso; a painstaking, large-scale, infrastructural improvement realized over a 20-year period between 1963 and 1983. More recently and of more limited scope we may cite such interventions as Bernard Lassus's somewhat exotic *auto-scapes* in north-western France; in the first instance the cutting of a road through an eroded rockscape in such a way as to create a geological park, in the second, the provision of narrow overpasses with which to maintain pre-existing patterns of animal movement across the barrier of an auto route.

The cultivation of landscape as a matter of ecological policy at a regional scale has almost become second nature in Germany, where the extension of Peter Latz's Emscher Park, which started as a demonstration project for the detoxification and reuse of obsolete industrial plants, has evolved over the last 15 years to become the model for expanding the park into a regional recreational area covering some 70 km on either side of the Emscher river. It is significant that Karl Ganser, one of the main architects of the Emscher reclamation programme, would come to regard the universal megalopolis as another 'brownfield' site in the making, one which would possibly prove to be even more resistant to decontamination and adaptive reuse.

As in much of Alvar Aalto's architecture, large and complex buildings may be rendered as though they were natural extensions of the topography in which they are situated. This paradigm was surely the primary motivation behind Arthur Ericson's Robson Square development, Vancouver (1983), wherein a megastructure comprising law courts and municipal offices was integrated with a parking garage in such a way as to assume the profile of a stepped escarpment. This last, laid out to the designs of the landscape architect Cornelia Oberlander, features a 300-foot-long (90-m) ornamental sheet of water which cascades down over the large plate-glass picture window enclosing the wedding registry. This artificial architectonic earthwork running through the centre of Vancouver has since been consummated as a main spine within the city by the medium-rise towers that have spontaneously arisen around its axis over the last decade. In this regard Robson Square has served as an urban catalyst in much the same way as Rockefeller Center drew the fabric of Manhattan around itself at the end of the 1930s.

A similar catalytic megaform was realized a decade later in Barcelona, in the form of the L'Illa Block, completed on the Avenida Diagonal in 1992 to the designs of Rafael Moneo and Manuel de Sola Morales. This 800-m-long complex housing a five-floor shopping galleria in addition to commercial frontage on the avenue, was handled as an integral part of a medium-rise slab, accommodating offices and a hotel. Built at the edge of Cerda's original *ensanche* and served by a multi-storey subterranean parking garage running beneath the complex for its entire length, the block was designed to respond to the scale of both the existing nineteenth-century urban grid and the random, *ad hoc* suburban development surrounding the historic core of the city. The stepped profile of this building enabled it to be read as a prominent landmark, particularly when seen from the inner suburban high ground overlooking the city. This mega-development effectively demonstrated de Sola Morales's concept of *urban acupuncture*; namely a strategically limited urban intervention, programmed and conceived in such a way as to augment an existing urban condition in a defined but open-ended manner. Unlike the all too common practice of siting shopping malls on the outskirts of cities in such a way as to undermine the pre-existing shopping frontage of small towns, this development serves to strengthen the existing commercial core and its established patterns of street use, while reinforcing the axial shopping frontage of the Avenida Diagonal.

Urban acupuncture was also adopted as a metaphor by the Brazilian architect-politician Jaime Lerner in order to refer to his introduction of an efficient public transit system into the city of Curitiba during his tenure as mayor of that city between 1971 and 1992. Among the most innovative aspects of this system is the use of doubly articulated 100-person buses, combined with elevated, totally glazed boarding tubes that facilitate the efficient boarding of such vehicles at each stop. Today this network comprises 72 km of designated bus lanes plus numerous other feeder lines. Over the same 20-year period the Lerner administration was also able to introduce many other socially beneficial services in the areas of public health, education, food distribution and waste management. At the same time, in spite of tripling the population of the city, they were able to achieve a one hundred-fold increase in the amount of green area per capita; a provision of 52 m^2 per person that now encompasses an extensive network of parks running throughout the city. This general upgrading of public facilities combined with the introduction of a high-speed bus system has recently been replicated in Bogota, Colombia, during the successive political leadership of Enrique Penalosa and Antanas Mokeus.

Sustainability

In his study *Ten Shades of Green: Architecture and the Natural World* (2000-2005), Peter Buchanan supplements his descriptive analysis of ten exemplary green buildings with ten precepts that cover a wide spectrum of sustainable practices from the optimization of natural shade, light and ventilation, to the use of renewable sources of natural energy; from the elimination of waste and pollution to the reduction of the amount of energy embodied in the constructional material itself. As he puts it: *The building material with the least embodied energy is wood, with about 640 kilowatt hours per ton. ... Hence the greenest building material is wood from sustainably managed forests. Brick is the material with the next lowest amount of embodied energy, 4 times (x) that of wood, then concrete (5x), plastic (6x), glass (14x), steel (24x), aluminum (126x). A building with a high proportion of aluminum components can hardly be green when considered from the perspective of total life cycle costing, no matter how energy efficient it might be.*

Statistics such as these should certainly give us pause, including the sobering fact that the built environment accounts for some 40 per cent of the total energy consumption in the developed world, comparable in fact to that consumed by automotive commutation and jet travel. Much of this profligate use is due to artificial lighting; some 65 per cent of our total electrical energy consumption being due to this, with air conditioning and digital equipment coming a close second. It is equally sobering that a large part of any contemporary land-fill is invariably made up of building waste; some 33 per cent of the average municipal waste stream in the USA.

In the face of these dystopic statistics, Buchanan's recommendations have a markedly cultural character, such as his advocacy of building according to the anti-ergonomic principle of 'long life/loose fit', as this precept was spontaneously integral to the load-bearing masonry structures of the past, bequeathing us a legacy of eminently adaptable buildings, mostly dating from the eighteenth and nineteenth centuries, many of which we have been able to put to new uses. This residual value is more difficult to achieve today given our minimal space standards and our commitment to the paradoxically inflexible, light-weight building techniques of our time.

Buchanan insists that every building should be closely integrated into its context. He thereby urges architects to pay as much attention to such interactive factors as micro-climate, topography and vegetation, as to the more familiar functional and formal concerns addressed in standard practice. Buchanan's eighth precept stresses the crucial role to be played by public transport in sustaining the ecological balance of any particular land settlement pattern, since urban sprawl, no matter how green it might be in itself, can hardly outweigh the energy consumed in the daily commutation by automobile from home to work and the accompanying environmental pollution that this entails. In opposing this entropic prospect, Buchanan stresses the public health benefits accruing to dense urban form that is well-served by public transport and is thus sustainable in the broader sense of the term.

One cannot conclude this brief overview of sustainable architecture without mentioning the research-based practice of the Munich architect Thomas Herzog, whose Halle 26 was built for the Hanover Fair of 1996. In this instance the achievement was as much tectonic as environmental, with the distinguished engineer Jorge Schlaich acting as structural consultant. In this regard the catenary roof of the building was as much determined by the need to erect the structure rapidly as by the environmental attributes of its section. The main support for the three-bay catenary roof, with each bay spanning 180 feet, was provided by three, 100-foot-high, triangulated steel trestles, with a fourth set somewhat lower. The wire cable structure carrying the roof was covered by two layers of wood, with gravel in between in order to add stabilizing weight to the catenary. The up-curving profile of the resulting section with a vent under the eaves serves to induce thermal uplift and exhaust stale air while fresh air is drawn into the hall via transverse triangular sectioned glass ducts spanning the trestles. To a similar end, the inner curve of the roof was used as a light reflector at night while the availability of natural light during the day was topped up by an anti-solar, glass panel let into the valley of the roof.

In the USA, where 2 per cent of the world's population consumes 20 per cent of the world's resources, there has been an understandable tendency to deny the reality of global warming, along with the maximized consumption of non-renewable energy to which it is directly related. This denial is evident in the reluctance of the American government to introduce and enforce progressive environmental regulations as a standard mode of practice. This obtuseness has been marginally condoned by architects on the grounds that sustainable design curbs their freedom of expression. Such an attitude is as reactionary as it is perverse, given that responding symbiotically to the exigencies of both climate and context has invariably served as a mainspring for tectonic invention since time immemorial; one that has been crucial to the maturation of a non-instrumental environmental culture rather than the other way around.

In the last analysis, going beyond the limited domain of architecture, the issue of sustainability begs the question as to whether capitalism itself is in any sense sustainable. As Martin O'Connor puts it: since the planet itself is materially finite this sets the limits as far as the future possibility for capital accumulation is concerned. The fact which the species does not want to face in our much vaunted consumer society is exactly this. But sooner rather than later we shall be forced to face it with the total elimination of oceanic fish, the growing shortage of water, the melting of the ice cap and the parallel scorching of the earth, and so on *ad infinitum*; the first strange fruits of our unsustainable hubris.

Kenneth Frampton's 'Architecture in the Age of Globalization' is an abridged extract from his new chapter for the fourth revision of his book *Modern Architecture: A Critical History* to be published by Thames and Hudson in Autumn 2007.

Martijn de Waal

Power Modernism

Chandigarh Modernism

When India and Pakistan were turned into modern nation-states, the Indian prime minister Nehru needed a new capital for the now divided state Punjab. This new city would be, as Nehru claimed, 'unfettered by the traditions of the past, a symbol of the nation's faith in the future'. It needed to demonstrate that India now had entered modernity, and would look forward rather than lean on its traditions. The foreign architect Le Corbusier was invited to design this city. At the beginning of the twenty-first century, many aspiring cities follow this same strategy: from Astana to Abu-Dabhi, international star architects like Norman Foster are invited to design iconic buildings or master plans that symbolize the embrace of modernity, and claim a position on the stage o which the international recognition race of world cities plays out.

Brasilia Modernism

Just like Chandigarh in India, Brasilia was planned to symbolize that Brazil had entered the era of modernity. However, no foreign architects were flown in, the design and architecture were thought up by Brazilian architects and planners with different cultural backgrounds. They used local traditions and architectural histories (such as the pre-columbic and Spanish colonial planning) to localize Le Corbusier's modernist theorie and rework them into the Brazilian context. Cou a similar approach of 'continuist modernism' be viable today as an alternative for the 'cities from zero'

...nisms

...'cities on the other side of the river' being build
...fast developing economies?

...Songdo Modernism

...n updated version of Chandigarh modernism,
...ting the demands of the information economy.
...ongdo is to be a new 120-million-square-foot
...evelopment, with 60 million square feet of pres-
...gious office space. It is built on a raised island
...ear the Korean coast and connected with a 6.4
...ile bridge to the Seoul-Incheon international
...rport. The developers not only designed the
...onic master plan, but also set up the legal frame-
...ork that turned this new city into a Free Eco-
...omic Zone that relieves companies from Korean
...ureaucracy and taxes and rewrites land-owner-
...ip legislation, and make it both a national and a
...enationalized symbol of 'faith in the future'.

Th
Fa
of
Fo

The Failure of the Formal   **Alfredo Brillembourg and Hubert Klumpner**

Power to the People?

One of the biggest problems in cities today is the failure of decision-makers to identify and contribute actively to a larger vision. Indeed, the absence of vision – both in the sense of foresightedness and of truly seeing one's surroundings – is part of a general abdication of responsibility: the inhabitants of large cities and those they elect both defer judgment and decisions to 'experts', on the assumption that the latter know best. To the contrary, we have found that projects conceived, promulgated, designed, and realized by the 'expert' architects and planners all too often are abject failures, because they are founded on formal nineteenth- and twentieth-century models and urban vocabularies. The urban and architectural theories and ideologies emerging from the university and from 'signature' architects fail precisely where they should be most intensely focused: on the city as a place for equal opportunities, urban culture, and policies in the service and the well-being of the citizens. The missing thread in the discussions of form and style and urban development is accountability to those whose lives are directly affected.

But global informal urban practices are transforming the city and its systems, upending the rules and models, creating new players and reconfiguring urban political power. For as long as people have migrated to the city from the countryside, newcomers have brought with them the village model – improvised, close-knit, interdependent, ad hoc. The barrio of Petare in Caracas is just one result of generations of such informal development: an entirely pedestrian city of nearly one million inhabitants, of unparalleled density, extra-legal infrastructure and governance systems, an exceptionally innovative way of assigning and managing property. Petare-dwellers practice sustainability not as an academic principle, but as a necessity, producing less waste and needing less energy than citizens of the formal city; making use of roof gardens, designing flexible 'growing' houses, using and reusing any and all available materials.

Where Have All the Planners Gone?[1]
The unfulfilled promise of Latin America's modernity was perhaps inevitable in light of the unprecedented size and scale of the urban explosion. The population of Mexico City, for instance, doubled five times over the last century. Much the same is true of

São Paulo, Buenos Aires, or Caracas – and of Beijing and Mumbai and other mega-cities as well. This growth, in turn, has produced a deficit in the physical and social infrastructure, ranging from housing to education. Venezuela alone is lacking 2.5 million housing units. In the absence of effective formal planning mechanisms, rural and family- or clan-based lifestyles and age-old informal practices – do-it-yourself design and construction, for instance, and the appropriation of unused or underused land by squatting – present the inhabitants, and us, with viable alternatives, as well as new ways of responding to sustainability and economics.

One concomitant of this contrast between formal and informal practices – between mere activity and actual accomplishment – is the divided city. There is global state-of-the-art technology and vast wealth, on one hand, and slum environments and abject poverty on the other. The widening social and economic gap is quite literally visible in aerial photographs of major Latin American cities: one can see the forces of innovation and of destruction at work. And as that gap increasingly manifests itself in soaring crime and political extremism, it produces further fault lines and fortifications, resembling those created by the laws of apartheid in Johannesburg, the de facto apartheid in Jerusalem, the gated communities of the USA.

If traditional regulated urban planning is no longer relevant, one must look first to the rapidity of change and the multiplicity of programmes in the informal city: working, warehousing, schooling, banking, betting, playing have made their place in the ghettos and transformed the urban house. Conventional zoning regulations, with their rigidity and hierarchies, cannot respond to the high-speed mutation of the American cities. The new city is flexible, generic, and malleable. The new environment privileges designs and planning that can respond and adapt rapidly to new programmes; is able to shift spaces, open new spaces, create new tactics; anticipates growth and change, seizes opportunity, does more with less.

There is No There There[2]

In the aftermath of September 11, 2001, the term 'global' gained new currency and the underlying concepts new urgency. We, too, talked about what it meant, but in more personal and professional terms, as architects who live and work in Caracas and for whom New York City is a second home. Eventually, we began putting our thoughts into writing, driven as least in part by the realization that, in the growing discourse about all things 'global' – the global city, the global economy, globalism – two elements seemed to us to be missing: the 'global slum' as a significant phenomenon, and the southern hemisphere's slums, or barrios, as one of its specific manifestations. We believed then – perhaps even more strongly now – that it was important to align the generalities and the breadth of the global discourse to the realities of the urban South and to the nature and role of architecture.

Pablo Souto / KSB, U-TT, La Vega

Informal Cities

Over the past years, we have continued our investigations and explorations, taking the original sketchy thesis about informality and the informal city and testing its utility as the foundation for a set of tools suitable for understanding and working in the contemporary urban setting. No small part of our objective is to create a consciousness about the need for profound change in attitudes and to generate cross-cultural, inter-generational debate. To that end, we have participated in the development and nurturing of a widening network of young professionals, who approach their work from an interdisciplinary perspective and process and who are 'architects' in the sense of makers, doers, catalysts, rather than in the traditional sense of 'designer'.

Among them are the three we selected to be represented in the biennale: Teddy Cruz, who works along the San Diego/Tijuana corridor; Jose Castillo from Mexico City; and Fernando

Parque Central

Melo, Marta Moreira, and Milton Braga of MMBB in São Paulo. Although their respective works are highly specific to site and circumstance, they have in common the invention and realization of their own projects, beginning autonomously rather than courting a client or commission. Working outside official institutions and the conventional client-architect-budget relationship, and analysing real-world social and spatial situations and responding with particular and specific programmes and strategies, these individuals and groups have abandoned the conventions of architectural and urban planning practice, blurring the boundaries between urban planning, urban design, art, and social and political activism.

As large as the goals may be, they – and we – deliberately employ micro-tactics, identifying small projects, working within communities and with their leaders, devising and testing particular solutions to arrive at more general principles applicable to any informal city. That approach, like that of the barrio dwellers themselves, is bottom-up: reusing, adapting, and modifying the existing infrastructure, and retrofitting and stacking generatively. What we seek ultimately is the development of an industrially-produced, interchangeable kit-of-parts that will serve as an essential quick-fix, an urban survival system for developing informal cities in urgent need of viable, affordable solutions. Far from eliminating architects, this approach enlists them in a bottom-up process of transformative design. We envision the development of a hybrid design strategy, in which architects, drawing on the hands-on expertise of the local population, create prototypes that are adaptable to various locations and conditions. The result of this process, we believe, would be an urban survival system of viable, affordable solutions for the development of informal cities.

Petare

Power of the Informal

Given the challenges of the urban South, form as a determinant, a starting point, an ideology, simply does not work. We are by no means suggesting that architecture for the contemporary city is or should be form*less*; rather, form arises from and is driven by need, circumstance, people, function.

In our use of the term, 'informal' does not mean 'lacking form'. Practices and results described as informal arise from within themselves and their makers, who are the end-users – the residents – themselves. The informal city is subject to rules and procedures potentially as specific and necessary as those that have governed official, formal city-making. It is by no means lawless, but it does occupy a grey area between legal and illegal transactions – and it is precisely that grey area that informal developers and architects working together can explore to great advantage. The processes of informality, like the informal city itself, can be elusive. If one looks at them from a distance, one searches in vain for an ordering principle, a clear beginning and end, for ways to separate the whole into comprehensible elements. But close up, patterns begin to emerge and a certain logic – unlike that taught by conventional architecture or planning – can be discerned.

Our interest in 'informal urbanism' has three points of origin:
• From a humanitarian standpoint, architects simply must come to terms with the fact of urban shantytowns and their problems. Professionals must engage in the social aspects of architecture and develop sustainable planning strategies that issues such as poverty.
• From a theoretical standpoint, the 'informal' can serve as the basis for studying adaptation and innovation. The informal city itself has enormous potential as a laboratory in which large-scale scenarios can teach and inform us, even as we direct our attention to their needs.
• From a design point of view, informality is a condition of complex, nonlinear systems in which patterns overlap, intersect, and mutate in unexpected ways. The informal city offers a generation of young architects a new way to consider and practice their art, to think differently about materials and their applications.

The informal city, long treated as an aberration or an exception to the standards of urbanism, is actually becoming the norm throughout the Global South, and it does so as an integral part of the global economy. Our research shows that in Caracas, a growing majority of the city's inhabitants live in informal zones, and 80 per cent of new housing is self-built. The improvisation that characterizes these zones resembles the 'plug-in, tune-up, clip-on' architecture of Yona Friedman.[3] What we have found in Caracas, and might well see elsewhere around the world, is a genuine community, one that is rapidly moving from resistance to action to gradual acceptance.

La Vega, Caracas

Forces of Inertia

Misconceptions about Informality
Though the term 'informal urbanism' has achieved text-book status, there remain three significant misconceptions as to its implications, which in turn prevent its potential powers from being realized:

• It is, in fact, the case that Informal urbanism has been a fact of life ever since the city has existed. One could argue that it is and always has been the inevitable by-product of changes in economies, of disasters both natural and man-made, of the human inclination to gather together. Sceptics conclude from this that, because slums have always existed, more a nuisance than a scourge, we have learned to live with them and therefore should continue to do so.

This argument ignores important transformations that began in the 1990s. Changes in political and economic life, together with the proliferation and availability of technology to ordinary citizens, have begun to erode the means by which governments have traditionally secured borders and boundaries and controlled information and access. Governments themselves also, perhaps inadvertently, participated in the resulting expansion of power: deregulation of previously closed or tightly controlled markets opened the doors to new players; while the essentials of the phenomena are common to the world's informal cities, it uniquely embodies the interface – perhaps collision – between the 'Global City' and the 'Global Slum'.

• It is also true that the informal city, or slum, is beset by poverty and its close cousin, crime. But it is a grave mistake to associate informality exclusively with criminality. By and large the activities of the informal city are not illegal, but extra-legal, operating outside the regulatory apparatus. It is also important to distinguish the global informality we see today – not only in Latin America but on virtually every continent – with its older expression: something temporary, transitional, small-scale, and concerned only with strategies for survival. The new informality is permanent, established, and large-scale. The contemporary informal city is the locus of employment and, though not for its inhabitants, of wealth: 60 per cent of the jobs in the Global South are located in the informal city.
• And, finally, there is the assumption that informal urbanism is an underground or fringe phenomenon, irrelevant to the actual

practices of urban planning and architecture. This is the most debilitating misconception for the future of cities themselves and for the professions, because it places informal practices outside the mainstream and robs them of their potential power to transform. It also tends to create false analogies, in which formal is to professional, stable, valuable as informal is to *un*professional, flimsy, worthless. It sets architecture with a capital 'A' – that which is studied in schools and relies upon received wisdom, ideologies, the search for 'innovation' and prizes – apart from the architecture practiced by those who live and build in slums. And it enables a particularly dangerous form of urbanism by making implicit moral distinctions that empower elitism.

The Academy and the 'Star' System
In the absence of utopia, architectural formalism is pointless

Afredo Brillembourg & Hubert Klumpner /U-TT,
Gimnasio Vertical, Baruta

and useless. While architecture in the Western world – the architecture of great wealth, great universities, and great names – applauds the attainment of 'purity', what it has in fact achieved is social irrelevance, the disengagement of the discipline and its practitioners from the essential task of defining the future of the city. Indeed, the education and training of architects are so far removed from real-world circumstances and challenges that many recent graduates are essentially unfit to practice their profession.

This is an extraordinarily dismaying state of affairs. Urban populations are confronting enormous challenges without the enlightened participation and support of architects; they need thinkers who ask the right questions and implementers who conceive real-world solutions to issues of scale, density, organization, planning, and programming. The discourse among urban components – social and physical living space; housing and work; public life and public space; and transportation and infrastructure – still employs the worn-out vocabulary of the modernist city.

We believe the city is in urgent need of hands-on research and of new and practical initiatives for development. Our advocacy for the engagement of architects in and with the informal city is intended as a rallying cry to our fellow professionals. Forget utopia; abandon 'purity' and idealism: successful architecture in the informal city is a matter of avoiding disaster, of averting collapse – its context is the urgency of need.

Agents of Change

How does, how should an architect work in this new migrant city, with all evident contradictions of wealth and poverty?

Most ordinary urban Venezuelans have neither the financial means to obtain market housing or to engage an architect or builder, nor the technical expertise to construct their homes on their own. But various informal, if well established and respected, agents have emerged with whom architects can work in and productively support the development of the barrios. The leader of the initial process of occupying – in effect seizing – the land is also the first agent, or developer, of barrio construction. Because such headmen, like Felix Carvallo of La Vega, emerge as natural leaders whom the community respects and trusts, they are sought out by other families for help in establishing a foothold. Carvallo and others have a singular talent for putting together knowledge with need and problem with solution, making them and the barrio committees they typically establish ideally suited to collaborate with architects, as teachers, students, and partners.

Surprisingly to some, the state, too, is an agent through which architects can engage with barrio dwellers and their committees. Although in theory and by law the state prohibits the illegal occupation of land, it tends to turn a blind eye when that occupation is undertaken by barrio leaders.[4] The state also gives tacit consent by helping individuals build on appropriated municipal and private land, hiring construction companies or identifying the users themselves as builders. In the past 55 years, this intermediary role has become an increasingly common practice and is by now sufficiently well-established to give architects a means of access.

And in what way have the urban realities of the southern hemisphere changed the way architecture is practiced in America?

We employ the 'power of powerlessness',[5] which is our ability as architects to exercise power in non-traditional modes of urban activism, designing quick, improvised applications. In contrast to established practices that conform to the organizational rules of the professional environment, the new practice of architecture must have an oppositional role. The architect today has to constantly prove that things can and should be done differently, by different people, with different goals. This new practice of Ditch Urbanism, as described by Michelle Provoost and Wouter Vanstiphout[6] 'is fundamentally different from Bottom-Up urbanism or from advocacy planning; it does not passively translate the will of the local people. It brings to the site a "view of the world", just not the one used by the official policy-makers or the sitting market-parties. And that is what makes these practices distinctly modernist.'

La Vega, Caracas

In the informal city, the citizen has the potential to become an agent provocateur, to engage with what we call 'performative architecture'. We see ourselves as initiators of processes, either in built form or abstractly, to set in motion a series of social practices. This performative role of the architect can help delineate the contours of a community and in turn inject a certain collectivity into a community. In this role, architecture also engages in a constant shaping and reshaping of the borders of the city by negotiating inclusions and legitimating exclusions.

The dependency on and underdevelopment of the informal city on the formal or planned city is characteristic. The excluded populations as a by-product of the value system of formal developments is not a final conclusion but moreover a commentary for further investigations. We like to question this notion as the basis of the informal city by underlining the general interdependency that exists among all cities regardless of their economic power. Cities as individual entities have in our view ceased to exist; we are dealing with a global urban phenomenon that has particular characteristic extensions, but ultimately is part of one global urban entity for the same reason, the global city and the global slum must be concerned with each other.

Malthus Was Right[7]

Their differences notwithstanding, cities such as Caracas, Tijuana, Mexico City, and São Paulo have in common their informal urbanization. It is a fact of twenty-first-century life, and it is global. Today, the world population is growing as never before, and people are moving as they never have before. It took 400 years to import 12 million African slaves to the new world; but in the past ten years alone, an estimated 30 million woman and children have migrated or been displaced in Southeast Asia. Crossboarder migration, which is only part of the picture, accounts for an estimated 700,000 to 2 million people each year. In 2004, the world counted 175 million documented international migrants, 3 per cent of humanity. Still more were internal migrants, drawn

from rural hinterlands to fast-growing urban and industrial zones. Another 20 million were refugees and displaced persons.

WHAT THEN SHALL WE DO?[8] Far from being irrelevant to the development of the informal city, architects are much needed. But they will have to be a different kind of architect, open to different ways of thinking, both about design and about the role and responsibilities of the profession in the social, economic, and political arenas. Consider, for instance, that in Cota 905, a district in Caracas, some 100 families have taken over a protected park area over the past six months, cutting down trees and building houses on a steep and precarious incline. The danger posed by the slope alone is greatly magnified by the all-but-inevitable mudslide in the next rainy season which, if it spares the settlers' lives, will surely leave them homeless.

The civic authorities are, in fact, contemplating measures that would enable them to anticipate future settlement needs and, rather than opposing all construction, assist settlers in identifying appropriate and safe sites, with adequate services. Who will help ensure that the homes, too, are safe? Who will help by teaching and demonstrating prudent construction techniques? Where are the architects?

At the Urban Think Tank, we propose alternatives to conventional architectural intervention, new guidelines for architects who are prepared to rethink their role in the city:
1. Apply what you already know is true. We all know, for instance, that policies on renewable energy sources and sustainable strategies should be in place. We need to act as though they already were.
2. Do not assume that design innovation – indeed, architectural excellence – and practice in the real world of the informal city or rural settings are mutually exclusive. Architecture schools and design practices can produce creative, workable, cost-effective structures and prototypes for lower-income communities. Consider the late Sam Mockabee's Rural Studio, affiliated with the Auburn University School of Architecture and located in Hale County, Alabama, one of the poorest regions in the USA. Since it was established in 1993, this design/build studio's students have designed and built more than 80 houses and civic projects, using sustainable design principles and found and donated materials, typically for less than $20,000 per project.[9]
3. Create incentives for the adoption of environmentally responsible products. Why not a free database of products that lower-income communities could sell directly, such as solar panels, dry toilets, and housing kits? One project in the south Indian state of Tamil Nadu involves the design, fabrication, and installation of very low-cost chimneys in villagers' houses, to combat the rampant lung disease arising from the heavy smoke of cooking fires.
4. Make a virtue of necessity. In many cities, the need for security, especially for homes, is unavoidable – but the ugliness and xenophobic messages of coils of barbed wire, walls topped with glass shards, and bars and gates are not. Security devices and structures deserve as much aesthetic as practical attention and should be created not as an afterthought but in the overall design context.
5. Share your knowledge, expertise, and advice with those with whom you work. The old adage – 'Give a man a fish, and you feed him for a day; teach a man to fish, and you feed him for life' – is still sound. Teaching local developers and residents the principles of sound construction techniques, the properties of different materials, the relationships between form and function gives long-term meaning and value to the architect's intervention in the community.
6. Help resolve issues of adequate and nutritional food by developing building types that incorporate food production. Green roofs, which could serve both to reduce heating and cooling needs and as kitchen gardens, require further investigation and refinement to make them more widely applicable and cost-effective.

7. Work on reducing bureaucracy in the profession, where it inhibits design innovation and the exploration of informal architectural practice, and in procedure-driven government agencies, so that permits for 'unconventional' buildings could be granted on a proposal basis.

8. Be proactive. Instead of waiting for a client's call or an RFP, make quick three-dimensional studies and offer to present and explain them, free of charge, to governments and local organizations – show them what they can achieve.

9. Above all, talk to non-architects, engage in discussions with activists in other disciplines, persuade everyone to become involved. It's time to stop waiting for governments to act and to complain when they don't. They can't implement revolutionary change on their own – and they can't conceive it without the profession.

It is time for professionals – architects, urban planners, social activists, and others – to confront the future by helping to build the common, social spaces of their cities from the bottom up; to interact forcefully but productively with politicians, policy-makers, and community groups; and to participate collaboratively in the construction of more equitable, workable and sustainable cities.

1   Pete Seeger, 'Where Have All the Flowers Gone?' (1961); the song became the anthem of the 1960s anti-war movement in the USA.
2   Gertrude Stein, on Oakland, California, in: *Everybody's Autobiography*, London: Heinemann, 1937), chapter 4.
3   Friedman 1999: 9-13
4   Hernando de Soto, in *The Mystery of Capital: Why Capitalism Triumphs in the West and Fails Everywhere Else* (New York: Basic Books, 2000), 55-56, states in the case of Peru, the Venezuelan State, 'in the face of the evident ineffectiveness of the legal system . . . had to resort to extra legal regulations, and specifically to invasion to create a housing project'.
5   Title which plays homage to Vaclav Havel's essay in 1978 by the same name, which influenced a generation of Eastern European dissidents to speak out against the state.
6   Michelle Provoost and Wouter Vanstiphout, Crimson Architectural Historian's article 'Facts on the Ground', *Harvard Design Magazine*, Fall 2006/Winter 2007, n. 25.
7   Malthusian principal based on the idea that population if unchecked increases at a geometric rate whereas the food supply grows at an arithmetic rate.
8   In the 1982 film *The Year of Living Dangerously*, the Chinese-Australian photo-journalist, Billy Kwan, despairing at the failures and brutality of the Sukarno regime in Indonesia, sits at his desk, typing over and over with growing speed and vehemence, 'What then shall we do? What then shall we do? What then shall we do?'
9   The Rural Studio's mission is to 'enable each participating student to cross the threshold of misconceived opinions to create/design/build and to allow students to put their educational values to work as citizens of a community. Students live where they work, in a poverty-stricken area, and work hand-in-hand with their clients, an exercise that 'refines the student's social conscience', teaching them first-hand 'the necessary social, cultural and technological concepts of designing and building'. The Rural Studio, School of Architecture, Auburn University, http:/cadc.auburn.edu/soa/rural-studio.

Perip
Land

Peripheral Landscapes
Negotiating with the Power of the Informal

Jose Castillo
Saidee Springall

Informality, as an urban phenomenon, has become a way of life in the context of Mexico City. Not only have informal practices changed the social and economic dynamics of the city, they have also influenced the production of urban space. It is estimated that over 60 per cent of Mexico City's urban form originated through a process of informality.

Informality refers to the practices (social, economic, political, architectural and urban), and the forms (physical, spatial) that various groups (dwellers, developers, planners, landowners and the state), undertake at the limits of the legal, the normative, the procedural and the regulated, not only to obtain access to land and housing, but also to engage in urban life. These practices are characterized by tactical and incremental decisions, by a complex and changing interaction among players, and by a distinct set of spatial strategies that produce a progressive, non-hierarchical urban space.

Informality has become a new geography in Mexico City; it operates at an expansive scale, transforming large territories, both central and peripheral, as well as at the micro-scale, transforming dwellings through programme and time, or economic protocols, on a daily basis. Informality operates at both the high and low ends of the economic spectrum, through bottom-up and top-down approaches. It involves everything from politics to architecture, from infrastructure and transport to a range of economic activities.

Informality is most visible in the area of housing provision. Each year in Mexico City, the formal sector constructs over 105,000 units of housing, while an almost equal number of units is built by the informal sector. The sheer scale of this phenomenon is, in itself, a challenge to traditional modes of city making. Aside from the power and magnitude of the phenomenon, informal urbanization has generated a series of mutations and creative surges in the practices of architecture and planning that cannot be ignored. Rather than witnessing the disappearance of the informal city, Mexico City has *become* informal.

During the past five years, for the first time in decades, the production of informal housing has decreased due to an accelerated pace of formal housing production. This formal growth is taking place adjacent to informal developments; the informal and the formal cities are happening simultaneously. New private formal developments are becoming, by plan or by accident, the largest gated communities in the city, with homogeneous streets, row houses and cul-de-sacs as the basis of urban design's lowest common denominator.

Contrary to an oppositional or simply dialectical model of the relationship between the formal and the informal, recent dynamics in the peripheries of places like Mexico City show more fluid processes between the two; the formal and informal coexist in a state closer to symbiosis than conflict. It would seem obvious that informal housing would strive to become 'formalized' by obtaining services and infrastructure, but more surprising, and less commonly known, is the way in which formal housing is transformed by the dwellers, through use, growth, and programme, achieving some of the messiness and 'para-legality' that characterizes informal housing. The apparently homogenous developments with specific low/middle-income iconography are transformed over time through mechanisms of subversion, negotiation and resistance to the rules that codify urban life in these communities. Adaptation becomes a mechanism for survival. The interesting aspect of these transformations within the planned developments is that they operate in a limbo between illegality and rule of law.

While seductive and even attractive in some of its physical manifestations, informality can neither be aestheticized nor thought of as an exclusively positive phenomenon. Some of its social, political and environmental manifestations are unarguably negative traits. In some cases they threaten to paralyze entire urban areas (such as the historic centre); they can produce authoritarian or even exclusionary social and political practices, and can infer environmental damage through action or omission, such as the occupation of flood plains or ravines, or the discharge of sewage into open-air canals, that other forms of planning can better address. Nevertheless, through its raw potential, the informal can give rise to new modes of acting with regard to urbanization.

The modes of engagement with informality begin with its acknowledgement as a legitimate and relevant force in city-making. The ability of the informal to provide conditions of growth, adaptability, flexibility of use and programme, or the economic transformation of the dwelling presents crucial lessons for traditional planning methods. In addition, the apparent polarity between that which is informal and that which is not, is played out in areas of urbanization other than housing. In other words, it is in the spheres of workplaces, public spaces and infrastructure that conflicts – and opportunities – arise between the formal and the informal.

This project presents three cases of informality in Mexico City, as paradigms in the production of the contemporary city. These cases are more than just polemical

The ambiguities of the formal (left) / informal (right) in Mexico City

Landscape

Avenue

Entrepreneur

Street names

Playground

Housing units

Bordo de Xochiaca, Neza

View of the Bordo Xochiaca and Texcoco Lake
View of Xochiaca and Neza towards the East from Chimalhuacan

representations of the city; they offer specific territories for the deployment of more engaging forms of planning and architectural interventions of/within the informal city today. The three sites are El Caracol in Ecatepec, Bordo Xochiaca in Neza and Xico in Valle de Chalco. Despite their adjacency to informal settlements of past decades, these sites are currently undergoing transformations through their interaction with larger scale and formal planning strategies. Furthermore, they coexist with other historical narratives relevant to the city as a whole: the transformation of post-industrial barren landscapes, the reuse of former (illegal) waste dumps at the edge of the city, and the interaction of urbanization with lake and volcanic landscapes.

The three sites selected are located on the eastern fringes of the city, an area with the highest population growth rates in the megacity, yet one historically ignored by traditional planning. By looking into these disregarded zones, developed through unfamiliar procedures, we hope to discover more effective techniques of engagement, design and transformation of the forces that construct the city.

The concept of negotiation is a privileged framework and strategy with which to understand the rapport between the formal and informal cities in these three sites. Negotiation today embraces a multitude of spatial and political realms and practices: of land tenure and conflict, of programme, of history, of geography, of the private and the public, of the professional, of the planned and the unplanned, of the physical and the social, of the infrastructural and the environmental. We aim to understand how in these dialectics of formal/informal transformations, new liminal zones or thresholds between the two can provide the space for new modalities of planning that negotiate the formal and the informal.

It would seem, from looking at these sites, that the only possible role for planning today in Mexico City's context of informality is to recognize its force as a player in city-making, to harness its negative effects and make the most of its

potentials. This involves achieving a level of intelligence that enables smooth movement among the realms of planning, landscape, infrastructure and architecture. It requires recognizing where bottom-up is more effective than top-down, where decentralized choices are more effective than centralized planning, and where they are not. Foremost, it involves recognizing the limits of control in the practices of architecture and urbanism, and their potential to operate as tools for social and economic welfare and empowerment.

Growth in Ecatepec, seen from the center of El Caracol
The dividing wall between formal and informal in El Caracol, Ecate

El Caracol, Ecatepec

205 Informal Cities Mexico City

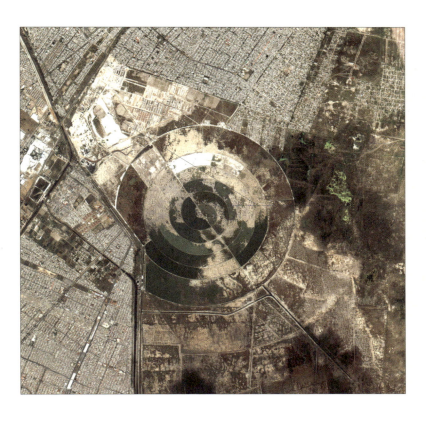

Xico, Valle de Chalco

View from Xico Volcano towards the southeast
View from Xico Volcano towards Tlahuac and Chalco Lake

Levittown Retrofitted
An Urbanism beyond the Property Line

Estudio Cruz
Teddy Cruz

The Political Equator

The post-9/11 world has produced a new, reconstituted global border between the First and Third Worlds – a division, freshly re-conceptualized by the Pentagon's New Map, between 'The Non-Integrating Gap' and the 'The Functioning Core'. Along this border we are witnessing how societies of overproduction and excess are barricading themselves in an unprecedented way against the sectors of scarcity they have produced out of political and economic indifference. On the one hand, the increasing migration of people across this global border is shaping an unprecedented illegal flow from the non-integrating gap, as the migrant communities from Latin America, Africa, and Asia move northward in search of the 'strong' economies of the functioning core. On the other hand, centres of manufacturing are being redistributed in the opposite direction, as the functioning core targets the non-integrating gap as the site on which to enact its politics of outsourcing and its search for the world's cheapest labour markets.

The dramatic images emerging from this political equator converge, and are intensified, through the prism of the current politics of fear manifested at the border between the USA and Mexico. As the US Congress passes a regulation to build 700 more miles of border wall, the fusion of antiterrorism and anti-immigration sentiments sets the stage for confrontations over immigration policy and the further hardening of social legislation in the American metropolis. Geographies of conflict such as the San Diego-Tijuana border are anticipatory scenarios of the twenty-first-century global metropolis; increasingly, the city is becoming the battleground where strategies of control and tactics of transgression, formal and informal economies, legal and illegal occupations meet.

Strategies of Surveillance: Tactics of Transgression

Despite the apocalyptic implications of a more fortified border with intensified surveillance infrastructure, the growing tension between the various communities of San Diego and those of Tijuana have elicited multiple insurgent responses. These responses have unleashed new opportunities for constructing alternative modes of encounter, dialogue and debate, sharing resources and infrastructure, recycling at the most outlandish levels the fragments and situations of these two cities, and constructing practices of encroachment into the increasingly privatized and controlled public realm.

A series of 'off the radar' two-way border crossings – north-south and south-north across the border wall – suggest that no matter how high and long the post-9/11 border wall becomes, it will always be transcended by migrating populations and the relentless flows of goods and services back and forth across the formidable barrier. These illegal flows are physically manifested, in one direction, by the informal land use patterns and economies produced by migrant workers flowing from Tijuana into San Diego, searching for the strong economy of Southern California. But, while 'human flow' mobilizes northbound in search of dollars, 'infrastructural waste' moves in the opposite direction, constructing an insurgent, cross-border urbanism of emergency.

This cross-border urbanism is made, for example, of nomadic disposable houses that literally move on wheels from San Diego into Tijuana, as do leftover materials and systems, including garage doors and rubber tires that are recycled into new spatial narratives and informal infrastructure. Most recently, this invisible flow was made visible when the general public was finally made aware of the thirtysome tunnels that have been dug in the last eight years, a vast 'ant farm'-like maze of subterranean routes criss-crossing the border from California to Arizona. An archaeological section map of the territory today would reveal an underground urbanism worming its way into houses, churches, parking lots, warehouses and streets. Not only were the fantastic images of cross-border two-way tunnels – all equipped with retaining walls, electricity, water extraction and ventilation systems – exposed, there was also the undeniable presence of an informal economy and density at work at the border.

From the Global Border to the Border Neighbourhood

The perennial alliance between militarization and urbanization is re-enacted at the San Diego-Tijuana border and later reproduced in many US neighbourhoods as an expanding social legislation of fear transforms the 11 million illegal labourers who live there into criminal suspects. What are the implications of these forces of control on the one hand, and of non-conformity on the other, in the reshaping of the American city? This project for the 2007 Rotterdam Architecture Biennale reflects on these trans-border urban dynamics, using the San Diego-Tijuana territory of conflict as backdrop to critically observe the clash between two patterns of development: the top-down discriminating forms of urban economic redevelopment and planning legislature (as expressed through dramatic forms of unchecked eminent domain policies supporting privatization and NIMBYism), on

Two-sector global divide

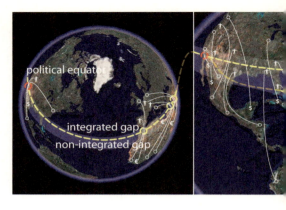

The border wall (sequential)
The border wall (telescopic)

Tactics of transgression: South-moving houses
Tactics of transgression: North-moving people

Two-sector global divide: integrated gap (First World) and non-integrated gap (Third World) bisected by 'the political equator', the cartographic band between the 25°N - 35°N longitude and centred on the 32°N longitude, along which the world's 'hotspots', critical thresholds, are located.

one hand, and the emerging American neighbourhoods made of immigrants on the other, whose bottom-up spatial tactics of encroachment thrive on informality and alternative social organizational practices.

This project primarily engages the microscale of the neighbourhood, transforming it into the urban laboratory of the twenty-first century. The control forces at play across the most trafficked checkpoint in the world have provoked the small border neighbourhoods that surround it to construct alternative urbanisms of transgression that infiltrate in the form of non-conforming spatial and entrepreneurial practices. This migrant, small-scale activism alters the rigidity of discriminatory urban planning of the American metropolis, and searches for new modes of social sustainability and affordability. The political and economic processes behind this social activism bring new meaning to the role of the informal in the contemporary city. It is not the 'image' of the informal that is interesting here, but the instrumentality of its operational socio-economic and political procedures. The counter-economic and social-organizational practices produced by non-profit social-service organizations (turned microdevelopers of alternative housing prototypes and public infrastructure at the scale of the site) within these neighbourhoods are creating alternative sites of negotiation and collaboration. They effectively attempt to transform top-down legislature and lending structures in order to generate a new brand of bottom-up social and economic justice that can bridge the political equator.

Casa Familiar: Practices of Encroachment

The most experimental work in housing in the USA is in the hands of neither private development nor government. It is instead in the hands of progressive, community-based, non-profit organizations such as Casa Familiar, which works in the border neighbourhood of San Ysidro, California. These types of agencies have been the primary social-service organizations engag-

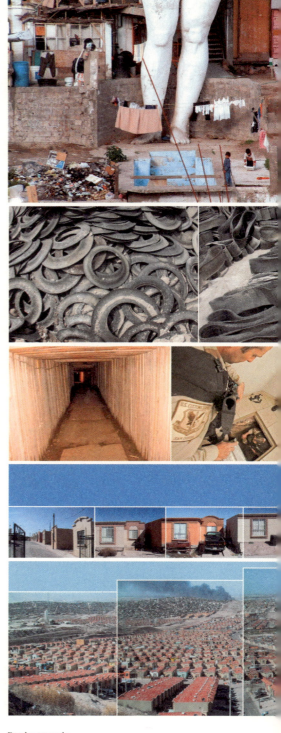

Favelas and informal infrastructure
Tires (re-deployed)

Border tunnels
Relocated mini-gated community
Gated Communities

213 Informal Cities Tijuana / San Diego

ing and managing the shifting cultural demographics caused by immigration within many mid-city neighbourhoods in the USA.

Designing Conditions, Designing Collaboration: AHOZ Micropolicy

Working with the premise that no advances in housing design in the USA can occur without advances in its housing policy and subsidy structures, our collaboration with Casa Familiar has been grounded on the shaping of counter-political and economic frameworks that can, in turn, yield tactical housing projects inclusive of these neighbourhoods' informal patterns of mixed use and density. In San Ysidro, housing will not consist only of 'units' spread indifferently across the territory. Here, housing is dwelling in relationship to a social and cultural programme managed by Casa Familiar. In this context, density is not just an amount of 'units per acre', it is an amount of 'social exchanges per acre'.

During the past five years, we have designed a micropolicy with Casa Familiar that can act as an informal process of urban and economic development for the neighbourhood, and empower the community of San Ysidro to become a developer of alternative dwelling prototypes for its own housing stock. This 'Affordable Housing Overlay Zone' AHO/micropolicy proposes that community-based non-profit organizations such as Casa Familiar can become mediating agencies between the municipality and the neighbourhood, facilitating knowledge, policy and microcredits. In essence, that these agencies will incrementally become informal City Halls, managing and supporting the shifting of socio-cultural demographics within many of these inner-city neighbourhoods.

Living Rooms at the Border

Living Rooms at the Border is a small housing project that emerges from the micropolicy and serves as a catalyst to anticipate San Diego's needed densities and mixed uses, while becoming a political instrument to enable Casa Familiar to further transform existing rigid zon-

Mid-city transformation (rings of suburbanization)

Levittown revisited

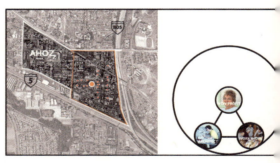

NGO + community/architect: research of existing neighbourhood conditions and workshop identification of affordable housing overlay zone (AHOZ)

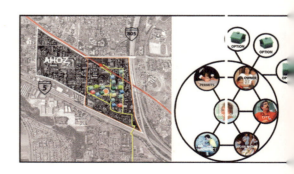

NGO + city: recognition and replacement approval (without penalty of nonconforming structures (those noncompliant with strict code and zoning) and mixed-use alley network designation

NGO/architect + city + homeowner: grant-assisted, personalized design process for addition/building renovation resulting in permits and pre-approved, standardized home-renovation plans

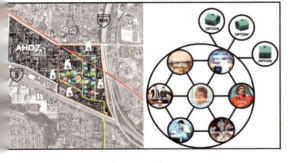

NGO + financial agencies: large affordable housing loans awarded to NGO and distributed to individual homeowners (transformed through sweat equity into developers) to defray construction costs

ing regulation for the border city of San Ysidro.

The informal negotiation of boundaries and spaces typical of this neighbourhood become the basis for incremental design solutions that have a catalytic effect on the urban fabric. On a small site where existing zoning allows only three units of housing, this project proposes, through negotiated density bonuses and by sharing kitchens, 12 affordable housing units, the adaptive reuse of an existing 1927 church on the site as a community centre, non-profit offices in the church's new attic, and a community garden that serves as social armature to support this community's non-conforming microeconomies and improvisational public events. Connected to the garden and the church, this armature is composed of a series of open-air rooms that contain electricity, serving as site for a variety of neighbourhood activities. The ambiguity of these spaces takes a different meaning as they are inscribed with social programme and community organization managed by Casa Familiar. The pairing of ambiguity and specificity is the essence of this project.

The tactical interweaving of dwelling units and social service infrastructure transforms the small parcel into a system that can anticipate, organize and promote social encounter. Furthermore, Casa Familiar injects microeconomic tactics such as time banking through sweat equity to produce alternative modes of affordability (barter housing units, exchange of rent for social service, and so forth). In a place where current regulations allow only one use, we propose five different mutually supportive uses, suggesting a model of social sustainability for the neighbourhood. This model conveys density – not as bulk, but as social choreography and neighbourhood collaboration.

Living rooms at the border

Watery Voids
Redefining the Power of Infrastructure

MMBB
Fernando de Mello Franco
Marta Moreira
Milton Braga

As this Brazilian metropolis continues to grow at a phenomenal rate, countless attempts to order the frantic production of built matter continue to fail. As a result, architects have begun to question the scope of their effective field of action, and to explore alternative strategies for impacting the built environment. Some have shifted their focus from buildings to infrastructural works, emphasizing their public value and systemic character. The project of infrastructure is a means that can empower architects: inserted into the city through the diffuse form of a network, infrastructural works can yield elements that help to reconfigure the systems to which they belong. This approach suggests a possible tactic for architectural intervention in the metropolis.

In the realm of our work, flood prevention in São Paulo, significant financial investments are predicted in what were formerly low-priority areas for public investments. In this context, we intend to work with the funds allocated to large infrastructural projects, redefining their paradigms. We aim to foster the 'power' to construct urban design value where previously only functional values were considered. This approach is based on the recognition that in São Paulo, infrastructure networks function as articulating elements on a territorial scale despite having a disaggregating effect on the local scale. The aim of the redefined paradigm – beyond articulating the services provided by the networks – is to link sectoral policies and build places suitable for urban life, while configuring images that refer to the cityscape, thus encouraging residents to establish effective relationships with the city.

The Technical Construction of São Paulo

São Paulo is a modern city largely constructed since the boom of industrialization that began at the end of the nineteenth century. This process demanded successive migratory inflows to supply the city with a workforce, setting off a vicious cycle of population growth. During the twentieth century, the metropolis grew from 250 thousand to 18 million inhabitants, comparable to constructing 35 new cities like the capital Brasília, on the same site, in a single century. The magnitude of this phenomenon resulted in the construction of the city by two opposing forces: on the one hand, selected investments in the modernization of its economic base; on the other, individual initiatives of a population seeking shelter, generally constructed in a spontaneous, 'informal' manner on the fringes of the legal city. The metropolis can be interpreted through the logic that guided the construction of the territory, privileging the productive sectors.

The implantation of large engineering systems on a hilly region converged with the strategic transformation of the fluvial plains of the São Paulo hydrologic basin, where roadways and water resources were associated with the availability of land that was both flat and cheap. São Paulo's transformation from an 'industrial city' to a 'contemporary city' was also enabled by this technical system, redoubling its importance. However, as a result of the area's uncontrolled process of urbanization, the urban soil became impermeable, particularly in the previous fluvial plains, which had played an important role in regulating the hydrologic flows. The result is a chronic flooding that affects the entire population. The residents of the areas near the watercourses live in a state of constant risk. Others suffer from traffic problems associated with the roadways built along the rivers.

When traffic congestion occurs on the main roadways, the problem spreads throughout the city, to the productive sector. As a factor that negatively impacts the urban economy, flooding is a significant political issue on the city's planning agenda. The government's previous concrete interventions in the sector provide exemplary opportunities for proposing alternatives to the hegemonic technicist view that has held sway in São Paolo's infrastructural projects.

Articulating Systemic and Local Concerns: The Network of *Piscinões*
The increasing lack of usable water sources requires that coordinated solutions be found for urban drainage, sanitation and water supply. This complex issue demands actions on both a macro- and a micro scale. Since 1990, these efforts have fallen under the scope of the State Plan for Water Resources (PERH) and the Macrodrainage Plan for the Upper Tietê Basin.[1]

One of the solutions proposed for the problem of flooding is the construction of a set of reservoirs to retain and regulate rainwater runoff. In Portuguese, this type of structure is called a *piscinão* (plural, *piscinões*), which translates to 'oversized swimming pool'. The main purpose of the *piscinão* is to collect water, delaying its discharge to the network of rivers and streams in the city, thereby reducing the risk of flooding. In short, the *piscinão* aims to substitute the original regulating function of the fluvial plains which, once overrun by urban development, became impermeable. There are currently 39 *piscinões* constructed out of a planned total of 131, which will hold 15.5 million cubic metres of water.[2] They are distributed among all the tributary microbasins of

Informal Cities
São Paolo

223

Informal Cities

São Paolo

Piscinões network

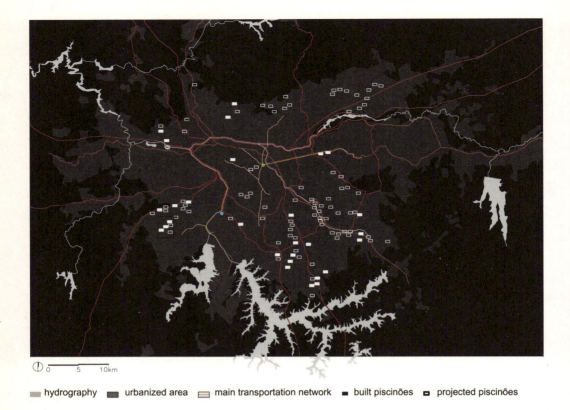

hydrography   urbanized area   main transportation network   built piscinões   projected piscinões

Piscinões Flooding points

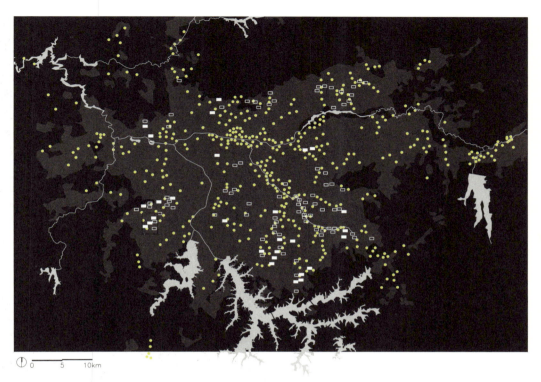

225 Informal Cities São Paolo

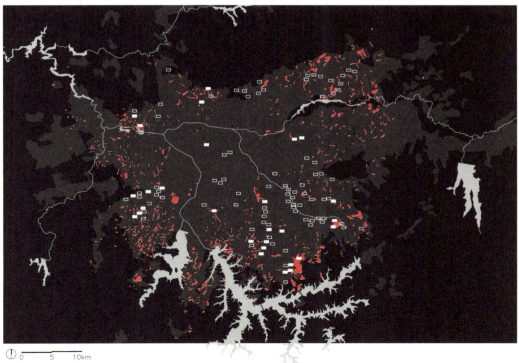

Piscinões Informal sectors

the Tietê River. Many are located near the city's 'informal' sectors. Dealing with the problem of flooding on a metropolitan scale will necessarily entail public investment in peripheral zones. The search for a fit between the metropolitan and local dimensions of this issue will therefore be the starting point towards any solution.

Spatially, the *piscinões* are excavations distributed in a diffuse pattern, temporarily filled during periods of rain. The rest of the time they are inactive spaces. These voids offer various possibilities for use if their construction is articulated in conjunction with the other plans for the city, taking into consideration needs for transportation, urban equipment and, especially, public space.

São Paulo's informal sectors are the most lacking in regard to public space. In these territories, where the dispute for urban land is often waged through violence, unoccupied areas remain. Generally used as soccer fields and for other collective activities, these spaces play a fundamental role in the construction of networks of sociability and belonging, strengthening the social bonds that offset life's adversities in the metropolis.

São Paulo's networks of vacant urban spaces can be consciously converted into opportunities for new networks of public spaces, to be reinserted into the urban fabric. Ultimately, we aim to transpose some of the frontiers of our metropolis by redefining the interfaces between the infrastructure and the locality, imparting to the built space the character of a place of dwelling.

1   For the PERH see: http://www.recursoshidricos.sp.gov.br/PERH.htm; for the macrodrainage plan see: http://www.daee.sp.gov.br/combateaenchentes/macrodrenagem/index.html.

2   Source: Departament of Water and Eletric Power (DAEE).

Programmed voids

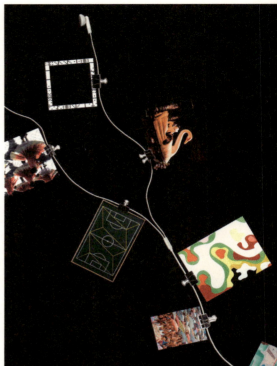

Piscinões network at Campo Limpo

y of the Dead festival in the central square of Cusco

adphone

Pedal boat at Tietê river – still of the play "BR3" Teatro da Vertigem, Evaldo Mocarzel / Casa Azul, 2006

The faithful at a mass given by Father Marcelo Rossi

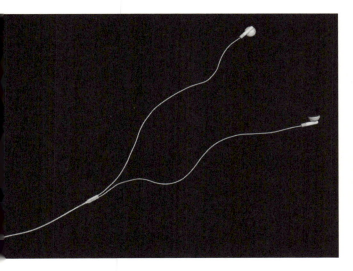

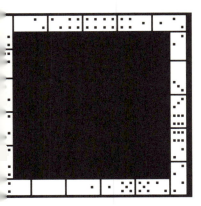

ninoes game

Futebol Neoconcreto 3, 2003

Study for the roof garden at the Ministry of Education and Culture Building – Rio de Janeiro, 37/45

Martijn de Waal

Powerification

Disneyfication

In an era in which media and transportation networks have uprooted the link between geographic place and identity, thematization has become a popular way of ascribing identity to certain places. This is an age-old process – Thomas Jefferson purposely chose the neo-classical theme of columns and timpani to grant the eighteenth-century New England towns of the newborn republic a respectable identity and have their architecture resonate the ideals of democracy. Disneyfication takes this process one step further. It not only provides a fictional and often nostalgic identity, but – its critics claim – also is purposely designed to break the contingency of public space that is characteristic of urban culture, replacing it with a domesticated family-friendly scenography of – often commercially controlled – pseudo-public spaces.

Unescofication

The redesign of parts of a city in order to be accepted in the Unesco World Heritage Programme. Usually this means preserving or restoring a slice of the city that is considered a picture postcard perfect cut-out of history. This might be an attractive strategy to preserve history and to attract tourists. By some it is also seen as a form of 'urbicide', since it freezes the city in history, in effect arresting the cumulative process of exchange and encounter that has shaped the city through the ages, and possibly halting further innovation or development of the city.

California Dreamification

Whereas urban theory often focuses on the importance of public space and encounter, for many middle-class citizens 'dwelling' is their number one priority. For many all over the world, the American-style gated suburb of single detached houses cum garage, garden and white picket fence is considered the ideal place to live, a status marker and a good investment in the future. In countries like China, new real estate developments are often marketed as 'authentic' copies of American suburbs, the Beijing suburb of 'Orange County', for instance, prides itself on being an exact copy of a Californian gated community. Many of these suburban developments are uniform zones, both architecturally, culturally and economically. Underlying forces are processes of parochialization in which people with shared identities flock together. There is also a financial logic driving the development of California Dreams all over the world: when sinking their life savings in real estate, prospective buyers are looking to secure their investment. Themed projects aimed at particular target groups with low levels of contingency and high levels of control are thought to be favourable for this.

Nowification

[t]he structural demolishment of historic buildings. We can distinguish between 'ideological nowification' and 'market nowification'. In the [for]mer, the ideology represented by the archi[te]cture of certain buildings has been deemed [ou]tmoded by or averse to the current regime. [R]emembrances of the past are erased in an [Or]wellian fashion, to make room for buildings [th]at celebrate a glorious and prosperous 'now' [an]d promise an even better future, 'brought to [yo]u by' current powers. These sometimes refer to [th]e demolishing process as the 'pulling out of rot[te]n teeth'. 'Market nowification' is the process in [wh]ich architecture is promoted in a fashion simi[lar] to technology gadgets: there is a continuous [ur]ge to update to the latest version, to continu[ou]sly update to the culture of the present now. In [ev]er shorter lifecycles, buildings with outdated [am]enities are demolished to make room for new [de]velopments that celebrate the branded lifestyles [of] today.

Sohofication

[Sin]ce Richard Florida published *The Rise of the* [*Cr*]*eative Class*, his book has made it to the bed[sid]e tables of civil servants all over the world, and [hi]s ideas into the zoning schemes from global cit[ies] to provincial backwaters. The idea is that in [th]e information age, the most value to the economy is added by a creative class of workers who tend to aggregate in cities that produce a high score on both his 'bohemian' and the 'tolerance'-index. In order to attract this talented and creative workforce, cities around the world encourage gentrification, trying to create their own Sohos. Old warehouses are converted into centres of creative entrepreneurialism, trendy boutiques and arty restaurants. Although this might be an effective way to boost the economy for a select number of cities, it can also lead to a one-sided policy in which the non-creative workforce and the locally rooted inhabitants are in effect removed, either through official rehousing policy or through rising real estate prices. And when gentrification truly sets in, many artists, galleries, clubs or dance troupes themselves can no longer afford to remain in the area.

Bronxification

The retreat of official structures like government programmes or police forces from urban zones that are deemed too rundown or dangerous to intervene in, creating urban slums and ghettos that give rise to informal and grey economies. According to some, the world thus falls apart in Dual Cities: the urban (theme) parks of Disneyfied, California Dreamified and Sohofied regions for those plugged in into the information age, versus the Bronxificated landscapes of despair for those who are thought superfluous.

Meditation on Ra Wire

Meditations on Razor Wire
A Plea for Para-Architecture

**Lieven De Cauter
and Michiel Dehaene**

Hyper-Architecture versus Infra-Architecture

Thinking the city in the twenty-first century requires thinking the periphery; a periphery which has become omnipresent, without a centre. The logic of centre and periphery is no longer one of interdependence and transfer, but of disconnection and extreme forms of unequal exchange: extraction. In raising the question of the city today, we cannot be blinded by the pep talk about the success of the city as nexus of the new creative economy. Despite the hype about 'mobility', 'smooth space' or 'the space of flows' and, of course, 'globalization', we live in 'striated space',[1] a world of control, division, disconnection and exclusion.

The centre-periphery logic has been replaced by the logic of dualization, between on the one hand the archipelago of secured, well connected capsules and on the other hand the 'ubiquitous periphery',[2] the landscape of endless townships of marginalized communities, a 'planet of slums'.[3] As opposed to this planet of slums, there is a universe of entertainment, of media, cyber games and theme parks: the simulation that comes before reality, 'hyper-reality'.[4] The reality of poverty, war and chaos is not represented; it does not appear in the images on our screens as it is 'unimaginable'. It is *infra-reality*. The extremes are linked: the more *infra-reality* rises, the more we retreat into *hyper-reality*.[5]

The archipelago of plugged in and secured capsular spaces increasingly produces a smooth sort of *hyper-architecture:* themed, spectacular and illusionist. Hyper-architecture is the product of the architect as the experience engineer within the experience economy. Architecture as social engineering (modernism) has been replaced by architecture as experience engineering or 'imagineering'. Koolhaas once said that the problem of our age is that there is no background left, there is only foreground, self-consciousness. Hyper-architecture has only foreground. In our world, architecture tends to be either pure logistics or purely décor. Its counterpart, formed by the enclaves of containment, comes in the form of *infra-architecture:* slums, ghetto's and camps. Infra-architecture, architecture reduced to its most minimal function of logistics – architecture as survival kit – corresponds to the 'infra-reality' of extreme poverty, chaos and war, as opposed to the hyper-architecture of glossy magazines, which corresponds to and expresses our hyper-reality.

The New Iron Curtain

Today capitalism is a system without a counter force, it has become transcendental. As a direct consequence of this, conditions of inequality rise, as capitalism is based on the asymmetrical accumulation of wealth.[6] The logic of transcendental capital produces ever fewer centres under the spell of hyper-reality and a ubiquitous periphery, always on the verge of the infra-real. The New Iron Curtain dividing North and South is the obscene, material marker of the split between the two realities: the fence in Ceuta embodying the rampart of 'Fortress Europe' and the fence on the Texas-Mexican border as the great divide between North and South America. The fact that the fences of Ceuta and Melilla, 'monuments' of respectively 7.8 and 10.5 km, are not really present in the European collective consciousness – after ten years of being in function and after hundreds of people trying to climb the wall (climaxing in the mass storming of October 2005), and after several thousand people having drowned trying to cross the Mediterranean – proves that it is infra-real, an invisible side of the global landscape. Seen from the Moroccan side, Ceuta is really a 'hidden city' behind the hills. On them one barely sees the discrete marks of a sort of new version of the Chinese Wall. In other words, the fence is the missing link between the hyper-real foreground of heterotopian enclaves and the background of abandonment.

This political geography is particularly clear on the New Pentagon World Map, in the divide between 'the functioning core' and 'the non integrating gap'. But it would be too simple to see these as homogeneous territories; what they are is archipelagos, and archipelagos inside other archipelagos. As a more abstract geopolitical concept, the global iron curtain should be conceived of as a set of forces that structure both the global world order and divide our cities. It creates the conditions which are left after the dismantling of the polis: people are either condemned to suburbs or to slums. In a city like Johannesburg this internal divide is most palpable.

The New Iron Curtain, the brutal logic of division of worlds, of inside and outside, marked with razor wire, is extended and replicated in the detention centres for asylum seekers and illegal migrants all over Europe. In a sense the new global divide becomes only clear when we conceive these detention centres as camps that are extensions of the fence between North and South. But this logic of 'capsularization' is also entering our everyday surroundings in many different ways. People withdraw into capsular, self-sufficient entities: fortified houses, condominiums, gated communities, enclosed malls, campuses, inward looking office blocks, atrium hotels, and all-in heterotopias,[7] often with hyper-real overtones.

Photograph of landscape with fence (anonymous, 2006)

The 7.8-km fence between Morocco and the Spanish enclave Ceuta lies hidden in the hills and is surrounded on both sides by no-man's-land that is forbidden military territory. Only sporadically and due to a few particular features is the fence actually visible. We can discern it on the left side of the picture as a tiny curve between a hill and a wood. There is a second, more visible belt, a ditch punctuated with small sentry houses. Beyond this belt, a few nineteenth-century towers mark the oldest line of defence. This photograph was taken from the Moroccan side. Ceuta lies over the hills – a forbidden, hidden city.

Underneath the iconography of fun there is 'an ecology of fear'. 'Going out' means going to all sorts of enclaves: theme parks, themed city quarters, festival markets, holiday villages, etcetera. The fearlessness of those who storm the fences of razor wire is the mirror of our fear, the fear of those on the other side of it. The more they become fearless, the more we are in the grip of fear. Normality is burned up in the process. The craze of the air-conditioned SUV's, the luxurious jeeps that invade our cities, is a clear allegory of this 'capsularization' or even 'militarization of urban space'. Razor wire, being the marker of the division line between the hyper- and infra-reality, will most probably be one of the most important features of the architecture and urbanism of the twenty-first century.

Photograph of the Ceuta fence by night (Ad van Denderen, go no go, foto # 12)

Picture by Ad van Denderen of the fence at Ceuta by night, taken from one of the few spots on the Spanish side from which the wall can be seen. Behind the wall, close to the sea, lies a Moroccan illegal village that has found its place in the strip of no-man's-land between the two running fences. The photo is part of the splendid series *Go No Go*, which documents the itinerary of illegal immigrants.

The Rise of Camps

If most hotspots in the archipelago could be called 'heterotopias', the black holes in the ubiquitous periphery we can call 'camps'. Indeed, the archipelago of secured and connected capsules has its dark counterpart, the archipelago of camps: the archipelago of order, wealth and security as opposed to the Gulag archipelago of detention centres, prisons, labour camps, refugee camps, military camps, secret prisons and outright concentration camps such as Guantánamo. The archipelago of camps is administered by the archipelago of order. The camp is the bio-political device which makes it possible to operate within the treacherous terrain outside of the network of well-connected premium worlds. Besides the proliferation of heterotopias that provide normality in the (atopic) network space – 'places to be' in the 'spaces of flow' – we see a proliferation of camp-like situations.

The concentration camp – the camp properly speaking – is the territorialization or embodiment of the state of exception, the place of 'the ban', the place of the 'bandit', the one who is banned outside the law: the *homo sacer*. It is the space where the law is suspended and inmates have neither civil rights nor human rights, and therefore it is the place where life becomes bare life. Bare life (*zoè*) is, according to a distinction made by Giorgio Agamben based on Arendt and Aristotle, a life stripped of its cultural form, of its civilized/civil character (*bios*).[8] Bare life corresponds to the private sphere (and the private parts) that should be hidden, *bios* to the public appearance. The camp is the situation in which the division between *zoè* and *bios*, between private life and public life, is suspended. It is the space where the city is annihi-

Photographs of the storming of the Ceuta fence in October 2005 (internet, 2007)

'October 2005. All around the world, television stations are broadcasting images of blood-smeared gloves that remain caught on barbed-wire fence, of young Africans in a daze, stumbling across the desert. . . . The fact that 19 were killed and hundreds injured in their desperate storming of the security fence that surrounds the exclaves – which were immediately heightened to an insurmountable 6 m – shocked the public less than the unbelievable decision to send the migrants into the desert and leave them there to die.' (2005-10-21, 'The new wretched of the earth' Boubacar Boris Diop, http://www.signandsight.com/features/425.html)

lated and the citizen stripped of his citizenship.

In the urban landscape we encounter more and more 'camp-like situations', where bare life is exposed. There are the homeless, people exposed to a lighter form of bare life and we observe the reuse of former tourist camping sites by fourth-world people who dwell in a permanently nomadic situation. Most important, of course, are the slums of the megacities of the South. Slums are not camps, but one cannot deny that the precarious informality at work in them exposes its inhabitants to the condition of 'bare life'.

Exposed to 'bare life' are certainly also the African immigrants that try to make it across the Mediterranean. They are also outside the law and are delivered to pure survival and often death. In that sense it is ineluctable to conclude that the famous/infamous *Bajesboten*, the 'Jail Boats' in Rotterdam for these and other illegal migrants, are ultimately offshore camps: extraterritorial

Photograph of the *bajesboten* in the port of Rotterdam
(photograph by Eun Kyung Lee)

The *bajesboten* in the port of Rotterdam, the offshore detention centres for illegal immigrants and asylum seekers, literally constitute extra-territorial non-places. The detainees get a brief airing in the metal cages on the quay. Although the boats lie close to the centre of Rotterdam, few people get to see this place, which makes it a sort of 'hidden city'. The barbed wire around the boats is in a way the continuation of the fence at Ceuta and the global Iron Curtain in general.

places, outside of the territory, outside the Netherlands, with on-land cages to air the inmates for a few minutes a day, the whole complex sealed with razor wire. This site is not only an extension of the fences separating North and South, inside and outside, but it is truly a 'hidden city', a blind spot in our urban landscape.

Heterotopia as Sanctuary

Heterotopia is, potentially, the opposite of the camp. A heterotopia is a sheltered space, closed off from the political and the economical sphere and safe-guarded against their respective intrusion or influence. The structure of the space of heterotopia is that of the 'sanctuary'. It is a refuge, a safe haven, a protected space. This structure becomes clear when we realize that heterotopias are spaces of the holy, of the holy days, the holidays. From grave yards to temples, theatres, cinemas, libraries, museums, saunas, holiday camps, brothels, and fancy fairs to our contemporary theme parks. The 'holiday' is a suspension – in time – of political and economical activities. Heterotopia, in the proper sense, is a time/spatial interruption, a refuge from the political and the economical. We adopt this as a more restricted (re)definition of Foucault's vast and encompassing concept.[9]

The camp is also a space that is neither economical nor political, however in a very different manner. As the space of the ban it is a space in which the very distinction between the economical and political, between the public and the private has been suspended. In heterotopia this crucial distinction on which every society since ancient Greece and all normality is based, is not suspended but 'diagonalized', sublated, as in a *catharsis*: a healing suspension of normality. If the heterotopia is the playground for otherness, for alterity, then the camp is the space where the other, all otherness, is abolished, annihilated (sometimes very literally).

The sanctuary, then, is the ultimate heterotopia: the absolute discontinuity of normality, of the legal order, for those who flee the legal order. It is a safe haven against the violence of society, legal or illegal. It is telling that in several European countries, groups of illegal immigrants go on hunger strike taking refuge in churches: by doing so they revived the ancient opposition between ban (camp, closed detention centre) and sanctuary. Our project is, in a sense, a plea for the re-creation of sanctuaries, heterotopian or not.

Para-Architecture as Strategy

There is nothing to be found for architecture in the camp, besides a gruesome confrontation with its abject underside. Even if we are fully aware that there is no way to make the camp, properly speaking, the object of architecture or urbanism, one of the chal-

Akropolis Redux by Kendell Geers

Akropolis Redux (the directors cut) (2004) by Kendell Geers defines a conceptual 'short-circuit' between heterotopia ('Akropolis redux' is a temple) and the camp (a violent machine of in/ex-clusion). The recurrent feature is the use of razor-wire. 'Barbed wire is for cattle, razor wire is for humans' as Kendell Geers once explained. (Kendell Geers in a presentation of his work at RITS filmschool, Brussels, September 2006)

lenges of the twenty-first century might nevertheless be to think about how architecture and urbanism can respond to the rise of camp-like situations, detention centres, refugee camps, transit camps, etcetera. If we find the camp both before and after the polis, architecture should always try to go beyond the camp.

The slum, the gated community, the ghetto, are all attempts to restore normality in the condition of implosion of normality, that is survival, the nature state, the real or imagined war of all against all. At the same time they are all self-defeating. We are looking for a type of script that deactivates these consuming oppositions. Besides hyper- and infra-architecture there might be an excluded third: let's call it *para-architecture*. Para-architecture is architecture that plays in a parallel world. In an age dominated by the extremes of hyper-architecture and infra-architecture, para-architecture might be a way to make architecture

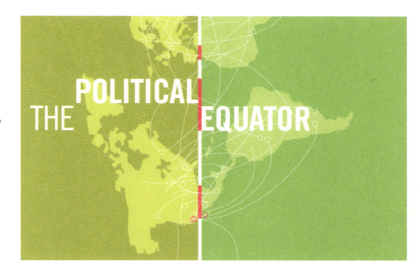

The Political Equator by Teddy Cruz.

This map by architect Teddy Cruz (see Informal Cities elsewhere in this book) links Ceuta with the Texas-Mexican border and by doing so defines the political equator, the division line between the global North and the global South.

again. Let's try and evoke three forms of para-architecture.

The first example is the most famous form of this sort of parallel architecture: the megastructure, the 'visionary' paper architecture of the 1950s and '60s. Paper architecture proposed a synthesis between the concrete and the abstract, between image and thought, between utopia and dystopia – from Yona Friedman's mobile architecture (1959) to the sublime immobility of *Exodus* (1972). Before it retired into the glossy magazines and museum collections this form of para-architecture constructed imagined heterotopias from where it could take the existing order under fire. Much of the visionary architecture of the 1960s is a critique of the modernist utopia, like the continuous monument of Superstudio or Archizoom's No stop city.

In *Exodus*, the project that marked the foundation of OMA, this is particularly visible. This manifesto for architecture transforms

World Map by Theo Deutinger

Walled World

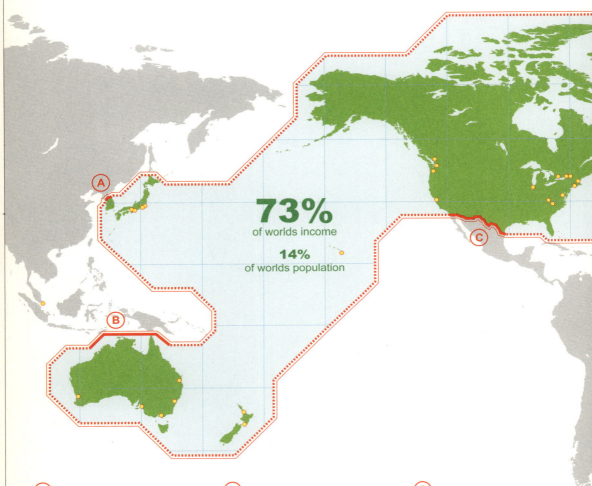

73% of worlds income

14% of worlds population

 The Demilitarized Zone (or DMZ)
in Korea is a strip of land running across the Korean Peninsula that serves as a buffer zone between North and South Korea. The DMZ was created in the ceasefire of July 27th 1953 and cuts the Korean Peninsula roughly in half. It is 248 km long and approximately 4 km wide.

 The Australian Defence Force
(ADF) conducts surveillance and response operations in Australia's northern approaches. Since September 2001 it doubled the number of days Customs vessels are at sea and increased flying hours for surveillance aircraft by 20 per cent. Under a proposed legislation from June 2006 all new boat arrivals would be transferred offshore to have their asylum claims processed.

 The United States–Mexico barrier
consists out of several separation barriers designed to prevent illegal immigration into the United States. The 3,140 km border between the United States and Mexico traverses a variety of terrains, including urban areas and deserts. The barrier is located mainly in the urban sections of the border which include San Diego, California and El Paso, Texas. Between 1998 and 2004, 1,954 persons are officially reported to have died along the US-Mexico border. On May 17, 2006 the U.S. Senate approved a possible extension what could be 600 km of triple layered-fencing and a vehicle fence.

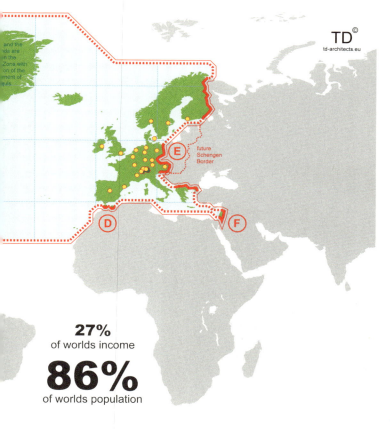

Accelerated through the fear from the attacks of 9/11 and all what followed, the so called "Western Society" is constructing the greatest wall ever build on this planet. On different building sites on all five inhabitable continents, walls, fences and high-tech border surveillance are under construction in order to secure the citizens and their high quality of life within this system.

The fall of the Berlin Wall was described as the historical moment that marks the demolition of world's last barrier between nation states. Yet it took the European Union only six years to create with the Schengen Agreement in 1995 a new division only 80km offset to the east of Berlin. Together with the wall in Israel, the US- Mexican border, the Australian Coast Defence and the DMZ in Korea, it makes part of a worldwide system that contains an exclusive society (14% of worlds population) with an average income of € 2.500,-/month versus the ones in front of the wall with an average income of only € 150,-/month.

27%
of worlds income

86%
of worlds population

○ World's top 50 cities with the highest "Quality of Life"
▬ High security border zone
⋯ Future Schengen border line
🌳 Switzerland voted in 2005 for the membership to the Schengen community and will become "Schengen country" soon

The Melilla border fence
is a separation barrier between Morocco and the Spanish city of Melilla. The razor wire barrier cost Spain €33 million to construct. It consists of 11 km of parallel 3 m high fences topped with barbed wire. Its height is currently being doubled to 6 m.

The Ceuta border fence
is a separation barrier between Morocco and the Autonomous City of Ceuta, in Spain. Construction of the €30-million razor wire barrier was financed by the European Union. It consists of parallel 3-metre fences topped with barbed wire.

Schengen Border
is an agreement among European states which allows for common policy on the temporary entry of persons and a border system. A total of 26 countries – including all European Union states except the Republic of Ireland and the United Kingdom, but including non-EU members Iceland, Norway, and Switzerland – have signed the agreement and 15 have implemented it so far.
The Republic of Ireland and the United Kingdom did not sign the Schengen Agreement but take part in the Schengen co-operation and use the Schengen Information System for law enforcement purposes.

The West Bank barrier
is a physical barrier being constructed by Israel consisting of a network of fences with vehicle-barrier trenches surrounded by an on average 60 meters wide exclusion area and up to 8 meters high concrete walls.
As of January 2006 the length of the barrier as approved by the Israeli government is 670 kilometers. Approximately 36% has been constructed, 25% is under construction, 20% has been approved but construction has not yet begun, and the remaining 19% awaits final approval

the Berlin Wall into an artificial paradise, a pleasure garden, a hidden city. It is iconic because it encapsulates the extremes: it is both a heterotopia and a camp; heterotopia: the baths, the park of aggression, the allotments; camp: the entrance is taken from scenes of a prison and the park of biological transactions, which is undeniably sinister with its conveyor belt from hospital to crematorium. It is and remains an extreme, 'aporetic' project: camp as heterotopia, heterotopia as camp.[10]

Today the very act of spending ones time making paper architecture is in itself an act of resistance by locating itself in a parallel world (on paper and in models), in the safe haven of *scholè*, free time, the time-space of obstinate dedication. If it chooses its objects carefully, paper architecture can 'diagonalize' the architectural wasteland between hyper-architecture and infra-architecture, by defining, as it were, 'short circuits'. We believe it

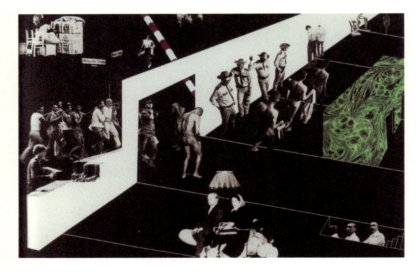

The reception area, from OMA: *Exodus or the Voluntary Prisoners of Architecture,* 1972 (collection of MoMa).

OMA: *Exodus or the Voluntary Prisoners of Architecture,* 1972. *Exodus,* OMA's legendary first project, is both a heterotopia and a camp. The following quote summarizes the sinister aspect of the project: 'The inhabitants of this architecture, *those strong enough to love it,* will become its voluntary prisoners, ecstatic in the *freedom* of their architectural confines.' (OMA, *Exodus,* our emphasis)

is important to critically revive this tradition. What is at stake is to give paper architecture its political charge/relevance again.[11]

A second strategy could be called *Détournement*, the old situationist trick to use existing strategies or materials against themselves or at least against the grain. It might be one of the very few viable strategies to operate against infra-architecture and hyper-architecture. We see examples in the work of Luc Deleu and T.O.P. Office; the projects of Joep van Lieshout and AVL, his heterotopian/utopian self-sustaining farm and, more recently 'Slave City'); Breughelview, the gated art community of Geert De Mot. Particularly grabbing is the work of the artist Kendell Geers, like his *Acropolis Redux (the directors cut)*: a temple made from razor wire. It is a shock, a short circuit: temple as camp, camp as temple.

It is not coincidental that these examples are mostly from the art world, or end up being hosted there. Experiments that move in the direction of the point at which heterotopia and camp coincide are best done in a controlled environment: the sanctuary of the museum, the free space of the exhibition. If this strategy of *détournement* can even be applied outside of this safe haven, in the real word, is not obvious. But it can supply provocative and inspiring counter-images, images that point at the heart of the *aporia* of our world.

The third strategy we have in mind is not really para-architecture, but rather *para-urbanism*. It consists of making safe havens as opposed to camps or camp-like situations. Our example is the low cost housing strategy *Kudha ki Basti*. A grassroots strategy developed in 1995 in Hyderabad, Pakistan but since duplicated on the edges of Karachi. Its main purpose is to be self-financing, thereby cancelling out both the effects of the local market,

Khuda Ki Basti

Khuda Ki Basti turns infra-architecture into para-architecture, using the strategies of the informal market to create conditions that again give individuals access to investment in their own environment. Like all infra-architecture, it does not lend itself to easy photographing, in spite of all its power – it's light, provisional, hardly there. Above - view from the first *Khuda Ki Basti* project in Hyderabad, Pakistan ten years after its initiation in 1985. Below (left) supply of affordable building material and technical assistance through the organization's 'building clinic'; (right) a typical row of self-built houses in *Khuda Ki Basti III* in Karachi, Pakistan.

but also the grip of external donor money, and the relations of dependence and long term financial obligations this comes with. To face this challenge the scheme has copied and inverted the basic mechanism used by the land-grabbing mafia which has 'successfully' provided housing for half of Karachi's population. The land-grabbing mafia brings people to unsecured land, provides the minimal means to have these people build houses, and leaves the problem of building infrastructure to an insecure future.

The *Kudha ki Basti* scheme follows the same logic of the land grabbers, except for the fact that it settles people on land that has been secured by the organization. People signing up for the scheme pay a minimal down payment for their plot and have to immediately settle on their land. If they don't, they loose their plot (to avoid that they sell it on). The new settlers build their house themselves. The organization provides basic technical assistance. The new occupants start by building a boundary wall and a toilet. It is the zero degree of architecture: two devices structuring the relationship between the public and the private; and between *zoè* and *bios*, between 'deep shit' and 'a room of ones own', between the brutal fact of excrements and the cosy refinement of 'interior life'.

Kudha ki Basti is a sort of 'Benevolent Camp', an encampment with a script that preserves the possibility to keep control over one's own life, preserves the hope that one day these places will no longer be mere campsites but will house something which resembles a city. The strategy works and is spreading. The critique could be that even if it tries to be a parallel urbanism, Kudha ki Basti remains infra-urbanism (or dirty realism): it ultimately accepts the unacceptable.

Border Oasis, by Office Kersten Geers David Van Severen (2005)

These two collages of the prize-winning project *Border Oasis* for a border crossing point between Mexico and Texas, is an excellent recent example of what could be designated as 'para-architecture': the border crossing as oasis, the metamorphosis of a place that symbolizes exclusion, fear and humiliation into a place where it is pleasant to stay. In this instance a camp-like situation is transformed into a heterotopian sanctuary.

Conclusion

We believe that para-architecture is a way to give architecture back its visionary power. As Venturi noted in *Learning from Las Vegas*, modernism and its afterbirths tried to save the world: 'total design conceives a messianic role for the architect as the corrector of the mess of urban sprawl.'[12] Para-architecture in contrast is only the small door through which the Messiah could enter (but mostly doesn't). Even if this sounds like messianic double Dutch, it cannot be denied that within para-architecture (both the classical and the more recent forms) there is a deep-rooted strategy of deactivation, non-participation. Well, interruption, suspension, revocation, discontinuity, standstill, reversal are all attributes of the messianic.

An image of this redeeming gesture could be the *Border-Oasis*, a project by Office for a border crossing at the Texas-Mexican border: the grim reality of the walled border and biopolitical control is redeemed by giving it the form of the heterotopian garden *par excellence:* the oasis. But, because of the beauty of this gesture, it will never be built. But it *could* be built (the architects insist), and in a sense it *should* be built. But it won't, because to transform the camp-like situation into a heterotopia would require utopian authorities. In other words: para-architecture is a long shot. But in the face of infra-architecture and hyper-architecture, what do we have to lose?

1   On the opposition between smooth space and striated space see: Gilles Deleuze and Félix Guattari, 'La Machine de guerre:traité de nomadologie', in: idem., *Milles Plateaux. Capitalisme et Schizophénie II* (Paris: Editions de Minuit, 1980).
2   Lieven De Cauter and Michiel Dehaene, 'L'archipel et le lieux du ban. Tableau de la ville désastre' (The Archipelago and the Ubiquitous Periphery. Snapshots of Disaster City', in: *Airs de Paris* (Paris: Centre Pompidou, 2007).
3   Mike Davis, *Planet of Slims* (London/New York: Verso, 2006).
4   Baudrillard might be forgotten, but his concept is back. It is one of the tools to understand our world, not only in high theory but also in popular culture, from *The Matrix* to Žižek. See Slavoy Žižek, *Welcome to the Desert of the Real: Five Essays on September 11 and Related Dates* (London/New York: Verso, 2002).

5   Lieven De Cauter, 'The Network and the Capsule', in: idem., *The Capsular Civilization. On the City in the Age of Fear* (Rotterdam: NAi Publishers, 2004).
6   See on this: Fernand Braudel, *La dynamique du capitalisme* (Paris: Flammarion, 1985); and Immanuel Wallerstein, *Historical Capitalism* (London/New York: Verso, 1993). The term transcendental capitalism is introduced in *The Capsular Civilization, o.c.*.
7   See on this Lieven De Cauter and Michiel Dehaene (eds.), *Heterotopia & The City. Public Space in a Postcivil Society* (London: Routledge, 2007).
8   Giorgio Agamben, *Homo Sacer, le pouvoir souverain et la vie nue* (Paris: Seuil, 1997), translated as: *Homo Sacer. Sovereign Power and Bare Life* (Stanford: Stanford University Press, 1998).
9   Lieven De Cauter and Michiel Dehaene, 'The Third Sphere: Towards a General The-

ory of Heterotopia', in: *Heterotopia & The City,* op. cit. (note 7).
10   See Lieven De Cauter and Hilde Heynen, 'The Exodusmachine', in: Martin van Schaik and Otakar Má el (eds.), *Exit Utopia. Architectural provocations 1956-76* (Munich/Berlin/London/New York: Prestel Verlag, 2005).
11   An example of that sort of architecture could be the bridge-city to Africa, an idea that yet has to be turned into architectural form. The bridge to Africa shows how para-architecture can point to the aporias of our contemporary world order. See on this Lieven De Cauter and Dieter Lesage, 'Re: the Myth of the Bridge. Connecting Ceuta and Gibraltar. An E-mail Correspondence', in: *Hunch*, The Berlage report, no.5.
12   Robert Venturi, Denise Scott Brown and S. Izenour, *Learning from Las Vegas* (Cambridge, MA: The MIT Press, 1972).

From Denver to Dainfern
Erasing the Power of Fear

blacklinesonwhitepaper
Kirsten Dörmann
Solam Mkhabela
Tumi Morule
Motsepe Architects
Fanuel Motsepe
Eric Lindenberg

The racial state in South Africa combined two technologies of power. In relation to blacks, both techniques of power and profit were, ever since the founding of Johannesburg, centered on the body: the individual body of the migrant worker and the racial body of the populace.
Achille Mbembe

In its 121 years of existence, the city of Johannesburg has been built four times over. This project is based on the hypothesis that it has always been a camping city. Over time, different forms of camps have been established for changing reasons.

Joburg is known as Jozi in daily life; Jovi 2010 is an initial collaboration of architects, photographers, a property economist and a social geographer who propose the adaptive reuse of city centre buildings to act as a trigger for the regeneration of the surrounding area as a mixed-use neighbourhood and support its village character.

POWER/SPACE

Apartness: *The quality of standing apart. Apartness is used as an urban planning instrument to segregate different groups of the population, based on social, economic, or cultural backgrounds or race.*

Examples of apartness include spontaneous segregation (Chinatowns) and forced segregation as political instrument of dominance and control (National Socialism, Germany; Apartheid Regime, South Africa).

Maps of Johannesburg from as early as 1897 – 11 years after the city originated as a settlement of tents – reveal the intentions of the municipal authorities to keep racial groups apart. Different areas clearly marked out for African, coloured, Indian and white residents were strongly supported by the mining bosses, the Rand lords. Life in the state of South Africa was based on the principles of the apartheid regime, which declared white people the superior race. Reserves and townships for the African population were part of the official urban planning schemes since the introduction of the Land Act in 1913. Later, the Group Areas Act of 1950 implied a particular urban planning framework which legalized and enforced consolidated residential areas for each racial group. Although the Group Areas Act was lifted in 1991, the settlement structure of the apartheid regime remained etched on the landscape.

Fear: *Basic human emotion aroused by impending danger, evil, or pain; one of a group of reactions in organisms with a long history of survival advantages for their owners.*

Johannesburg's first free elections in 1994 turned the political and social worlds of the population upside down. The racial police state turned into a democracy, with free access to space for everyone and huge economic discrepancies. Crime rates increased to the highest in Africa. Whites fled to the north of the city or out of the country, many leaving their properties vacant. Today, fear is one of Johannesburg's main design parameters; inhabitants of all races and cultural groups are extremely attentive to their surroundings. Invisibility, control and various forms of private security extend the historical urban script of segregation.

Faith: *Faith can be placed in a person, inanimate object, state of affairs, proposition, or body of propositions such as a religious creed.*

Economic greed and the persistent vision of a better life drove hundreds of thousands of immigrants to the 'city of gold'. National, regional and international migrants have, since the beginning, shaped the hidden spaces of Johannesburg within and beyond state powers. This resulted in a multiple power system of rural, tribal, colonial, religious and racial origin.

Botho/Ubuntu: *Botho/Ubuntu is a traditional African philosophy and active part of everyday life that offers an understanding of the individual in relation to the world. It can be translated as 'I am because we are'.*

The practice of *botho/ubuntu* develops and maintains a cohesive society within a sustainable environment and has officially been recognized as part of legislation since 1997, when the South African National Assembly passed the White Paper for Social Welfare.

RECORDING

From Denver to Dainfern is an audiovisual recording of Johannesburg's contemporary camping landscape, juxtaposing two extremes from the poor south, where a lot of people live, and the rich north, where most of those people work. Camping is understood as the activity of setting up shelter for temporary use for a body of persons.

Denver is a group of hostels for male trans/national migrants and the surrounding informal settlements that host a

Johannesburg started off as a settlement of tents and developed into the biggest city of the continent within 20 years, outside of which a specifically South-African form of encampment developed, usually referred to as a 'location' or 'township', where non-whites had to reside pre-1994.

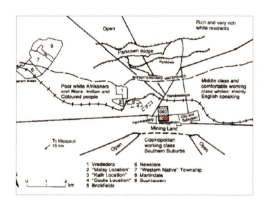

Early map of racial segregation

Consolidated residential areas for each race group had to be separated by buffer zones, which could be strong natural barriers (rivers, valleys), strong man made barriers (railways, highways) or, if neither of these is available, open spaces of specific dimensions.

Islands. Arial view from Denver to Dainfern, indicating major islands and specifying the making of today's boundaries

251 Hidden Cities Johannesburg

Dainfern: Residences, Golf Estate Perimeter wall, seismic sensors, electric fence, reinforced steel bars 10ft down, private security, passcards, surveillance cameras

Fourways Mall. Commerce. Perimeter fence, private security, surveillance cameras

Design Quarter. Commerce. Perimeter fence, private security, surveillance cameras

Bryanston Wedge + Grosvenor Crossing. Commerce. Perimeter walls, electric fences, private security, surveillance cameras

Bryanston Country Club + Bryanpark. Golf estate. Perimeter walls, electric fences, private security, surveillance cameras, membership

Peter Place. Commerce, business. Walls, fences, private security, surveillance cameras

Sandton, Morningside, Sandown, Nelson Mandela Square, Sandton City. Residences, commercial + business hub. Walls, fences, private security, neighbourhood security organisation, surveillance cameras

Alexandra. Residential in/formal. Trade in/formal. Established in 1913 as 1st black township. Fenced spine running in the middle of Louis Botha Avenue (N11) bordering Standton, fences bordering Kew to be key closed at night. Inverted security.

Randburg, Cramerview, Peter Place, Sanlam Centre, Crossroads, Randburg City, Piazza Centre. Commerce, business. Walls, fences, private security, surveillance cameras

Craighall, Delta Park, Blairgowrie Plaza, Valley Centre, Craig Park Centre, The Colony. Residences, commerce, business. Electrified fences, walls, private security, surveillance cameras

Kelvin View, Marlboro, Kramerville, Wynberg. Industrial strip. Planned as buffer zone by the apartheid regime. Private security

Hyde Park Corner, Lancaster Centre, Hyde Square, Dunkeld West. Residential, commerce, business. Walls, fences, private security + surveillance cameras

Commercial, business, sport, residential. Melrose Arch, Illovo, Atholl, Oaklands, Wanderers, James + Ethel Gray Park. Gates within gates. Walls, electric fences, private security, surveillance cameras, closed circuit television

Rosebank Mall. Commercial, business. Walls, private security + surveillance cameras

Killarney, Saxonwold, Forest Town, Parktown. Commerce, business, residences. Perimeter walls, electric fences, private security + surveillance cameras

High End Residential Estate + Sport Amenity: Houghton Estate, Houghton Golf Club. High end Residences, sport. Perimeter walls, electric fences, private security, surveillance cameras, membership

Roedean, St Johns, King Edward, WITS, Johannesburg Hospital. Private + public institutions, office parks. Walls, fences, private security, surveillance cameras, membership, SAPS.

Betrams, Lorentzville + Judith's Paarl. Mixed use. Absentee landlords, ever increasing drug, criminal and sex industry. Protected by drug lords + slum lords

Hillbrow, Berea. Mixed use. Absentee landlords. High density apartment complexes striving with drugs + sex industry. Protected by drug lords + slum lords.

Downtown Jozi: Newtown, CBD. Business. Headquaters. Residences. Squatters. 50% empty. Metro police, private security, surveillance cameras, drug lords, slum lords, shack lords + makeshift walls

Denver, Jeppe, Malvern. Industrial spine wedged between rail line + M2 freeway with single sex hostels and shack farms. Criminal activities include drugs, fire arms, prostitution + car chop shops. Protected by the indunas, drug lords + shack lords

The headlines of *The Star*, Johannesburg's oldest newspaper, feed public paranoia on a daily basis, displayed on street poles all around the city.

Fear : Jozi 1000 voices. Personal data confronts official crime statistics. In the process of the project, 1000 people are asked about their crime experiences. Is the city as really dangerous as its image? This recent and updated crime portrait is mapped out between Denver and Dainfern.

From Denver to Dainfern: film stills of Johannesburg's controversial horizon

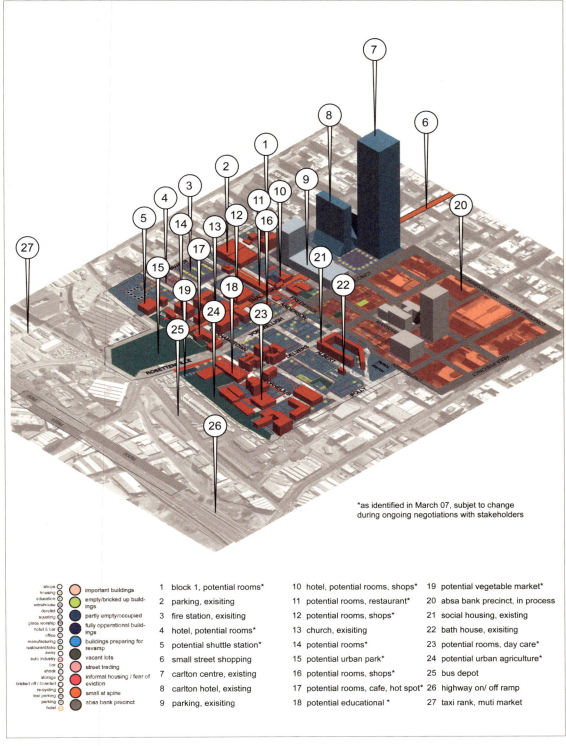

	important buildings	1	block 1, potential rooms*	10 hotel, potential rooms, shops*	19 potential vegetable market*
	empty/bricked up buildings	2	parking, exisiting	11 potential rooms, restaurant*	20 absa bank precinct, in process
	partly empty/occupied	3	fire station, exisiting	12 potential rooms, shops*	21 social housing, existing
	fully opperational buildings	4	hotel, potential rooms*	13 church, exisiting	22 bath house, exisiting
	buildings preparing for revamp	5	potential shuttle station*	14 potential rooms*	23 potential rooms, day care*
	vacant lots	6	small street shopping	15 potential urban park*	24 potential urban agriculture*
	street trading	7	carlton centre, existing	16 potential rooms, shops*	25 bus depot
	informal housing / fear of eviction	8	carlton hotel, existing	17 potential rooms, cafe, hot spot*	26 highway on/ off ramp
	small st spine	9	parking, exisiting	18 potential educational *	27 taxi rank, muti market
	absa bank precinct				

Strategic Spaces: circa 18,000 m² of usable space is identified on which to build homes and jobs under the umbrella of a B&B organization: *ndawo yami*, or my place, with regards to urgently needed accommodation for the World Cup in 2010. South Africa will be the first country in the history of the FIFA World Cup where bed & breakfast accommodations will receive official accreditation.

population of 34,000 people, mainly from Kwa Zulu Natal, hidden between highway and industry, officially about to be forgotten.

Dainfern was originally the most expensive gated residential golf estate of Southern Africa, ready for occupation in 1992, two years before the first free elections were held. It was the safest haven around in which to buy a house.

The journeys from Denver to Dainfern cross in the inner city, where the operation Jovi 2010 is starting to develop.

Inner City
Between Denver and Dainfern, the inner city of Johannesburg has been nearly completely repopulated since 1994, with little evidence of architectural change.[1] Having been zoned as strictly 'white' for more than three decades, its colour code after the abolition of racial zoning has become black and coloured.
   Nigerian drug lords, cross-border traders, street prostitutes and ordinary business people share the spaces of the previously 'forbidden city'. Some banks have kept their headquarters operational. The chickens in the street are reminders of village life. Because of vacancy and fires, destruction and unlawful occupation, no one knows how interior spaces really look. In close proximity, the Carlton Hotel plans its comeback as the country's finest hotel in anticipation of the World Cup in 2010. The inner city tries to regenerate itself. The pressure is on.

PLANNING

Jovi: Safe Space
Jovi is an area of 36 city blocks in Marshalltown, the southeast border of downtown Johannesburg. It is being investigated for possible re-habitation. More than 50 per cent of Marshalltown is officially empty. Secretly, more than half of those 'empty' structures are being occupied. Threatened to be *dainferized*, Marshalltown is turning *denverish*. Operation *Jovi* is acting within those extremes. By 2010,

Left: A 'tenant' of an abandoned building off Kruis Street with a black chicken that will be slaughtered for an ancestral ceremony of the traditional healer who also resides in the building.

Right: Utata has been living in the city for more than 15 years. He is about to brush his teeth. The only access to water is a communal tap outside the rooms. However, the favourite colour of clothes of the community is white.

Bantu Spot, between Polly and van Wielligh Street, is one of Johannesburg's urban secrets. Built on the entrance of a former gold mine, between a bus depot and the initial city edge, it operates as a low budget gated community, with two controlled entrances that slip the observers eye if not attentive. Bantu residents have no access to water; they collect it in drums on a day-to-day basis. They cultivate an abandoned piece of land to grow food for the whole community. Just before these pictures were taken a candle caught fire and burned down half of the shacks. Sisi and other residents had to start rebuilding them before nightfall.

Left: Cross-border traders who got caught in a raid of a Chinese restaurant, which did not have the permit to sell a specific kind of fish and cigarettes. Even if not the initial targets of the raid, they risk losing everything for nothing in situations like this.

Right: A lot of traders from different African countries cross in Delvers Street/Marshalltown, where many buildings have been abandoned by their landlords and serve now as shelter to desperate salesmen looking for a space to sleep and store their goods.

255 Hidden Cities Johannesburg

1,000 rooms are proposed to be built in existing structures under the umbrella of *ndawo yami* or *my place*. The development of the area is based on an urban design scheme, developed in accordance with city officials, that introduces basic pedestrian access and green public space. The project touches on the huge lower-income housing backlog of the country and on urgently needed accommodation for the World Cup in 2010. It invites current inhabitants to apply for *rooms*.

Camping Design Guidelines
Jovi accepts the existence of ruling powers and acts carefully within their boundaries. Design guidelines developed with the advice of a property economist and a social geographer form the framework for development and are illustrated in a design guide: How to . . .

To propose a mixed-use, mixed-income, non-gated, urban neighbourhood with pedestrian access and green space might sound very ordinary, looking at comparative models in the northern hemisphere. However, it seems to be the most radical approach to envision within the South-African context in times where normality of that kind does not exist.

1 Mphethi Morojele, *Presence and Absence, Transitional Space in the Post Apartheid Metropolis*, 2006.

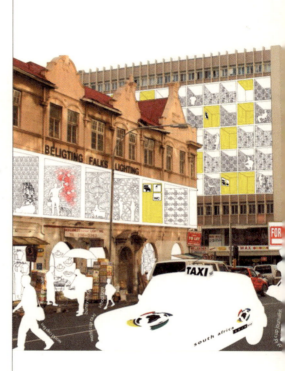

 ply for a room  pay for a room  design a room  build a room 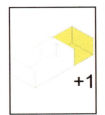 add a room  have a guest

sicelo yokuthola ikame londlu | ukukhola ikame londlu | ukuhlela indlu | ukwakha indlu | ukwakha enye indlu | ukuba nesimenywa

Cité de Refuge
Inverting the Power of Separation

Office Kersten Geers David Van Severen
Kersten Geers
David Van Severen

Qu'est-ce que l'architecture? La définirai-je avec Vitruve l'art de bâtir? Non. Il y a dans cette définition une erreur grossière. Vitruve prend l'effet pour la cause. Il faut concevoir pour effectuer. Nos premiers pères n'ont bâti leurs cabanes qu'après en avoir conçu l'image. C'est cette production de l'esprit, c'est cette création qui constitue l'architecture, que nous pouvons, en conséquence, définir l'art de produire et de porter a la perfection tour édifice quelconque. L'art de bâtir est donc qu'un art secondaire, qu'il nous parait convenable de nommer la partie scientifique de l'architecture.
Etienne-Louis Boullée, Essai sur l'art

Cité de Refuge #1
Any project on Ceuta today is one of sublime projection; however precisely articulated, it can be nothing more than a conjecture. But the only way to deal with the reality of Ceuta is to make a project that confronts it head on. This is as much a political reconsideration as it is a re-evaluation of the architecture of the city and its power. The city-island of Ceuta is a testing ground on which to explore the concept of the city in its most radical and stripped-down state – as a conscious decision, a political form.

Throughout history, the Mediterranean region has functioned as a constellation of city-states organized around fortresses, free havens or trading communities. Greek and Phoenician settlements that incarnate the zero degree of the city as state were often understood as points of power in relation to the hinterlands they tried to control. Nevertheless, they attempted to establish conditions of mutual influence. Invariably, the historical Mediterranean city consisted of a walled centre of political or religious power (its political frame), surrounded by 'sprawl' – an accumulation of the elements of real life: harbours, markets, and more or less permanent inhabitants.

The current situation is new, but not entirely different. The Mediterranean Sea is surrounded by states with inland centres of power, but it no longer serves as the epicentre. Instead, it has become the natural border between continents, or more precisely, between rich and poor, between the first and the third worlds. This border has risen to symbolic proportions with the erection of a 6-m-high razor wire fence between the Spanish enclaves (Ceuta and Melilla) and Morocco. The image of the iron curtain springs to mind, but in this case, the fences stop people from entering the formalized territory of Europe. While Europe is on the one hand evolving toward an ephemeral state, this border makes tangible the antithesis – the concept of Fortress Europe.

This project does not treat Ceuta as a problem to be solved, nor does it pretend that the issues related to the border can be untangled. Nowhere, however, are the borders of Europe so tragically concrete; hence nowhere is there such a rich opportunity to make them so (tragically) beautiful. This project rearranges the elements of the neutral zone into an architecture powerful enough to pursue the ever-present conditions of separation and border. As a result, the neutral zone – the zone between two continents – is understood as a place of transit. This condition has become such a powerful magnet for uncontrolled sprawl that it requires nothing more than a deliberate framing, or containment, in order to formalize the bare life of the border.

This city is a city of interiors: that is the ultimate consequence of its location on neutral territory. The central market plaza is its spatial type. It takes the pragmatic desire for separation – a wall – to the level of a formal project: space is framed by the typical mass generated by the border-institutions and its administrations, thus creating a central square. The square functions as neutral territory, a backdrop in front of which life endlessly unfolds. It rearticulates the activity that previously occupied the area *around* the border crossing as *city life*.

Cité de Refuge #2

The city defines an inner square of 482 x 482 m. The building is 90 m high. It is positioned in the hills of the North African continent — between Ceuta and Tanger, between Spain and Morocco, between Europe and the World.

The square is framed by a colonnade. The colonnade defines the four inner façades of the infrastructural building of the border crossing. The inner order houses the vertical circulation of the building. The outer façade is organized as pragmatically as possible. The thick wall houses all diagonal infrastructure of the border *machine*. In between the outer perimeter and the inner façade, a mere 1.2 million m² of floor area is available. Blue taxis enter the city at the 30-m level. A road towards the city meanders along the mountain range, following the accidental track prepared by the control towers and the double fence.

The blue taxis enter the building's circular driveway after a quick check (leaving a country has always been easy), and drive down through the double wall to arrive in the crowded courtyard. The courtyard is a market place, cut on one side by a loose sand beach facing the water. Boats embark at the opposite side. The colonnade cuts off a portion of the

Border infrastructure and seashore view towards Morocco

Europe

Africa

Ideogram of the Mediterranean Sea

261 Hidden Cities | Ceuta

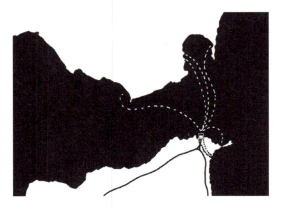
Ideogram of the crossing

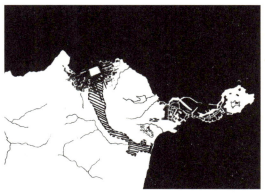
Ideogram of the neutral land – border zone

territory with a slice of sea and a giant square. The columns organize all of the direct vertical access to the endless accumulation of parasite programs in the building: inside are ducts, elevators and stairs. One can find the Salvation Army somewhere between the twelfth and thirteenth floors. The hallways on these floors provide little glimpses of the sea and the silhouettes of another continent. Support organizations inhabit offices at the colonnade passage, next to shops and would-be shops. Pedestrian gates are organized in the outer wall thickness. The passageways to the boats are located under the colonnades. Cars drive in directly from the 30 m level, down the ramp, and into the embarkation section. They seem hardly to touch ground. A leftover piece of sand, populated by beach huts, appears almost lost in contrast to the vivid and crowded marked square. Blue taxis find their way through the crowds.

The city's square is a surface where nothing is really organized. The infrastructure of the terminal is found within its borders; the machine is arranged in its margins. The building's outer façade is decisively unarticulated; its significance perhaps lies in its expression of sheer mass. It acts as a fixation-point for any development on either territory. Inside, the space is arranged with architectonic rigor and silent irony: the building displays that which it cannot handle. In between the walls, it is a slick and technocratic machine, loosely infiltrated with whatever activity it allows. Outside it endows the landscape with a monumental presence of pure pragmatic organization – a giant bridgehead.

'Ring-road (Findeq, Ceuta)', Bas Princen, 2007

Cité de Refuge: Perspective 1

Cité de Refuge: axonometry

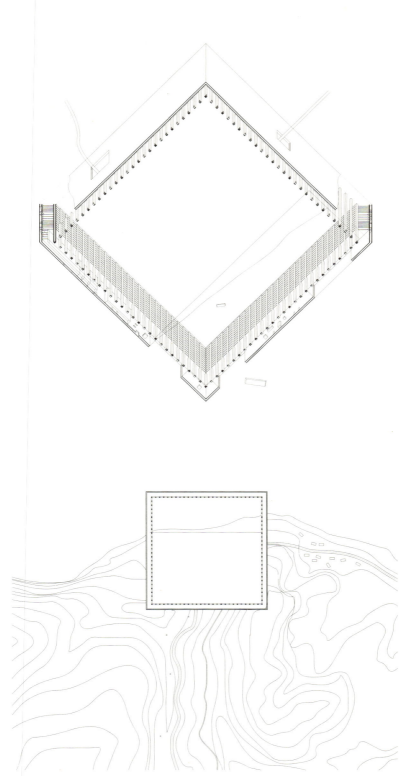

Cité de Refuge: plan 1 : 10 000

Cité de Refuge: Perspective 2

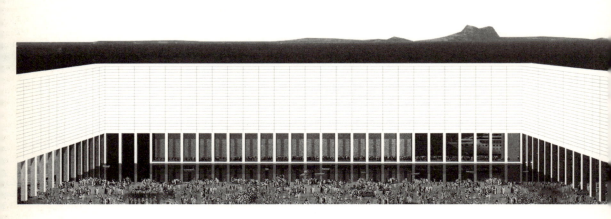

Cité de Refuge: plan of the ground floor

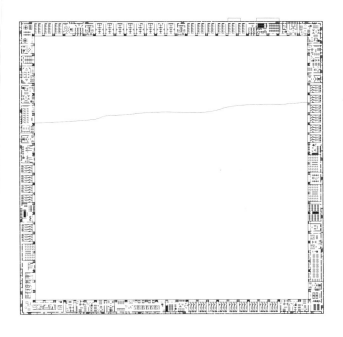

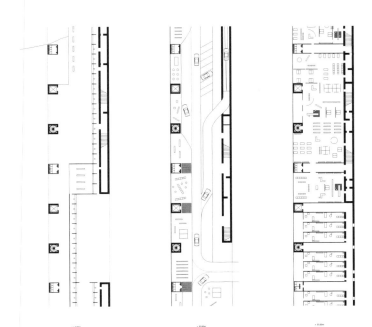

Cité de Refuge: typical floor plans (0 m / 30 m / 33 m)

Conte
Neolib
Urban

Contesting Neoliberal Urbanization
The Right to the City

Roemer van Toorn

'Architecture is political in the manner it makes reality visible by means of its own organization and form, and gives social direction. Afterall Architecture influences our sensorium of being, our experience of a spatial constellation, how we move through space, what we imagine a city to be.'

Contesting Neoliberal Urbanization

In his article 'The Right to The City'[1] Henri Lefebvre explains that the city should be understood as an oeuvre – a work in which all its citizens can participate in the public sphere. He claims that publicity in the city needs a thick heterogeneity, the constant attraction of new immigrants and spaces of density. The city is where difference lives and where the struggle with one another over the shape of the city, the terms of access to the public realm and even rights of citizenship constantly have to be renegotiated. Out of this struggle; the city as a work – as an oeuvre, as a collective if not singular project – emerge new modes of living, and new modes of in- and cohabitation are produced. In the bourgeois city the oeuvre is alienated, says Lefebvre. Capitalism's totalitarian demand to individualize everything results in the breakdown of social relations; not knowing how to keep individuals together as a collective. Now that the individual has taken precedence over the community and the fittest prosper, this has devastating consequences on the vast majority of people everywhere as explained by the different curators in this biennale catalogue.

In fact – as David Harvey has shown[2] – the reorganization of international capitalism through neoliberal individualism should be understood as a political project which wants to re-establish the conditions for capital accumulation and to restore the power of economic elites. The interest of this dominant neoliberal class and its sets of economic interest is not after making the city a site for the cohabitation of differences.[3] As neoliberal prime minister Margaret Thatcher famously declared: there is 'no such thing as society, only individual men and women' – and she subsequently added 'their families'. All forms of social solidarity were to be dissolved in favour of individualism, private property, personal responsibility, flexibility and family values. 'Economics are the method, but the object is to change the soul.'[4] Neoliberalism seeks to bring all human action into the domain of the market. More and more spaces are made *for* us and not *by* us, says Don Mitchell.[5] And its 'creative destruction', remarks Harvey, destroys not only prior institutional frameworks and powers (even challenging traditional forms of state sovereignty) but also division of labour, social relations, welfare provisions, technological mixes, ways of life and thought, reproductive activities, attachments to the land and habits of the heart. 'A contradiction arises between the seductive but alienating possessive individualism on the one hand and the desire for a meaningful collective life on the other,' remarks David Harvey.

According to Lefebvre, people have the right to the oeuvre. Moreover, this right is related to objective needs, needs that any city should be structured toward meeting: 'the need for creative activity, for the oeuvre (not only of products and consumable material goods), the need for information, symbolism, the imaginary and play.'[6] Lefebvre remarks that the right to the city is the right to urban life, to renewed centrality, to places of encounter and exchange, to life rhythms and time uses, enabling the full and the complete usage of moments and places. The right to inhabit, to use value free of exchange value. The right for appropiation way beyond ownership, the right to housing in opposition to the right to ownership, etcetera. Lefebvre wrote his article in 1968 and since than a lot has changed, but his claim: 'The Right to the City', is more urgent than ever in our urban age. The task for everybody involved in creating our urban environment today is how we can re-invent an idea of the city in opposition to the terrorism of the endless (sub)urbanization that neoliberalism prefers to advocate.

Talking about the Right to the City concerns a politics of space that is about struggle, debate and dissonance in the public sphere. Architecture cannot, of course, conduct parliamentary politics. Spatial constellations can deliver no advice on how to vote or convey messages about social and political problems. Architecture is political precisely because of the distance it takes from these functions. But architecture can be political in the way in which, as a space-time sensorium, it organizes being together or apart, and the way it defines outside/inside relations within the city. Architecture is political in the way that it makes reality visible by means of its own organization and form, and gives social direction. After all, architecture influences our sensorium of being, our experience of a spatial constellation, how we move through space, what we imagine a city to be.

Many neoliberal cities today – such as the Corporate City, and The Spectacular City with its Hidden City full of informal creativity – do construct conditions full of contradictions that bring about heterogeneous combinations, but these heterogeneities don't 'automatically' mobilize an emancipatory political agenda. Every collective situation in the Spectacular and Corporate City is objectified and therefore no longer makes a difference, no secrets are unlocked or new possibilities opened, neither does it lend itself to a polemic about our controversial reality. Neoliberalism is not interested in the politics of heterogeniety, but in policing – controling – reality, preferably a reality full of chaos. By policing, neoliberalism normalizes everything as quickly as possible, avoiding any kind of disagreement or discussion. What has been lost is the fact that a system replete with heterogeneity can also raise urgent matters without consensus, without already wanting or being able to provide the ultimate answer. Citizens come to the city to be free, cities are messy. And freedom is messy, and often dangerous. The alternative is bureaucratic order, which raises the question whose order? Many architects, bureaucratic institutions and politicians want the urban experience to be cosy, tidy, green, and designed without any form of dissonance or challenge. Although the sprawl of urbanization today is full of unintended heterogeneities, it doesn't propogate anxiety, while a true city is full of anxiety: contradictions that stimulate progression, like in William Blake's 'Proverbs of Hell': 'Opposition Is True friendship.'

In this third International Architecture Biennale Rotterdam, 14 architecture offices together with the eight researchers will show that the cohabitation of juxtapositions existing in our extreme reality can be a starting point for the establishment of new social political connections. Instead of the closed city of (sub)urbanization dominated by private interests, fear and order, a world full of gated communities, and desert and camps, the urban and architectural proposals in this biennale opt for porous (mediating) collective systems in which the power of neoliberalism is exposed, contested, and relations between strangers become possible through different formations of dissent (dissonance). The problem they face is not political architecture – the grand-narrative of neoliberalism – but how to make the architecture of the city political again.

The Architect as Public Intellectual

According to Edward Said[7] the intellectual is an individual with a specific public role in society that cannot be reduced simply to being a faceless professional, a competent member of a class just going about her/his business. The central fact says Said, is that the intellectual is an individual endowed with a faculty to represent, embody, articulate a message, a view, an attitude, philosophy or opinion to, as well as for, a public. And this role has an edge to it, and cannot be played without a sense of being someone whose place it is to publicly raise embarrassing questions, to confront orthodoxy and dogma (rather than produce them), to be someone who cannot easily be co-opted by governments or corporations, and whose *raison d'etre* is to represent all those people and issues that are routinely forgotten or swept under the carpet. Traditional intellectuals of academia uphold eternal standards of truth and justice that are precisely not of today's world. Architects in pursuit of practical solutions cannot behave like traditional intellectuals, but could be called organic intellectuals[8] who work inside a discipline, able to use their expertise, and to organize space through their material practice.

All architects involved in this IABR entitled *Visionary Power* try to operate as public intellectuals – they may disagree about how to reach their goal, apply different expertise's and operate in different locales; they do have the following in common:
- Once you know whose side you're on, you also know who your enemy is. The architects in this exhibition not only know their enemy by heart, but also show its true face. In neoliberalism the search for truth goes on as an endless conversation from which the force of power (the enemy) is absent and where reason and persuasion seem to prevail. Political and economical conflict are transformed into a matter of opinion: the story is told that the better you are informed and the more 'enlightened' the public is, the closer you can get to the truth. Knowing your enemy means that you decide whose side you're on, it is not just a matter of collecting data and opinions. Being a public intellectual is based on awareness that proper political questions always involve decisions, which require making a choice between conflicting alternatives.[9]
- Facing marginality – escaping the corruption of the real – or accepting the conventions of commercial practice is not what a public intellectual is after. Contemporary cities and urban structures – from Dubai to Mexico City – demonstrate that the complex interactions of desire, density and commerce that characterize the urban field, will consistently exceed the predictable expectation of critical discourse. Public intellectuals are curious about a degree of deviance right from within the system: a 'Cheating in the mix'.[10] That is why all research includes mapping; a kind of projective mapping that is based on matters of concern: information (data) that helps mobilize a progressive agenda. Complicity and negotiation with our extreme reality is seen as the only option for change. After all, the space of the city is in continual flux, dynamic and self-regulating. It is no coincidence that Roberto Unger assigns a specific role to the uncovering of the wild contingency of the city: 'If the triumph of certain institutions and ideas was relatively accidental, their replacement can also be more easily imagined as realistic.'[11]

- Instead of celebrating the paradigm of difference, the public intellectuals in this exhibition look for truth; a multiple truth that engages the urgent issues of contemporary society. The urgent question is: how can you make a city democratic again in the face of totalitarian individualization. Not (yet again) culture as entertainment, but the politics of space is what's at stake; an urban and spatial politics mobilizing the history of the civil city, its contemporary dynamics and possibilities from within its local territory under global influences.
- Instead of prioritizing the pure, solid, functional and objective qualities of the self-referential architectural object, they explore what kind of experiential and relational qualities their formations in space activate by means of its aesthetics (form) and organization.
- The question this IABR raises is not: is populism bad or good (its in all of us), but what kind of political logic [12] of the popular – the one of the public sphere – can be constructed in our contemporary cities? For many of us the popular has a negative connotation. Populism is depicted as anti-elite, cheap, irrational, folkloristic and dangerously superficial. But what we share as a group is of essential importance for every society. Whatever political system you choose, a democracy or dictatorship, they all have to deal with a certain idea of the collective, how that could be a leading principle for the city.

Different Political Strategies

Once the architect operates as a public intellectual – contests neoliberal urbanization by advocating progressive alternatives for the city – that doesn't tell you as yet which political strategy a practitioner prefers or which method (and expertise) according to the architect is most effective; that again depends on certain beliefs and the specific urban territory the architect operates upon. Let's look into some of the biennale architecture projects, and their curators, to better understand which political strategies have been developed and how they believe neoliberal urbanization could be contested by conjectures which install an idea of the city reconfiguring the notion of the *citoyen* in opposition to the cocooning superindividual.

For the sake of clarity imagine a continuum that shifts from institutional authority to guerrilla tactics, with in between the political position of the pirate. Within this spectrum you can locate all the different ideological positions of the 14 projects on the city contesting neoliberalism. Some approaches hold on to the power of form: the authority of architectural monumentality; an absolute idea of architecture,[13] others are neither interested in the image nor the form of architecture, they concentrate, from the ground up, on participation and invent complex empowering systems of self-organization; sometimes against, or elsewhere cheating in the mix. Let's look at a few of them[14] to better understand where they stand and what they produce.

1) Counter-Institutional Architecture. Negative Critique
With their plea for para-architecture, Lieven De Cauter and Michiel Dehaene, the curators of the Hidden City, research how architecture and urbanism can respond to the rise of hidden cities such as camp-like situations, detention centres, refugee camps, and, for instance, transit camps. With their para-architecture they look for imagined heterotopias from where the existing status quo of neoliberalism can be put under fire.

They look for a kind of paper architecture that exposes and makes legible the extremes of our neoliberal society. This apporach is most evident in Border Polis, designed by Office Kersten Geers David Van Severen at the city of Ceuta. With the Centro Direzionale in Turin by G. Polesello, A. Rossi and L. Meda of 1962 in mind, they designed a camp/prison/sanctuary of horrific beauty. Fortress Europe shows its true face: defending its Western privileges against all 'strangers'. It is an architecture that tells the truth to power, knowing that it cannot solve the tragedy of exclusion. Instead of celebrating the foreground of the Spectular City or Corporate Zone, with its middle-class 'paradises' fetishizing individual desires, De Cauter and Dehaene dismantle the good looks (lifestyles) of suburbanization by exposing what normally stays hidden from view in the Western urban land- and mediascape. Instead of hiding or resolving conflicts, they believe that architecture under control of neoliberalism should tell the truth to power by a kind of messianic non-participation, suspension, reversal, even standstill. The philosopher Theodor Adorno's advise that, if the everyday world is corrupt, there is only one thing that the aesthetic experience can do: distance itself from reality in order to guarantee a pure aesthetic promise exposing the real contradictions. Such a negation of reality – by means of a strong, almost absolute, aesthetic gesture in architecture – is meant to arouse resistance and rebellion in the political field against the institutionalization of the status quo.

2) Institutional Architecture. The City as Political Form

While De Cauter and Deheane tell the truth to power – shelter the oppressed, expose and represent its horrific face in the hope that one day the neoliberal city will be overthrown – Pier Vittorio Aureli and Martino Tattara– with their Capital Cities research – investigate how architecture as an urban artefact – by its intrinsic architectural discourse – can counter the neoliberal culture of individualism where the idea of *civitas* has been lost. What ever happened to our metropolitan consciousness, the city as theatre of political debate and class conflict? Why should we celebrate a generic habitat of absolute individualism – a culture of sprawl of only incidents – based on the supremacy of mobility? These are the questions the Capital Cities research tries to answer by investigating how true form – the one of monumentality representing power and the idea of the horizontal plane (platform) for collective action – can generate a civic space of appearance and confrontation. The research on Moscow (by Alexander Sverdlov) investigates how a collective idea of the city can be generated through prefabricated housing projects for the masses. While in Moscow the aesthetic order of monumentality is tested in mass housing, the project in Beirut researches with different means (rotating festivals, cedar evolution, a thick infrastructure of tents, etcetera) how the enactment of conflict by activities on different platforms in the open city of Beirut – in opposition to appeasing strategies such as the one of Disneyfication and mediterranization – could turn the city into a political platform.

Both Counter-Institutional and Institutional Architecture challenge the market and declare that it should be over. They both favour monumental, often monochrome (black or white), severe, empty and void spaces where only life itself is allowed to be colourful, human and joyful. The institutional architectural poetry promoted by De Cauter and Dehaene embodies the trauma of our existence: the impossibility of the real. The invisible walls and fences between the haves and the have-nots get physical in all their horrendous truth. Aureli and Tattara are not so much after exposing power in all its negativity, their politics are of another kind. They look for redemption instead of exposing trauma. It is no coincidence that they look for spaces of coexistence and cohabitation in which the different powers come together and fight their battle of life. Instead of choosing a side, the city can be nothing else than a battlefield of different powers. That is the only democratic and public truth architecture can represent and make appear. Aureli and Tattara's city architecture is not after overthrowing power, having a new world in mind such as De Cauter and Dehaene do, but gives the different powers – present in the city – the right to the city. They can write their oeuvre in all their purity, anger, honesty and vulnerability in relation to each other. All this on the basis of an almost eternal architectural truth: an architecture of formal rhetoric, monumentality, type and abstraction; how urban design can be the prime contributor to the formations of the city, also acknowledging the limits of architecture that it never can bring revolution on its own.

In most cases true trans-national economical and political power[15] is hidden from view – there are no representations of truth, platforms of public presence for debate or demonstration – our collective desires in neoliberalism are redirected into endless individual lifestyles and persuaded by beautifully designed architectural experiences. Both De Cauter and Deheane and Aureli and Tattara show us neoliberal power's true face. De Cauter and Dehaene are after breaking consent: they oppose the neoliberalist city, while Aureli and Tattara institutionalize disagreement to overcome the dictatorship of individualization in the city. Instead of setting up a discourse which tries to set up a *we* against a *them*, Aureli and Tattara and De Cauter and Dehaene are after a vibrant democratic culture where a Left and Right politics expose their ideology and fight their battle.

3) Guerrilla Architecture. The Power of the Immediate
The curators Alfredo Brillembourg and Hubert Klumpner – working in the poor neighbourhoods of Caracas – don't fight the neoliberal system with conventional architecture; the authority of design, the drawing board, legitimate architecture histories or the expertise of a physical planning department. Instead of such an institutional approach – believing in the 'truth' of the formal language of architecture, or the power of institutions – they use the tactics of guerrilla warfare. Guerrilla tactics are not a regular force. It is a method of unconventional combat which operates from within informal culture, empowering local populations without the need for any uniform style. It is based on the reflexive capacity of the immediate, the inventive power of people, manipulating and negotiating existing conditions. What seems guarded in these guerrilla tactics is immediacy, the unknown, that untreated bolus of direct experience, those lines of flights that cannot be reflected by any dialectical opposition as we have seen in the projects of De Cauter and Dehaene and Aureli and Tattara. So freedom is not something you have to establish outside reality – by being critical towards society – but can be developed through practice experiments in a world divided between privilege and poverty. In their work, the border between urbanism, architecture, design, art, film and social work is blurred. They could care less how they are labelled, as long as their projects really do improve the reality of the poor, the one of everyday life. Even when their work consists of physical objects, these are at most tactic manipulations of political landscapes. Their built work is after changing the political status quo in such a way that more things become possible in our actuality. They employ

micro tactics with a macro ambition, identifying small projects, working with communities and their intelligence: reusing, adapting, and modifying existing infrastructures by making them more viable and affordable.

In fact two kinds of humanity are activated in the Informal City projects. One the one hand there is the focus on the city of Johannesburg as a place for equal opportunities, urban culture and policies in the service and wellbeing of the citizens. On the other hand the informal city research by Teddy Cruz shows that the informal city provides answers to how we in the field of housing can overcome the worldwide problem of cocooning: in others words, how we can de-individualize our many gated communities. What Cruz discovered on the micro scale of the neighbourhood in Tijuana, are micro heterotopias that are emerging within small communities; in the form of non-conforming spatial and entrepreneurial practices, defining a different idea of density and land use, setting forth a counterform of urban and economic development that thrives on social encounter, collaboration and exchange. The trans-border urban dynamics at play across the most trafficked checkpoint in the world has provoked the small border neighbourhoods that surround it to construct alternative urbanisms of transgression. In Teddy Cruz's research we can detect how guerrilla tactics can arrive at Piratical Architecture.

4) Piratical Architecture. Cheating in the Mix

'A piratical architecture' according to curator Keller Easterling, 'does not evaluate the integrity of expression or the regrettable urge to reform. It intervenes in the patterns of believers and cheaters, evaluating the ability of masquerades to leverage change.'[16] According to Easterling, architects are well-trained to pirate in their own career: they have multiple voices, tactics, and a political craft to deploy self-promotion, but for the rest the discipline reinforces the boundaries of its own world – its autonomy as an art form within which to write monologues that preserve its integrity. Aureli and Tattara and De Cauter and Dehaene prove that institutional architecture – the convention of form – can expose and even confront power on the urban scale of the city. Speaking the truth to power is not what Guerrilla Architecture is after. With Guerrilla Architecture the intelligent nature of the informal – the anarchistic survival system of everybody beyond the normative of the institutional – is mobilized to survive the terror of the status quo. No symbolic fight, but direct humanitarian action, repeating what is destroyed even if the means are minimal. With piratical architecture we have to do with an attitude that tries to find luck on the sea. Liberation and convention, liberation and cliché (commodification) travel together in piratical architecture. Institutional Architecture looks for truth, either the one of justice against neoliberalism or the political Form of the City. Guerilla Architecture is a kind of 'Médicins Sans Frontiéres', whatever the system, it fights with the people for survival and primary justice through immediate action. Pirates do not only manage to survive any system, but are also able to play the system and even enjoy its extravaganza and luxury. They fight the system with its own means, its own schizophrenia, without regretting its often corrupt attitude. What they share with the guerrilla is its anti-authoritarian nature. Their weapon is the multitude, the one of immanence, while Institutional Architecture opposes the multitude through the institutional authority of architectural form and the alternative shelters.

When Rafi Segal and Els Verbakel showed their research on New Jersey for a Future Urbanism, they screened the raw opening stills (probably filmed with a handycam) from the American television series 'The Soprano's'. We see New Jersey from Tony Soprano's car window, as he tries to be a good family man on two fronts – to his wife, kids and widowed mother – and as a cape in the New Jersey mob. New Jersey is Sprawl City par excellence – the backyard, garden city making the Corporate Zone a success. Instead of ignoring the suburban setting of New Jersey altogether, Segal and Verbakel read, interpret, and intervene like pirates dissecting, recombining and synthesizing what progressive spaces could emerge from within Suburban City New Jersey.

Institutional and Guerilla Architecture shies away from the power of spectacle within place. Any spectacle is politically incorrect, too corrupt or just not to the point according to them. But as John Urry correctly remarks 'spectacle-ization is necessary in order for places to *enter* the global order, to somehow be 'recognized'.[17] Places depend upon performances, such as *flâneurie*, photographing, running, shopping, swimming, sunbathing, talking, reminiscing, reading, playing or listening to music, surfing, eating, partying, drinking, collecting, climbing and so on. Piratical Architecture doesn't ask itself the academic question if spectacle-ization is good or bad. The question is not defining the truth – as a public intellectual you cannot afford yourself that kind of luxury when you have to transform reality. The question is what kind of specatle-ization you can construct given a certain situation. How you can re-imagine the idea of heritage beyond Disneyfication for instance. How tourism can be the unexpected motor of cityness in Rome as (baukuh), or how you can make a better World Heritage City by escaping the regulative power of the UNESCO in Innsbruck, overcoming the risk of freezing a city in a history that never happened in the first place.

From Political Cities to making Cities Political

To make political cities is not that difficult. Even when you avoid the political you will be a child of your time; embodying and representing the political and ideological implications of the status quo. To be politically active – making cities political in opposition to just surfing the waves of neoliberalism – demands that the architect operates as a public intellectual, rethinks the profession, and reinvents what it means to be socially engaged today. That's why the political practices shown in this publication are not so much after a practice of dissent – an element that has the function to express an a-priori discontent and dissent – but rather use confrontation and dissonance within the current neoliberal system as a 'method' to affect the public's imagination and help to improve the real conditions of urban life. All architects in this IABR operate as public intellectuals, confront the neoliberalist terrorism of suburbanization through alternatives, are concerned with how our cities in the twenty-first century can be a place for the world citizen. These are not visions that reject reality, but ones concerned with different realms of emancipatory politics that develop alternatives based on what we urgently need in our contemporary society.

1   Henri Lefebvre, *Writings on Cities*, english translation introduction and editorial arrangment by Eleonore Kofman and Elizabeth Lebas (Oxford: Blackwell Publishers, 1996), French original: Le droit a la ville, published in 1968.
2   David Harvey, *A Brief History of Neoliberalism*, Oxford, Oxford University Press, 2006).
3   The traditional idea of the city no longer exists. Under pressure from the neoliberal market economy, the idea that architecture can serve the public interest has been undermined. Economic and private interests are rated more highly than cultural and collective values. Not only does the economic logic of property developers and investors determine the city's landscape, the city council, too, acts as property developer and investor. In so doing, the government follows the market regime and the public task becomes a derivative of market-orientated thinking. While the Modern Movement sought to improve the world with its architecture primarily from a social perspective, today it is about plans that attempt to give the city a better competitive position vis-à-vis other cities in the world. And superarchitects – preferably with star status – are engaged in order to promote the economy of a city with a stunning design.
4   Quote by Margaret Thatcher taken from the Internet: http://www.saidwhat.co.uk/quotes/political/margaret_thatcher
5   See also Don Mitchell, *The Right to the City: Social Justice and the Fight for Public Space* (New York: The Guilford Press, 2003); and Setha Low and Neil Smith, *The Politics of Public Space* (New York: Routledge, 2006).
6   Lefebvre, op. cit. (note 1).
7   Edward Said, *Representations of the Intellectual*, The 1993 Reith lectures (New York: Vintage Books, 1996).
8   After Antonio Gramsci, *The Prison Notebooks: Selections* (New York: International Publishers, 1971).
9   See Carl Schmitt, *The Crisis of Parliamentary Democracy (Studies in Contemporary German Social Thought)*, translation Ellen Kennedy (Cambridge, MA: The MIT Press, 1988); and Chantal Mouffe, *On The Political* (New York: Routledge, 2005).
10 Keller Easterling, *Enduring Innocence. Global Architecture and Its Political Masquerades* (Cambridge, MA: The MIT Press, 2005).
11 Roberto Unger, quote taken from *Sites and Stations. Provisional Utopias. Architecture and Utopia in the Contemporary City*, edited by Stan Allen and Kyong Park (New York: Lusitania Press, 1996).
12 Ernesto Laclau, *The Populist Reason* (New York: Verso, 2005).
13 Pier Vittorio Aureli, unpulished PhD disertation 'The Possibility of Absolute Architecture – a study on architectural form from Bramante to Mies' (Delft/Rotterdam: TU Delft/Berlage Institute, 2006).
14 When writing this article most of the projects were far from finished. My analysis is based only on the texts submitted.
15 The grand narrative of neoliberalism.
16 Easterling, *Enduring Inocence*, op. cit. (note 10).
17 See John Urry elsewhere in this catalogue.

Martijn de Waal

Power Cities

Garage City

The reappearance of a cottage industry of home-based entrepreneurs, albeit more likely based in the garages of sprawling exurbia and sheds of metropolitan shanty towns than in some pastoral countryside. In some countries this idea is hard-wired to
a paper-boy-to-millionaire myth in which determined self-made inventors knock up
the new new thing from their garages, ousting the ossified 'dinosaurs of big business' who 'just don't get it anymore'. Here, informal ingenuity trumps the formalized, creativity-strangled bureaucracies of big business.

In other places, it is more a survival strategy or way of life, focusing on small niches or hyperlocal services neglected as too risky or not lucrative enough by big business. For instance, in Mexico City many suburbians turn the garages of their master-planned estates into workshops, small restaurants, hair salons, or the base for permanent garage sales, resembling the grey economy of the informal settlements that surround them, breaking the clear separation between the formal and informal economy.

Barrio City

The barrios – also known as the slums, the favelas, the shanty towns, the derelict inner cities, the *banlieus* – are often described as antagonistic to the official city – and thus everything the 'official city is not: no social institutions, legal framework, monuments, jobs, public spaces, or state monopoly on violence. However, many of these informal settlements, such as the Caracas barrio of Petare, have become permanent destinations for its settlers, and have developed their own institutions, social relations, job markets, neighbourhoods, identities and even political base, sometimes parallel to, sometimes extra-juridical from, sometimes overlapping with official society, creating a way of life that partially takes place outside the legal frameworks of official society, but certainly not outside any political, cultural or economic framework.

Squatter City

On Sundays, the Hong Kong financial district – the territory of the blackberry-crowd for the rest of the week – is turned into a giant picnic ground/open air church for Philippino housekeeping maids. After the recent Israeli-Lebanese war, white refugee tents appeared in the gentrified and recently commercialized downtown of Beirut, its residents seeking both refuge from the war and publicity for their protests. At other times an archaeological research site and tourist destination in central Rome is usurped by marchers against some cause or another. In all these examples, the function of city space is produced rough the performance of its inhabitants. They ve the power to 'squat' all kinds of spaces for creational, countercultural or political usage, us producing the city through bottom-up social ocesses rather than through top-down planng.

ittle Somewhere lse City

ith the rise of the Global Village-phenomenon mes the rise of global villages. In their adopted untries and cities, many cultural or ethnic oups dispersed in their diasporas around the rld, do not only seek a place to dwell, but often o long for their own parochial domain and mbolic spot in the skyline, that both recognizes eir identities and affirms that they belong – be Muslims putting up minarets in cities across rope or the century-old phenomena of Chitowns and Little Italys around the world. The me can be said for some lifestyle identities – for stance the gay community marking its presce with rainbow flags in San Francisco's Castro strict. These instances of skyline politics and e creation of local 'colonies' can be played out in th a progressive and a conservative way. In the ter case, cultural groups seek to connect with eir global communities, isolating themselves m their local surroundings. In the former, the ocess of identity formation is a process of negotiating: mixing up customs from their origin with the practices from their new home countries.

Butler City

The idea – from the perspective of the consumer – of the city as a 'butler' that serves up a personalized menu of infrastructural services (transport, housing, access to electronic networks) to paying customers. Through electronic technology the butler (embodied by infrastructural companies and government agencies) is able to keep track of the exact amount of services consumed – be it kilometres travelled on toll ways, or kilobytes transported on the electronic highway. The city in its entirety is formed by the aggregate of these service packages, purchased by consumers with the required spending power.

As Stephen Graham and Simon Marvin have pointed out, this is a clean break from the ideal of modernist urbanism, that can best be understood as the successive rolling out of infrastructural networks, guided by the principal of 'universal access'. That ideal not only created the public grids of roads, electricity, sewage and other utilities, meant to emancipate and connect all citizens alike. It thereby also produced the idea of an inclusive urban community of citizens to whom these grids belonged, rather than a society of consumers to whom these services are sold as marketable products.

Epilogue

Emblems of the City *after* the End of History Joachim Declerck

The end of history will be a very sad time. . . . The worldwide ideological struggle that called forth daring, courage, imagination, and idealism, will be replaced by economic calculation, the endless solving of technical problems . . . and the satisfaction of sophisticated consumer demands. In this post-historical period there will be neither art nor philosophy, just the perpetual caretaking of the museum of human history. I can feel in myself, and see in others around me, a powerful nostalgia for the time when history existed. . . . Perhaps this very prospect of centuries of boredom at the end of history will serve to get history started once again.
Francis Fukuyama, 1989[1]

Not even twenty years ago, and only months after the fall of the Berlin Wall, the American philosopher and political economist Francis Fukuyama declared 'the end of history'. The decisive reforms in both China and the Soviet Union towards a more or less controlled form of market economy imply, according to Fukuyama, the end of the global ideological duel between liberalism and communism and the 'unabashed victory' of the former over the latter. This 'triumph of the West, of the Western *idea*' speaks from the 'total exhaustion of viable systematic alternatives to Western liberalism'. According to Hegel's view on history, what actually drives it exists first in the realm of *human consciousness* and *ideas*, understood in the sense of 'larger unifying world views', and only then in the material world. Therefore, even if we witness, today again stronger than a decade ago, the remainders of communist political systems, the fact that liberalism has no alternative at the level of ideology proves the totality of its victory. And, when history culminates in a moment in which an *idea* of society and state are victorious, history, according to Hegel, has reached its end.[2]

Economic liberalism, or what has now taken the form of 'global capitalism', has proven to be extremely successful in spreading around the world. Unlike any previous phase of capitalism – a societal model that originated around the beginning of the sixteenth century – its late twentieth-century manifestation is transcendental[3] in nature: there is no possible understanding of the world if not by starting from neoliberal capitalism; there is nothing outside of capitalism. The inevitability of liberalism is what makes us literally experience 'the end of history'. The last decades of the previous century and the beginning of the twenty-first century will be remembered for the dramatic shift of power from the public to the private. And politics, or the profession of *visions* on how a society of people inhabits its territory, is reduced to a debate on the degree to which the permanent inequality generated by capitalism should be 'corrected' – or in other words, how the spending power of the consumer can be increased.

    Global capitalism not only marginalized politics, but also the very context of architecture and the city. Parallel to the decline of politics – understood as *visions* on the 'polis', a term that brings together in one word both *civitas* (the city of people) and *urbs* (the city of stones)[4] – globalization has caused a significant disconnection of civilization from its direct spatial setting. *All That Is Solid Melts Into Air*[5] is the title of Marshall Berman's essay on the experience of modernity that suggests the essential shift away from space as a signifying element of society. The supposedly total disconnection between our physical context and the experience of contemporary culture – symbolized in the contemporary nomad and the consumer – finally allows contemporary man to free himself from the burdens of physical constraints and to live a radically 'modern' existence. It is indeed this widely shared conviction that the 'truth' of our globalized postmodernity is not to be found in the specificity of places, but in the all-encompassing global network of flows of information, goods and people that significantly altered the order of our world, and the respective roles of architecture and urbanism. The city, which had always been one of the most complex manifestations of civilization, ceases to be the physical expression of the society it accommodates. And architecture, confronted with the absence of a significant role for the city beyond the generic, is torn between endlessly mapping the complex manifestations of the nearly natural organism of globalization – see the numerous books on the city and globalization – and the decoration of what is left of the city with architectural sculptures or 'iconic buildings'.[6]

It is around the start of the new millennium that the heroic image of globalization's emancipatory force starts to fall apart. Let's go back to the agile debate that followed the publication of Francis Fukuyama's essay in 1989. One of the main critiques pointed at his profound conviction that the dispersion of liberal democracy around the world answers an expectation that is assumed to exist in the different agglomerations of the world's civilization. While acknowledging the existence of a significant part of the world that did not participate in the hegemony of liberal democracy and economy, Fukuyama was convinced that freedom and a modern life was what these populations, too, were finally after.[7] And, according to Fukuyama, liberal democracy is the best conceivable social-political system for fostering freedom. It is this strong belief in the unifying force of globalization and of liberalism that characterized the 1990s, while it rapidly 'melted into air' at the beginning of the third millennium. This is a sensation that Fukuyama himself quite literally lived during the past years: he was one of the architects of the neoconservative 'Project for a New American Century'[8] and hence a fierce defender of the US invasion in Iraq – supposedly aimed at installing liberal democracy in the heart of the Middle-East. But perhaps the fact that Fukuyama has now left the ship of the neoconservatives and openly criticizes the idea of actively and forcefully spreading liberal democracy across the world,[9] symbolizes the clear death of the fiction that the worldwide dispersal of liberalism is inevitable and positive. Instead of merely studying the agile and pervasive force and speed of globalization, our consciousness has started to adapt to the painful duality of the world, to exclusion and the consequential migration as significant factors of the current world system. This polarization upon which Fukuyama only moderately touched in his 1989 essay has now become the perspective through which we collectively understand the world: Western society is increasingly protecting the acquired wealth in its suburban landscapes and generic global cities against the rapidly growing and migrating global South.

But could we not take this one step further? Wouldn't it be logical to assume, at a moment – now! – that the combined impact of global warming and demographic explosion alter the very nature of the world system, that what we are collectively witnessing is the emergence of a relevant 'exterior' to liberal democracy? In about 40 years, half of the world population will live in informal cities, the backside and by-product of the triumph of the Western *idea*. Could this not mean the end of the hegemony of liberal capitalism over the world and the city? If more than half of the world population finds itself excluded from the benefits of the dominant system, and when ecological changes urge us to rethink the way we inhabit the territory of the globe, are we then not close to arriving *after* the end of history? Maybe a new *human consciousness* or *ideology* has not yet been shaped, but we cannot neglect that the prospect of both exploding cities and climate change could – and should – trigger a new start of Politics and instil a renewed structural role to the physical context of the world's civilization. Politics will again be concerned with the way in which the physical footprint of society – the habitat – is able to represent a shared social, political and cultural project – the context in which also economy will find its next life.

The city, as the physical framework and place of world civilization *after* the end of history, constitutes the challenge for the current generation of architects and politicians. The much-repeated dictum says that by 2050, two thirds of the world population will be living in cities. The fact that, following this same statistical prophecy, most of the European continent would be considered 'city' clarifies the extent to which a redefinition of its *idea* is urgent. We can no longer accept to see the city as a neutral canvas or territory upon which different actors paint. The result is the current landscape of accidental sculptures that fails to embody a true *vision* of the polis. Future *visions* will resemble neither of the twentieth-century caricatures of urbanism: the 'scientific' modernist and ordered city, and the post-modern neoliberal utopia of the 'subjective' consumerist city. The physical context of the city is the place where architecture will address the multitude of citizens – the contemporary *mass* of a truly globalized world. It is the place where architecture will represent, as emblem of a new *idea*, the city *after* the end of history.

1   Excerpt from the concluding paragraph from: Francis Fukuyama, 'The End of History?', *The National Interest* (1989) 16.
2   Ibid.
3   Lieven De Cauter, *The Capsular Civilization. On the City in the Age of Fear* (Rotterdam: NAi Publishers, 2004), 41-42.
4   The description of 'polis' is borrowed from ibid., 7.
5   Marshall Berman, *All That Is Solid Melts Into Air* (New York: Penguin Books, 1988, first published in 1982).
6   For an in-depth analysis of the phenomenon of 'iconic building', see Charles Jencks, *Iconic Building. The Power of Enigma* (London: Frances Lincoln, 2005).
7   Francis Fukuyama, 'A Reply to My Critics', *The National Interest* (1989) 17.
8   For more info, see www.newamericancentury.org.
9   Francis Fukuyama, 'After Neoconservatism', *The New York Times*, 19 February 2006.

Biographies

arquitectura 911sc is a practice of architecture and urbanism based in Mexico City and co-founded by Saidee Springall and Jose Castillo. Springall and Castillo both studied architecture at the Iberoamericana University in Mexico City and at Harvard's GSD. The firm has won several competitions including those for the expansion of the Spanish Cultural Center in Mexico City and for the new CEDIM campus in Monterrey. Among their built works are more than 20 Porrua bookshops, the SA236 Housing, and the JS32 offices.
Their work and research has appeared in *Praxis Journal*, *Arquine*, *2G*, *Domus*, *Architectural Record* and *Bomb*. Castillo teaches and lectures both in Mexico and abroad and has curated a number of exhibitions including Mexico City Dialogues at the Center for Architecture in New York City, NY and participations at the Rotterdam (2005), São Paulo (2005), Venice (2006) and Canary Islands (2007) Biennales.

a-u-r-a (architecture, urbanism + research agency) is a German-Mexican office, based in Neu-Ulm, Germany, co-founded by Marisol Rivas Velázquez and Christian Schmutz. a-u-r-a incorporates design as well as research on various scales ranging from architecture to urbanism and back. Research is considered as an integrative part of design and as nothing without design.
Marisol Rivas Velázquez studied architecture at the ITESM, Monterrey and the Berlage Institute, Rotterdam.
Christian Schmutz studied architecture at the University of Stuttgart, the Technical University of Graz and the Berlage Institute, Amsterdam/Rotterdam. Between and after their studies they worked in offices in Austria, Germany, the Netherlands, Mexico and Belgium. Parallel to their professional practice Marisol and Christian have been visiting professors at ITESM, Monterrey, TU Munich and currently they are researchers and assistant professors at the Institute of Design of Leopold-Franzens-University in Innsbruck.

Pier Vittorio Aureli is an architect and educator. After graduating cum laude from the Istituto di Architettura di Venezia, Aureli obtained a doctorate in urban planning, a master's degree at the Berlage Institute, and a PhD at the Berlage Institute/Delft University of Technology. His theoretical studies focus on the relationship between architectural form, political thinking, and urban history. Aureli teaches at the Berlage Institute – where he is unit professor and responsible for the 'research on the city' programme. Currently he is a visiting professor at the Architectural Association in London, Columbia University in New York, and Delft University of Technology. Aureli has lectured and published worldwide, and he is currently working on a book entitled *The Possibility of Absolute Architecture* – a study on architectural form from Bramante to Mies. Together with Martino Tattara he is the cofounder of DOGMA, a non-professional architectural collective centred on the project of the city. Very recently, DOGMA won the first prize in the international competition for the new Administrative City for 500,000 inhabitants in the Republic of South Korea, and in 2006 received the Iakov Chernikhov Prize for the best emerging architectural practice.

bad architects group is an internationally-orientated architecture office operating from Innsbruck, Austria, co-founded by Ursula Faix and Paul Burgstaller. The office collaborates with bad-architects.network, an emerging internet-based network of young architects, co-founded in May 2004. Next to designing projects for intelligent clients, bad architects group is devoted to developing new tools for exploring the phenomena of the urban condition in the digital age and has exhibited and published several projects, such as 'nEUtral' (*Magazine on Urbanism*) and together with bad-architects.network 'DE-tro-IT' (gfzk Leipzig, Germany). bad architects group will lecture on urban design at the University for Business and Technology in Prishtina, Kosovo, starting in fall 2007.
Ursula Faix, studied architecture at the Technical University of Vienna. Prior to founding bad architects group she collaborated with several offices among which Massimiliano Fuksas in Vienna and Rome. She is a lecturer at the Institute for Urban Design and Regional Planning, University of Innsbruck and has published articles in, for instance, *Graz Architecture Magazine* (GAM) and *Archplus*.
Paul Burgstaller, studied architecture at the University of Innsbruck. Prior to finishing his studies and founding bad architects group together with Ursula Faix, he collaborated with several offices among which Behnisch & Partner, West 8 and Office for Metropolitan Architecture. He is giving lectures and guest critics at various universities.

baukuh was founded in January 2004 by Paolo Carpi, Lorenzo Laura, Silvia Lupi, Vittorio Pizzigoni, Giacomo Summa, Pier Paolo Tamburelli, Francesca Torzo and Andrea Zanderigo. baukuh is based in Genoa (Italy). Baukuh produces architecture.
No member of baukuh is ever individually responsible for a project. Design is based on a rational and explicit process of making. baukuh has no stylistic dogma. Design depends on public knowledge, namely the architecture of the past. Starting from this heritage, it is possible to solve all architectural problems.

blacklinesonwhitepaper was founded as a north-south collaboration by Kirsten Dörmann, Solam Mkhabela and Tumi Morule in 2002. It is now based in Johannesburg, South Africa. **Kirsten Dörmann** graduated from the Technical University of Aachen and the Berlage Institute, **Solam Mkhabela** studied at the Cooper Union and graduated, as did **Tumi Morule**, from the University of Cape Town. blacklines focuses on sustainable urban development, urban design and urban narratives.

Lieven De Cauter studied philosophy and the history of art. He published several books: on contemporary art, experience and modernity, on Walter Benjamin and more recently on architecture, the city and politics. He teaches philosophy of culture at several art schools and universities: currently at the Department of Architecture of Leuven University, the media school RITS and the dance school PARTS (Brussels) and the postgraduate school for architecture, Berlage Institute (Rotterdam). His latest book is *The Capsular Civilisation. On the City in the Age of Fear* (2004). He was initiator of the B*Russell*s Tribunal on 'the Project for the New American Century' and its responsibilities in the invasion of Iraq. He is also co-founder of the 'platform for liberty of expression', that fights antiterrorism legislation. He is co-editor with Michiel Dehaene of *'Heterotopia and the City. Public Space in a Post-Civil Society'* to be published by Routledge in the spring of 2007.

Princeton University Center for Architecture, Urbanism and Infrastructure was established at the School of Architecture as a research centre providing a collective site for an increasingly important area of interdisciplinary research on urban issues. The Center offers a focused venue for sharing existing collective research, while also providing a platform for expanding it, approaching urbanization not only as a global phenomenon of physical and cultural restructuring – but as a spatial effect in itself, of distributed networks of communication, resources, finance and migration that characterize

and influence contemporary life.
The contribution to the Rotterdam Biennale is lead by **Rafi Segal** and **Els Verbakel**, both practicing architects and PhD candidates at the School of Architecture. The project team involves students in the Master of Architecture programme: Yan Chu, Ajay Manthripragada, Marc McQuade, Ryan Neiheiser, Kate Snider, Michael Wang. The Director of the Center is Mario Gandelsonas and the Dean of the Architecture School is Stan Allen.

Teddy Cruz's work dwells at the border between San Diego, California and Tijuana, Mexico, where he has been developing a practice and pedagogy that emerge out of the particularities of this bicultural territory and the integration of theoretical research and design production. Teddy Cruz has been recognized internationally in collaboration with community-based non-profit organizations such as Casa Familiar for its work on housing and its relationship to an urban policy more inclusive of social and cultural programmes for the city. He obtained a Master's in Design Studies from Harvard University and the Rome Prize in Architecture from the American Academy in Rome. He has recently received the 2004-05 James Stirling Memorial Lecture On The City Prize and is currently an associate professor in public culture and urbanism in the Visual Arts Department at UCSD in San Diego.

Joachim Declerck studied architecture and urban planning at Ghent University, Belgium, and obtained his master's degree at the Berlage Institute in 2005, where he was engaged in the research programme on capital cities. He is currently working as an independent architect and as assistant professor at the Berlage Institute. He co-edited the publication *Brussels – A Manifesto. Towards the Capital of Europe* and was co-curator and coordinator of the exhibition 'A Vision for Brussels'. He is co-curator of the International Architecture Biennale Rotterdam 2007. He publishes regularly on the role of architecture and urban design in building the city, and is a member of the editorial board of *OASE*.

Michiel Dehaene studied architecture in Leuven, urban design at the Harvard Graduate School of Design and completed his PhD at the Leuven University with a dissertation on the influence of 'Civic and Regional Survey' on the development of British Town Planning in the first half of the twentieth century. He is a lecturer in urbanism at the Eindhoven University of Technology and is a member of the research group OSA at Leuven. He is co-editor with Lieven De Cauter of *Heterotopia and the City. Public Space in a Post-Civil Society* to be published by Routledge in the spring of 2007.

Keller Easterling is an architect, urbanist and writer from New York City. Her book *Enduring Innocence: Global Architecture and its Political Masquerades* (MIT, 2005) researches familiar spatial products that have landed in difficult or hyperbolic political situations around the world. A previous book *Organization Space: Landscapes, Highways and Houses in America* applies network theory to a discussion of American infrastructure and development formats. A forthcoming book, *Extrastatecraft*, examines global infrastructure networks as a medium of global polity. Easterling is an associate professor at Yale University who received her Masters of Architecture from Princeton University.

Kenneth Frampton is Ware Professor of Architecture at the Graduate School of Architecture, Planning and Preservation, Columbia University, New York. He is the author of the canonical historiography *Modern Architecture: A Critical History* (London, first published 1980). Other publications include *Studies in Tectonic Culture: The Poetics of Construction in Nineteenth and Twentieth Century Architecture* (Cambridge Mass., 1995), the monograph *Le Corbusier* (London, 2001), and *Labour, Work and Architecture. Collected Essays on Architecture and Design* (London/New York, 2002).

FÜNDC BV is a Rotterdam-based architecture office, co-founded by **Paz Martin** and **César García**, both graduated architects from Spain. Their objective is to improve the architectonical product by becoming an unified source of design solutions in the fields of urban planning (Kolenkit Urban plan, Amsterdam, with UUD), art installations (Bloodsushi bank, Migros Museum, Zurich, with Alicia Framis), graphic design (Bridge procedures with SNTG), interior design (Getxo Hotel with LKSstudio). FÜNDC is currently building in China (Restaurant 13, 1,500 m², Shanghai), Spain (New Cultural Center, 15,540 m², Madrid). They have taught at Delft University of Technology, IBK Innsbruck and Politecnico di Milano and have published articles in *DOMUS, A+U , L'ARCA, ARCAM, EVD, YEA*. FÜNDC's work has recently been exhibited in Shanghai (Creative week), Amsterdam (Wonderland, ARCAM gallery), Belgrade (8th Triennale of Architecture) where they were awarded the gold honourable mention.

Jeffrey Inaba is the founder of INABA, a consulting and architecture firm based in Los Angeles. He is the programme director of SCIFI, the postgraduate studies programme at SCI-Arc, the Director of C-Lab, a think-tank at Columbia University, and the Features Editor of *Volume Magazine*. The IABR project was realized by INABA: Jeffrey Inaba (Principal), Ben Konen (Project Architect), Haydee Avila, Dionysia Daskalaki, Moira Henry; Environmental Engineers: ARUP, Steve Done, Karen Mozes and Video and Motion Graphics Designer: David Vegezzi.

IND (Inter.National.Design) is a recently born architecture office based in Rotterdam.
Co-founders Felix Madrazo (Mexico) and Arman Akdogan (Turkey) met at the Berlage Institute during their master's degree and have collaborated ever since on a regular basis. Their relationship developed as Turkish and Mexican backgrounds coincided again in popular Dutch office backgrounds. Their collaboration increased after they won the International Vanguard Competition for Housing in Ceuta in 2007, construction expected 2008. Currently they run architecture and urban projects in Amsterdam, Moscow, Istanbul and Ceuta.

Arman Akdogan studied architecture at the Mimarsinan University in Istanbul, Turkey. In his professional carrier he has collaborated with offices based in Istanbul such as Arkizon and Ecarch since 1994. From 2000 to 2002 he followed the master's programme at the Berlage Institute in Rotterdam. After graduation he worked for several international architecture offices in both Holland (OMA and West 8 in Rotterdam). He established his own (www.armanakdogan.com) practice in Rotterdam in 2005. He is a co-founder of IND (Inter.National.Design) He is currently directing various architectural and urban planning projects.

Felix Madrazo is co-founder of Supersudaca (www.supersudaca.org). With Supersudaca he received the Best Entry Award at the Rotterdam Architecture Biennale in 2005 with a study on the impacts of tourism in The Caribbean. Also with Supersudaca, he won the best research proposal at the Bienal Iberoamericana de Arquitectura with a study of PREVI. He worked for OMA in Rotterdam and Alberto Kalach in Mexico City. He was a fellow of the Kulturstiftung with studies of informality in Caracas. Currently he is involved as author and co-editor of the Supersudaca book Al Caribe (PCF-Actar).

Martin Mutsclechner studied architecture at the University of Innsbruck. After his graduation in 1997 he worked for different architectural offices in Italy and Austria. In 2000 he applied for a postgraduate study at the Berlage Institute in Rotterdam. After his graduation in 2002 he opened his architectural office www.stadtlabor.org and worked as a teacher, first as a guest professor, later as an assistant professor at the architecture faculty of Innsbruck. He is currently working on the realization of several projects and is involved in urban research.

Gabriele Mastrigli is an architect and critic living in Rome. He studied at the University of Rome 'La Sapienza' and at the RWTH Aachen (Germany). He investigates the relationship between architects' designing and writing, researching publishing as a critical form of architecture – the main subject of his PhD dissertation. Since 1998 he has been teaching Theory and Design at Ascoli Piceno School of Architecture and has been a visiting lecturer and guest critic at Cornell University,

Ohio State University, Penn State University and the Berlage Institute Rotterdam. He is a regular contributor to the national daily *il manifesto* and its cultural supplement *Alias*. His articles and essays have been published in *Arquitectura Viva*, *Domus*, *Log*, *Lotus international*, *Volume* and the Chinese magazine *World Architecture*. In 2006 he published *Junkspace*, an anthology of Rem Koolhaas's recent writings (Quodlibet). Since 2000 he has been a consultant to the Italian Ministry of Culture's Department of Contemporary Art and Architecture.

Vedran Mimica was born in Zagreb, Croatia, in 1954, and was granted a diploma as an architect-engineer (1979) from the University of Zagreb, Faculty of Architecture. Upon graduating he attended several post-graduated courses, in a Diocletian palace in Split (1979-1981), in Plecnik's Ljubljana (1984) and at Delft University of Technology (1985-1986 and 1990-1991). Vedran Mimica joined the Berlage Institute Amsterdam as project coordinator in January 1991. Currently he is Associate Dean at the Berlage Institute, responsible for creating the educational programme, composing the curriculum and guiding research activities.

He has been a lecturer, visiting critic and examiner at numerous schools of architecture all over the world. He organized a series of workshops and projects in Zagreb, Split, Sarajevo, Ljubljana, Belgrade and Tirana, as an attempt to redevelop cities in southeast Europe after a large-scale catastrophe caused by the war in former Yugoslavia. Currently he is a project leader of Matra Social Transformation Programme for Central and Eastern Europe of the Netherlands Ministry of Foreign Affairs in the project 'Croatian Archipelago New Lighthouses'.
He is active as a writer on architecture and architectural education in *Domus*, *Hunch*, *Architectur Aktuell*, *Architecture-Seoul*, *Man and Space-Zagreb*, *AB-Ljubljana* and *Oris- Zagreb*.
Mimica is a regular member of numerous national and international architectural competitions. He is extensively engaged in the curatorial activities such as the Croatian exhibition as well as the Berlage Institute exhibition at the 10th Venice Biennale.

He is a head of the curatorial team for the 3rd International Architecture Biennale Rotterdam 2007.

MMBB is a firm headquartered in São Paulo, founded in 1996 by **Fernando de Mello Franco** (1964), **Marta Moreira** (1962) and **Milton Braga** (1963), architects who graduated from the Universidade de São Paulo, Brazil between 1986 and 1987.
The wide range of projects they have worked on most notably include public and institutional projects with an urban dimension. In them, they focus their investigation on the systems of urban mobility and the management of water resources, aiming to impart architectural value to the infrastructural interventions.
They have also been active in the cultural and academic context, participating in and/or organizing cultural events and exhibitions, as well as engaging in teaching and research.
The firm has participated in the Biennales of Lima, Havana, Quito, São Paulo and Venice, as well as other exhibitions. They have published works in various international magazines, and in the books *Coletivo* (Cosac&Naify, 2006), *Ainda modernos? Arquitetura Brasileira Contemporânea* (Nova Fronteira, 2005) and *Brazilian Modern Architecture* (Phaidon, 2004).

Motsepe Architects was founded by Fanuel Motsepe in 2005. It is based in Johannesburg, South Africa. Fanuel graduated from the University of Cape Town. For the IABR, he is working with Eric Lindenberg, who graduated from the University of Witwatersrand. M.Arch's work is inspired by space and place-making philosophies in indigenous and contemporary South Africa.
Consulting partners: Mirjam Patz, Max Voigt, Lerato Maduna/Market Photo Workshop, Ishmael Mkhabela, Prof François Viruly.

Office Kersten Geers David Van Severen was founded in 2002 by David Van Severen and Kersten Geers. The office is based in Brussels.
David Van Severen graduated in Architecture and Urbanism from the University of Ghent, Belgium and the ETSAM in Madrid, Spain. He worked as an architect for Stéphane Beel Architects in Ghent, Xaveer De Geyter Architects in Brussels and for Atelier Maarten Van Severen. He currently teaches at Ghent University.
Kersten Geers graduated in Architecture and Urbanism from the Ghent University, Belgium and at the ETSAM in Madrid, Spain. He was a project leader for Maxwan Architects and Urbanists and Neutelings Riedijk Architects in Rotterdam until 2005. He currently teaches at Delft University of Technology and Ghent University and is visiting critic at the Berlage Institute in Rotterdam.
The office has won several international competitions, among which a border crossing in Mexico, a New Administrative Capital in South Korea (in collaboration with DOGMA) and a new Centre for Contemporary Art in Brussels. It is currently working on a wide range of different projects.
The IABR project is Office 35. Project team: Kersten Geers, David Van Severen, Jorrit Sipkes, Steven Bosmans, Michael Langeder, Asli Cicek. Special thanks to Lieven de Cauter

Alexander Sverdlov is a co-founder and partner of SVESMI, Rotterdam/Moscow. After graduating from the Berlage Institute in 2002, he worked at different offices in the Netherlands such as Neutelings Riedijk , West 8 and OMA/AMO. He was a part of the Shrinking Cities research by the German Cultural Foundation. He taught and lectured in various schools in Europe. SVESMI was founded by Yuri Grigoryan, Anastasia Smirnova and Alexander Sverdlov in 2006. With branches in Moscow and Rotterdam, SVESMI develops architecture powered by cultural collisions between European and Russian conditions.
Project Russia is a leading Russian architectural magazine. Established more than ten years ago by Bart Goldhoorn, it became a major mirror of rapidly changing Russian architectural culture.
Alexander Zelikin graduated from Moscow Architectural Institute. Since 2001 he runs prj_Z, his own practice in Moscow.

Martino Tattara studied architecture at the IUAV in Venice and at the Berlage Institute, from which he graduated in 2005. During his studies at the Berlage he participated in the research programme on capital cities, investigating Tirana and Brussels. He is currently a PhD candidate in Urbanism at the IUAV in Venice. He is cofounder of DOGMA, an office based in Rotterdam.

Roemer van Toorn is an architect, critic, photographer and curator. After graduating from Delft University of Technology, he published *The Invisible in Architecture* (1994) in collaboration with Ole Bouman; in this acclaimed encyclopaedic manifest he dissects the varied range of cultural, economic, political and philosophic outlook within the contemporary architectural discourse with the aim of outlining the different positions and issues of today's architecture.
As professor, he runs and coordinates the Projective Theory programme at the Berlage Institute and is a researcher at the Delft School of Design run by Prof. Arie Graafland at Delft University of Technology, while at the same time pursuing a career as an international lecturer. He has been the editor of several issues of the annual publication *Architecture in the Netherlands*, as well as an advisor of the magazine *Archis*(*Volume*) and *Domus*. As author and photographer he also contributes to many other publications. His photography work has been exhibited in Winnipeg, Los Angeles and was part of the exhibition *Cities on the Move* curated by Hou Hanru and Hans-Ulrich Obrist. In October 2004 his photos on the Society of The And have been exhibited at *Archilab The Naked City* curated by Bart Lootsma. Currently he is working on a publication as part of his PhD research (Berlage Chair) at Delft University of Technology: *Fresh Conservatism or Radical Democracy? Aesthetics as a Form of Politics*. Forthcoming in 2008 is his photo book *The Society of The And*, which will include, besides texts by himself, articles by Stefano Boeri, Jeffrey Kipnis, Thomas van Leeuwen and Bart Lootsma.

The Urban Think Tank (U-TT) was founded in 1993 by Alfredo Brillembourg and, in 1998, Hubert Klumpner joined as partner. It is a multi-disciplinary design practice dedicated to high-level design on a variety of subjects concerned with contemporary architecture and urbanism.

The philosophy of U-TT is to deliver innovative and sustainable solutions through the combined skills of architects, civil engineers, environmental planners, landscape architects, and communication specialists. In 2006, the book *Informal City: Caracas Case* (edited together with Kristin Feireiss) was published by Prestel, Munich. The Gimnasio Vertical™ was presented at the *10th Architecture Biennale in Venice*.

Alfredo Brillembourg received his master's degree in Science in Architectural Design from Columbia University in 1986. In 1992 he received a second architectural degree from the Universidad Central de Venezuela (UCV) and started U-TT as an independent practice in Caracas. Since 1994 he has been a guest professor at the University José Maria Vargas, the University Simon Bolivar, the Central University in Venezuela and a guest design review critic at Columbia University GSAPP, Harvard GSD and the The Irwin S. Chanin School of Architecture of The Cooper Union.

Hubert Klumpner graduated in 1993 from the University of Applied Arts in Vienna in the Master Class of Prof. Hans Hollein. He received a master's degree in Science in Architecture and Urban Design from Columbia University. He has been a guest professor at the Universidad Central de Venezuela (UCV). Since 2001 he has been the urbanism consultant of the International Program for Social and Cultural Development in Latin America. In 1998 he joined the Urban Think Tank as partner in Caracas.

John Urry is Professor at the Department of Sociology, Lancaster University, Lancaster, LA1 4YD. He was educated at Cambridge, with a BA/MA in Economics and a PhD in Sociology. He has since worked at Lancaster University where he has been Head of Dept, Founding Dean of the Social Sciences Faculty and University Dean of Research. He is also a Fellow of the Royal Society of Arts, Founding Academician, UK Academy of Social Sciences, Member (1992) and Chair UK wide Research Assessment Panels (1996, 2001), and has an Honorary Doctorate from Roskilde University.
He has published about 35 books and special issues, with his work being translated into 14 languages, and has lectured in circa 30 countries. His is currently Director of the Centre for Mobilities Research at Lancaster that has extensive links throughout the world relating to the study of physical movement and its interconnections with the 'virtual' and the 'imaginative'. Recent books include *Sociology beyond Societies*, Routledge (2000), *The Tourist Gaze. Second Edition*, Sage (2002), *Tourism Mobilities. Places to Play, Places in Play*, Routledge (2004), *Performing Tourist Places*, Ashgate (2004), *Automobilities*, Sage (2005), *Mobile Technologies of the City*, Routledge (2006), *Mobilities, Networks, Geographies* (2006), *Mobilities*, Polity (2007).

Martijn de Waal is a writer and researcher based in Amsterdam, the Netherlands. His main focus is a PhD-project at the Department of Practical Philosophy at the Univerity of Groningen. He studied as an exchange student at UC Berkeley and worked as a free-lance reporter in Silicon Valley for Dutch Media during the dot-com boom days.
De Waal delved into new media theory at the department of mediastudies at the University of Amsterdam and worked as advisor, organizer, writer or researcher with different organizations and companies, such as Submarine, the Dutch Fund for Cultural Broadcasting, the Dynamic City Foundation, V2, Hivos, and the Mondriaan Foundation.
Martijn de Waal's writings and thoughts have appeared in national newspapers and magazines in the Netherlands, and have been broadcast on National Public Radio. He published *Amerika, toets 1 voor Paradijs (America: Dial P for Paradise)*, 2002.

WORK Architecture Company is a New York-based firm dedicated to the exploration of shape and ideas; and committed to research through practice. Recent projects include a headquarters building for Diane von Furstenberg, a Master Plan for the BAM Cultural District in Brooklyn and the re-conceptualization of Anthropologie's retail stores. Publications include research projects on Dubai and Eco-Urbanism – an investigation into the potential sustainability at the urban scale. WORKac was selected as part of the 2007 Architectural Record Design Vanguard and was chosen for New York City's Design Excellence programme for public projects in 2007.

Amale Andraos received her master's degree from the Graduate School of Design at Harvard. She is currently an adjunct professor at Harvard University's Graduate School of Design and at Princeton University's School of Architecture. **Dan Wood** received his master's degree from Columbia University's Graduate School of Architecture. He is currently an adjunct professor at Princeton University's School of Architecture and was the 2006 Trott Professor of Architecture at Ohio State University.

Yimin Zhu studied architecture in Xi'an Institute of Metallurgy and Construction Engineering in the middle of the 1980s in China. He attended the Berlage Institute in 2000 after working as an architect in China for more than ten years and graduated in 2002. In the same year he founded DOGMA Office with Pier Vittorio Aureli. He is currently running DOGMA Office Guangzhou while teaching at the South China University of Technology. In correspondence with the most brutal, intensive and dramatic changes of society, his practical works aim to search for an alternative dimension of spatial productions on the condition of capitalist globalization and to negotiate between the fragmentary urban/social landscape of China by means of built forms. Projects that have been realized include a museum for the collections of the Great Cultural Revolution era during the 1960s in Chengdu and an office building in Luoyang.

Sharon Zukin is Broeklundian Professor of sociology at Brooklyn College and the Graduate School of the City University of New York. She has written about cities, culture, and the economy since the early 1980s, focusing on *Loft Living* in New York City (1982), on emerging *Landscapes of Power: From Detroit to Disney World* (winner of the C. Wright Mills Award, 1991), and on *The Cultures of Cities* (1995). Zukin has also written a critical cultural history of shopping, *Point of Purchase: How Shopping Changed American Culture* (2004) and co-edited *After the World Trade Center: Reshaping New York City* (2002), besides doing research on France and the former Yugoslavia.

Credits

Capital Cities

The City as Political Form
Pier Vittorio Aureli & Martino Tattara
Project elaborated within the "Research on the City" program at the Berlage Institute.
Project Team
Pier Vittorio Aureli (Research Director)
Martino Tattara (Research Director)
Adolfo Despradel Catrain
Elena Gissi
Sahil Abdul Latheef
Miha Pesecs
Lama Sfeir
Melisa Vargas Rivera
Yvette Vasourkova
Juan Bernardo Vera Rueda
Zhong Ping Wu
Shanshan Xue.

Astana versus Almaty
Project Team
IND (InterNationalDesign)
Arman Akdogan
Felix Madrazo
with
Martin Mutsclechner
Collaborators
Sophie Panzer
Rudie Nieveen
Tesa Spoelstra
Special thanks to
Pars Kibarer for his bright insight on the topic
Madina Dzhunusova & Ilnur Arslan for their constant assistance in Kazakhstan;
Emina Beslagic for contacts;
Mikhail Evstafiev & Saule Buldekbaeva of The Organization for Security and Cooperation in Europe for kindly allowing us to use their photograph bank.

Cadavre Exquis Lebanese
Project Team
Worc Architecture Company
Amale Andraos
Dan Wood
Rami Abou Khalil
Fred Awty
Mikkel Bøgh
Paul Coudamy
Sam Dufaux
Julianne Gola
Thomas T. Jensen
Merete Kinnerup Andersen
Christo Logan
Fadi Mansour
Ana Cristina Vargas
Research and Photography
Dina Debbas
Marc Mouraccade
Nada Raphael
Pierre Sarraf
Rayyane Tabet

Moscow Prefabricated
Project Team
Alexander Sverdlov (SVESMI), Rotterdam
with
Project Russia
Alexander Zelikin
Jorrit Sipkes
Photography
Ekaterina Golovatyuk
Alexey Narodnitskiy
Sergey Sitar
Alexander Sverdlov

Corporate Cities

The Zone
Keller Easterling
Catalogue en exhibition images
Satya Pemmaraju
Kohn Pederson Fox
AllianceTexas
Exhibition
Zone timeline
E. Sean Bailey
Yale University School of Architecture
Video transfer
Karl Mascarenhas

Moore's Law Meets Sustainability
Project Team
INABA
Jeffrey Inaba (Principal)
Ben Konen (Project Architect)
Dionysia Daskalaki
Haydee Avila
Moira Henry
Yi-han Cao
Jesse Madrid
Sustainability Engineers
ARUP
Steve Done (Principal)
Karen Mozes
Video and Motion Graphics Designer
Yi-han Cao
Jesse Madrid

The New City of Luoyang
Project Team
Yimin Zhu (SCUT Guangzhou)
with
Lu Zhang
Dong Zhao
Participants
Wei Wang
Yihong Ding
Shui He
Yijun Qian
Zhuoer Song
Boyi Sun
Yuan Tian
Liya Ye
Lu Zhao
Special thanks to
Guolin Ma, Guoen Li (vice director general of Luoyang urban planning bureau) Luoyang urban planning bureau for kindly allowing us to use the planning information and photographs of the new city of Luoyang.

Garden State/ Backyard City
Project Team
Princeton University Center for Architecture, Urbanism and Infrastructure
Rafi Segal (Team Leader)
Els Verbakel (Team Leader)
Yan Chu
Ajay Manthripragada
Marc Mcquade
Ryan Neiheiser
Kate Snider
Michael Wang
Director of Center
Mario Gandelsonas
Dean of School
Stan Allen

Spectacle Cities

The Power of Spectacle
John Urry
Special thanks to
Tom Urry

The Power of Unesco World Heritage
Project Team
bad architects group
Paul Burgstaller
Ursula Faix
Collaborators
Karin Woergoetter
Nicolas Ebner
Video Editing
krost audiovisual
Special thanks to
Martin Mutschlechner
Arnold Klotz
Wolfgang Andexlinger
Johannes Niedertscheider (tiris)
Supported by
Bundeskanzleramt Sektion Kunst (Bernd Hartmann)
Amt der Tiroler Landesregierung Abteilung Kunst (Erwin Koler, Verena Baeumler)

Reintroducing the City in Havana
Project Team
a-u-r-a (architecture urbanism + research agency)
Marisol Rivas Velázquez
Christian Schmutz
FÜNDC BV (architecture + design consultancy)
Paz Martín
César García
Photography
Christian Schmutz
César García Guerra
Special thanks to
Prof. Mario Coyula-Cowley
Prof. Miguel Coyula & the people of GDIC (Grupo para el Desarrollo Integral de la Capital)
Prof. Dr. Rubén Bancroft Hernández
Prof. Dr. Orestes del Castillo
Arch. Maikel Menendez
Arch. Volker Kleinekort
Arch. Inger y Federico Reiners
Juanjo, Roberto Jr., Pipo, Patricia, Roberto Sr., Clarisa, Sandra, Jóse

Roman Holiday
Project Team
baukuh
Paolo Carpi
Lorenzo Laura
Silvia Lupi
Vittorio Pizzigoni
Giacomo Summa
Pier Paolo Tamburelli
Francesca Torzo
Andrea Zanderigo
with
Romolo Ottaviani
Martin Sobota
Collaborators
Beatrice De Carli
Ettore Donadoni
Photography
Francesco Jodice
Giovanna Silva
Special thanks to
Comune di Roma: Walter Veltroni (Sindaco), Mario Cutuli (Responsabile per l'architettura dello staff del Sindaco), Mariapia Garavaglia (Vice Sindaco), Caterina Saccaro (Ufficio Turismo),

Livia Omiccioli (Servizio Bilancio)
Soprintendenza Comunale ai Beni Culturali di Roma: Eugenio La Rocca (Soprintendente), Giovanni Caruso, Roberto Meneghini, Elisabetta Bianchi, Riccardo Santangeli, Paola Virgili, Lucrezia Ungaro, Antonio Mucci
Parco Regionale dell'Appia Antica: Francesca Mazzà, Caterina Rossetti, Andrea Bonamico
Soprintendenza per i Beni Archeologici di Roma: Angelo Bottini (Soprintendente). Direzione Generale per l'Architettura e l'Arte contemporanee del Ministero per i Beni e le Attività culturali DARC: Margherita Gruccione (Direttore), Elisabetta Virdia. spacexperience | stalker, 2a+P, MA_A, MP2S, unpacked, Clementina Panella e Alessandro Vanzetti (Dipartimento di Scienze Storiche, Archeologiche e Antropologiche dell'Antichità, Università degli Studi di Roma "La Sapienza"),
Renato Funiciello e Arnaldo De Benedetti (Dipartimento di scienze Geologiche, Università degli Studi di Roma Tre), Sebastiana Allegrina, Carlo Brizioli, Mattia Darò, Lorenzo Franchini, Stefano Giussani, Cecilia Guida, Italo Insolera, Gabriele Mastrigli, Emanuele Stefani.

Informal Cities

Failure of the Formal
Alfredo Brillembourg & Hubert Klumpner
Urban Think Tank Films
Alfredo Brillembourg & Hubert Klumpner
John & David Frankfurt
Thanks to
Claudia Heinzl

Peripheral Landscapes
Project Team
arquitectura 911sc
Jose Castillo
Saidee Springall
Video and Motion Graphics Design
Plasmatic Concepts, Los Angeles, CA
Sarah Lorenzen and David Hartwell
Design and Research Team
Juan Carlos Tello
Guillermo Delgado
Eduardo Ezeta
Norma Maldonado
Juan Jose Acevedo
Gimena Lara
Ariela Rodriguez

Supported by
Secretaría de Relaciones Exteriores
Embajada de México en los Países Bajos
Consejo Nacional para la Cultura y las Artes
Fomento Cultural Banamex
Royal Philips Mexicana

Levittown Retrofitted
Project Team
Estudio Teddy Cruz
Teddy Cruz
Andrea Dietz
Adriana Cuellar
Jota Samper Escobar
Mariana Leguia
Jesus Limon
Gregorio Ortiz
Alan Rosenblum
Casa Familiar
Andrea Skorepa
Luz Camacho
David Flores
Parc Foundation
David Deutsch
Megan Wurth
Andy Sturm

Watery Voids
Project Team
MMBB
Fernando de Mello Franco
Marta Moreira
Milton Braga
with
Gabriel Manzi
Lucas Girard
Manon Fantini
Marina Sabino
Collaborators
Armando Tobias de Aguiar
Renato Cymbalista
Renato Tagnin
Photography
Lalo de Almeida
Nelson Kon
3D Model
Aleks Braz
Special thanks to
Ministry of External Relations
Brazilian Embassy in Haia
DAEE - São Paulo Department of Water and Electricity
LUME - Laboratory of the Metropolitan Urbanism, Faculty of Architecture and Urbanism of the University of São Paulo

Hidden Cities

Meditations on Razor Wire
Lieven De Cauter
& Michiel Dehaene

From Denver to Dainfern
Project Team
blacklinesonwhitepaper
Kirsten Dörmann

Solam Mkhabela
Tumi Morule
Motsepe Architects
Fanuel Motsepe
Eric Lindenberg
Graphics+ Design Development
Mirjam Patz, Max Voigt
Social Geography
Ishmael Mkhabela
Property Economy
Prof François Viruly
Photo Essay
Lerato Maduna/ Market Photo Workshop, Photojournalism and Documentary Photography Programme, supported by Getty Images
How to . . . support
planact, Mike Makwela
Denver/ Dainfern Informants
Mathews Baloyi, Masimba Sasa, Puwai Mpofu, Mpilonhle Mpilonde: Jo Veary with RHRU, University of the Witwatersrand
Film Final Mix
Jurgen Meekel
Voiceover
James Wangala
City Records
Mbali, Chrisula, Shimane, Sparks, Lerato, James
Fear Survey Consultancy
Kieke Grootenhuis
General
Participants of fear survey and *ndawo yami* design workshop

Cité de Refuge
Project Team
Office Kersten Geers David Van Severen
Kersten Geers
David Van Severen
Jorrit Sipkes
Steven Bosmans
Michael Langeder
Asli Cicek
Photography
Bas Princen
Office Kersten Geers David Van Severen
Special thanks to
Lieven De Cauter
Richard Venlet
Roeland Dudal
With support of
Department of culture, Flemish Community

Illustration Credits

Lalo de Almeida and Nelson Kon *222-223*
Arman Akdogan *35 b. c., 35 b. r., 37 t., 37 b.*
arquitectura 911cs *200, 201, 203 b., 205 b., 207 b.*
a-u-r-a and FÜNDC BV *156-158*
bad architects group *145 r., 145 r.*
M. Báez y G. Barrasa and C. Schmutz *154, 155*
BR3 Teatro da Vertigem, Evaldo Mocarzel/Casa Azul, 2006 *227 t. r.*
Milton Braga *227 t. l.*
Alfredo Brilembourg & Hubert Klumpner / U-TT *192-193*
George Brugmans *191, 195*
BASE aerofotogrametria 2001 | GOOGLE EARTH 2007 *226 b.*
baukuh *164-167*
blacklinesonwhitepaper and Motsepe Architects *251-253, 256-257*
DAEE | CESAD *224, 225t.*
DAEE | LUME |CESAD *225 b.*
Ad van Denderen *236*
Theo Deutinger *242-243*
L'Espresso, summer 2001 *18*
Estudio Cruz *210-217, 241*
Fotos Fontenelle *26*
Kendell Geers *240*
Gli obelischi di Roma, Cesare D'Onofrio, Rome: Bulzoni, 1967 *24 b. r.*
Inaba *90-93*
Francesco Jodice *168-169*
Nelson Kon *220-221, 227 c. l.*
Lerato Maduna/ Market Photo Workshop *254-255*
Marcelo Min *227 c. r.*
Alejandro Martinez & Eun Kyung Lee *238*
Burle Marx *227 b. r.*
M. Menendez *153 t.*
Office KGDVS *246, 247, 260, 261, 264-267*
OMA *244*
Damian Ortega *225 b. c., 227 b. l.*
OSCE-Mikhail Evstafiev *35 t., 35 b. l.*
Satya Pemmaraju *77*
Bas Princen, Courtesy Van Kranendonk Gallery, Den Haag *262-263*
Princeton University *104-111*
C. Schmutz *152 b., 153 b.*
Schönbrunner Schloßgesellschaft, whc.unesco.org *146*
Massimo Sestini, courtesy of the Italian National Police *19*
Giovanna Silva *162-163*
Pablo Souto / KSB-U-TT *187-189,*
Alexander Svredlov *54-57*
Martino Tattara and Pier Vittorio Aureli *27, 29-31*
Tiroler Kunstverlag Chizzali GmbH *144 t., 145 t. l., 144 b., 145 b. l.*
whc.unesco.org *146-147 b., 149 b.*
Work Achitecture Company *46-49*
www.google.de *147 t., 149 c.*
www.google.earth *203 t., 205 t., 207 t.*
www.signandsight.com/features/425.html *237*
www.youtube.com *149 b.*
Yimin Zhu *98-101*

Colophon

Visionary Power
Publication

This publication appears parallel to *Visionary Power*, one of the main exhibitions of the third International Architecture Biennial of Rotterdam (IABR). This third edition of the IABR entitled *Power – Producing the Contemporary City* is curated by the Berlage Institute and held from 24 May to 2 September 2007 in Rotterdam.

This publication has been made possible thanks to the generous support of the the Netherlands Architecture fund.

Edited by
Christine de Baan (International Architecture Biennale Rotterdam)
Joachim Declerck (Berlage Institute)
Véronique Patteeuw (NAi Publishers)

Text editors
Jennifer Sigler (architects' contributions)
Salomon Frausto (prologue)

Copy-editing
D'Laine Camp

Graphic Design
Thonik

Publisher
Eelco van Welie (NAi Publishers)

© 2007 the authors, the researchers, the architects.
© 2007 NAi Publishers, Rotterdam.

All rights reserved. No part of this publication may be reproduced, stored in a retrieval system, or transmitted in any form or by any means, electronic, mechanical, photocopying, recording or otherwise, without the prior written permission of the publisher.

For works of visual artists affiliated with a CISAC-organization the copyrights have been settled with Beeldrecht in Amsterdam. © 2007, c/o Beeldrecht Amsterdam
NAi Publishers is an internationally orientated publisher specialized in developing, producing and distributing books on architecture, visual arts and related disciplines. www.naipublishers.nl
info@naipublishers.nl

It was not possible to find all the copyright holders of the illustrations used. Interested parties are requested to contact NAi Publishers, Mauritsweg 23, 3012 JR Rotterdam, The Netherlands.

Available in North, South and Central America through D.A.P./Distributed Art Publishers Inc, 155 Sixth Avenue 2nd Floor, New York, NY 10013-1507, Tel 212 6271999, Fax 212 6279484.

Available in the United Kingdom and Ireland through Art Data, 12 Bell Industrial Estate, 50 Cunnington Street, London W4 5HB, Tel 208 7471061, Fax 208 7422319.

Printed and bound in Belgium

ISBN 978-90-5662-579-5

Visionary Power
Exhibition

Curators
Joachim Declerck
Vedran Mimica

Exhibition Management
Christine de Baan
Marlin Kornet

Exhibition Design
Daan Bakker,
DaF Architecten

Exhibition Construction
Landstra & de Vries
Bart Cuppens Tentoonstellingsbouw

Film Interviews
Rob Schröder

Graphic Design
Thonik

Lettering
Rocka

Lighting
Focus Showequipment bv

Editors
Els Brinkman
Joeri de Bruyn

Translation
D'Laine Camp

Audio Visual
Video Schaay B.V.

Researchers:

Capital Cities
The City as Political Form
Pier Vittorio Aureli
& Martino Tattara

Corporate Cities
The Zone
Keller Easterling

Spectacle Cities
The Power of Spectacle
John Urry

Informal Cities
Failure of the Formal
Alfredo Brillembourg
& Hubert Klumpner

Hidden Cities
Meditations on Razor Wire
Lieven De Cauter
& Michiel Dehaene

Participating Offices:

Capital Cities
Astana / IND (Inter.National. Design)
Beirut / WORK Architecture Company
Moscow / Alexander Sverdlov

Corporate Cities
Busan / INABA
Luoyang / Yimin Zhu
New Jersey / Princeton University Centre for Architecture, Urbanism and Infrastructure

Spectacle Cities
Innsbruck / bad architects group
Havana / a-u-r-a & FÜNDC BV
Rome / baukuh

Informal Cities
Mexico City / arquitectura 911sc
Tijuana/San Diego / Estudio Cruz
São Paulo / MMBB

Hidden Cities
Johannesburg / blacklinesonwhitepaper & Motsepe Architects
Ceuta / Office Kersten Geers David Van Severen

3rd International Architecture Biennale Rotterdam

Board
Mr. drs. L.C. Brinkman, chairman
A.Th. Duivesteijn, vice-chairman and secretary
Ir. J.M. Schrijnen, treasurer
Drs. S.J. Stuiveling
Drs. A.T. Meijer
Drs. L.H.M. Kohsiek

Director
George Brugmans

Head of Programme
Christine de Baan

Head of Production
Monica van Steen

Head of Communications
Rinske Brand

Visual communication
Thonik

Coordinator PowerLounge
Michiel Schwarz

Exhibitions Producer
Marlin Kornet

Researcher / Project Assistant
Sophie van Ginneken

Project Assistant
Sylvia Lodewick

Project Assistant
Sabrina Basten

Communications Advisor
Laura Liem

Communications Assistants
Kim Kraan
Chantal Kradolfer

Office Assistant
Jacqueline Arnell

Web Editor
Harry den Hartog

Berlage Institute
Curator

Curatorial Team
Vedran Mimica
Joachim Declerck
Rients Dijkstra

Director
Rob Docter

Producer
Francoise Vos

Graphic Designer
Mick Morssink

Broadcasting
Salomon Frausto

With the Kind Support of

City of Rotterdam
Ministry of Housing, Spatial Planning and the Environment
Ministry of Education, Culture and Science
The Netherlands Architecture Fund
Rotterdam 2007 City of Architecture
Video Schaay